AF292443

VENICE WITH TURNER

Ian Warrell

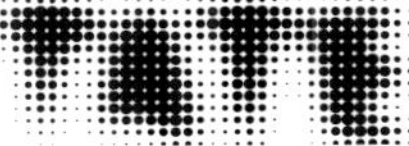

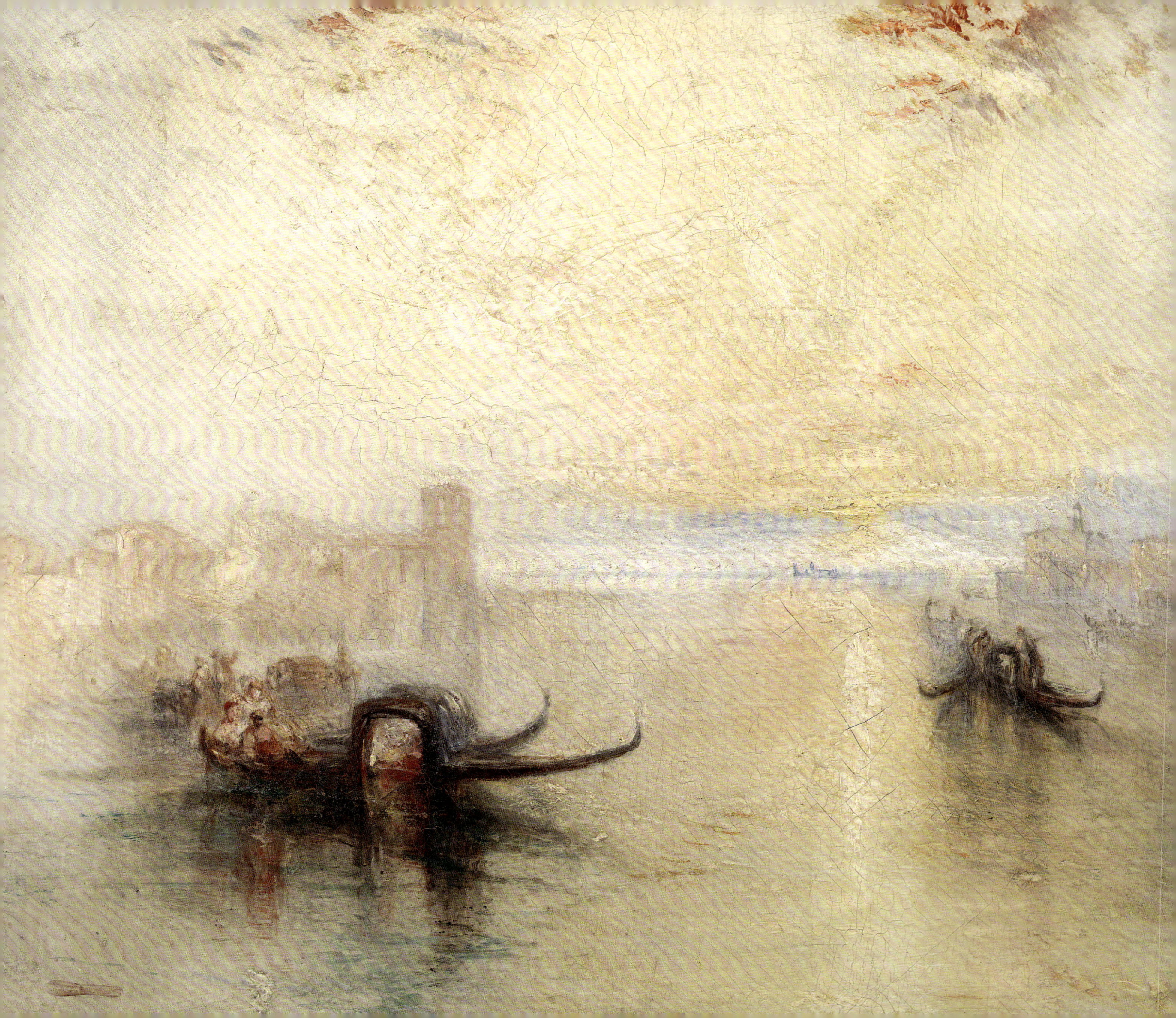

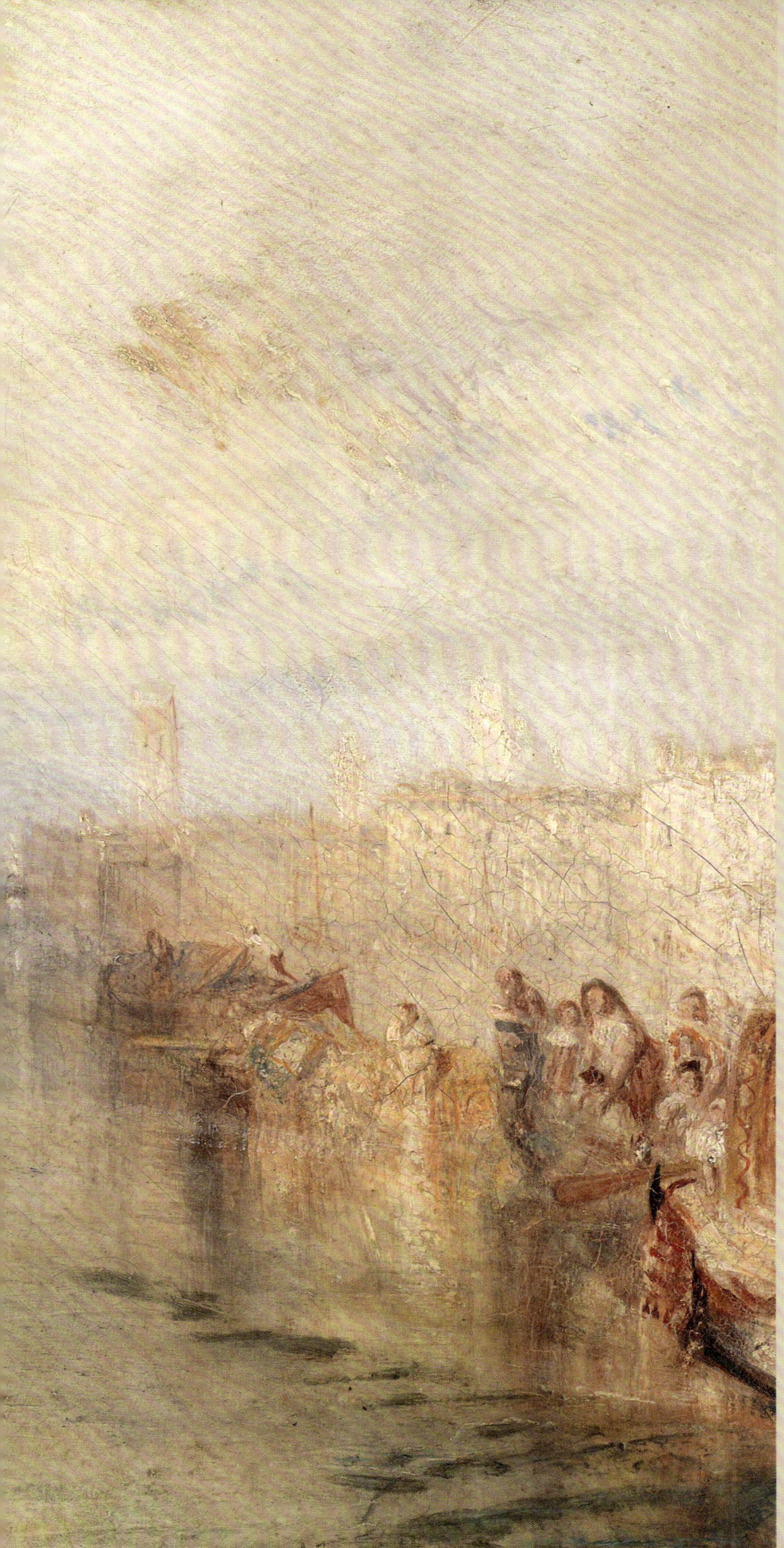

St Benedetto, Looking towards Fusina
exhibited at the Royal Academy in 1843
Oil paint on canvas, 62.2 × 92.7

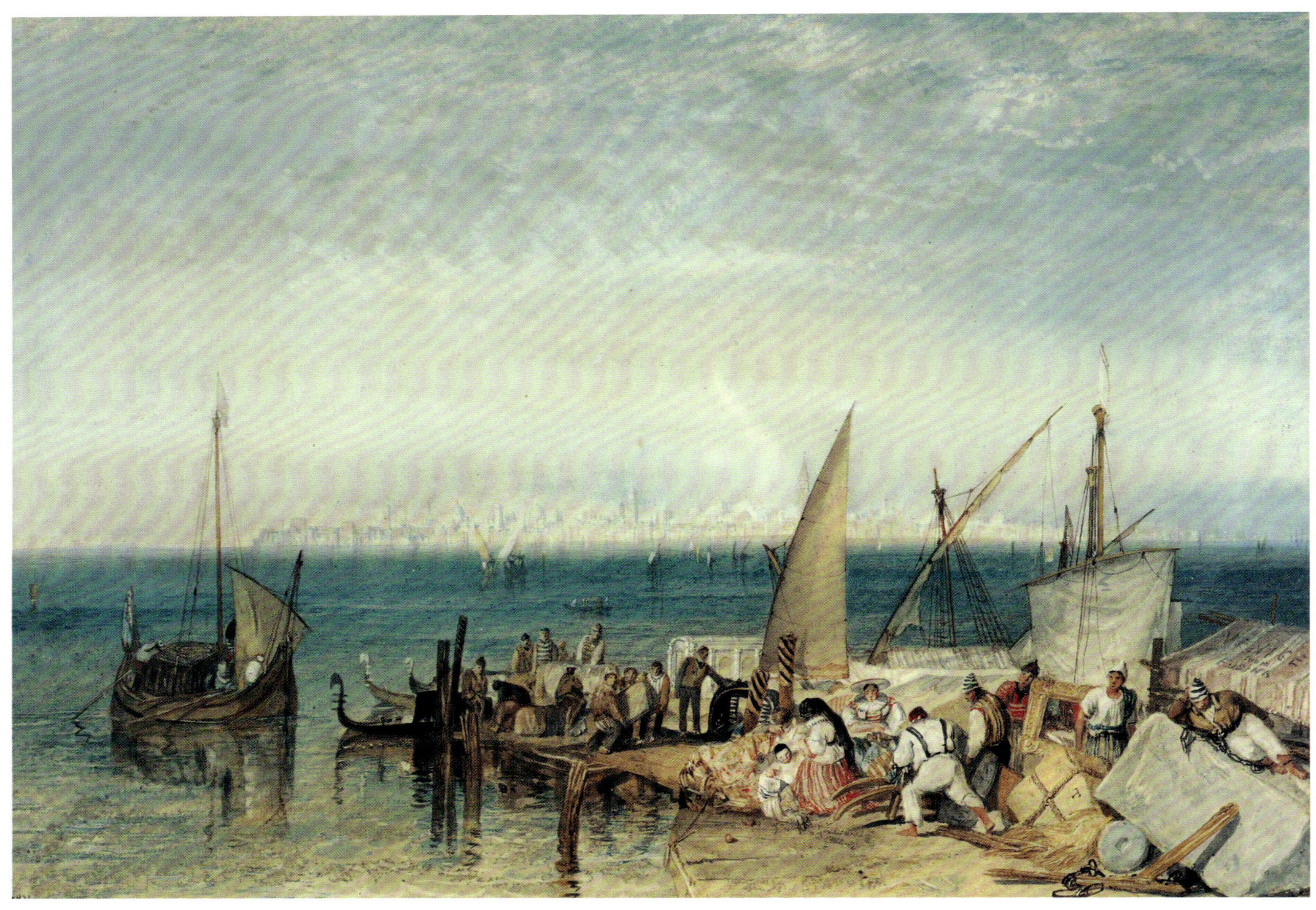

Venice from Fusina c.1821
Watercolour, 29.1 × 41.4, Private collection

Introduction

Turner's views of Venice are among the most enduring responses to that spectacular but uniquely fragile city: as colourful and vibrant as Canaletto's scenes; as wistful as Guardi's skilful impressions; as mysterious as Whistler's nocturnes; and as resonant as Monet's late souvenirs. Given the continuing appeal of this aspect of Turner's output, it is remarkable that he actually exhibited only twenty-five pictures of Venice in his lifetime.[1]

Those paintings were generally quickly snapped up by collectors at a time when much of his work was controversial and remained unsold. But it was only after Turner's death in 1851 that the true extent of the impact of Venice on his imagination became plain. From the mid-1850s onwards, the watercolours he had painted in sketchbooks, and on a variety of loose sheets of paper, were gradually brought to light, offering a vision of Venice that captured both the shimmering sunlight on water and stone, and more elusive effects, half-seen at twilight and throughout the spell of a Venetian night. This much more substantial body of work, amounting to around 150 watercolours, and perhaps a thousand pencil sketches, preserves the artist's more personal encounter and it is all the more notable because it results from just three short visits that cumulatively total barely four weeks in the city.[2]

Like other artists, it took Turner a while to find his own way of engaging with Venice. For his generation, the city had already been comprehensively defined in the crisply exacting images of Canaletto (1697–1768), which provided the template, as well as the standard for all followers to match. Inevitably, therefore, the compulsively competitive Turner jousted with the shadow of his celebrated predecessor in his first Venetian subjects, appropriating subject matter and approximating the Old Master's style (see p.11). Yet, as a British artist, his attitudes to, and his experience of, this most visually captivating of cities were also conditioned by literary responses. These spanned from Shakespeare to Lord Byron, whose descriptions of Venice in the final canto of 'Childe Harold's Pilgrimage' (1818) frequently hover implicitly, if unspoken, in the works Turner created. Arguably the most significant sentiment Turner adopted was Byron's evocation of an idealised Venice, suspended out of time – where the moon and the sun simultaneously inhabit the sky – and where past and present co-exist, imperceptibly intermingled.

Turner and Byron never met in Venice itself; for when Turner visited the city for the first time in 1819, the exiled poet was away. In any case, as an established name himself, then aged forty-four, Turner had no desire to be chaperoned around, even by such a famous (actually somewhat infamous) compatriot. His arrival on 1 September was accidentally inconspicuous because the local officials who were required to record all visitors mistranscribed his surname as 'Curner', a crucial detail only stealthily unearthed in the last few years.[3]

Turner was remarkably well prepared for his visit, having long dreamed of making a tour of Italy. He arrived in Venice carrying a notebook annotated with a list of practical recommendations of suitable lodgings and where to find key artworks among those places considered worth visiting. The useful (but not infallible) annotations had been provided by another author, James Hakewill, who had toured Italy a few years earlier. When publishing an account of his travels in 1818, Hakewill had commissioned Turner to translate his monochrome sketches into richer, more artful pictures. The process of collaborating on the project evidently resulted in pleasurable discussion that shaped the scope of Turner's tour. Hakewill, in fact, encouraged him to leave Venice until the latter part of his journey, as a final burst of sensory extravagance, after spending much longer in and around Rome.[4] But Turner could not resist the appeal of Venice as he pressed south during the first part of his route through Italy.

In a stay of around a week, he sketched extensively in four notebooks, carefully observing the distinctive shapes of Venetian boats, before diligently working his way up the Grand Canal, in addition to a thorough study of the great civic buildings around the Piazza San Marco. Wherever he went in the city, he sought out the paintings of Venetian artists like Titian (c.1488/90–1576), Veronese (1528–1588) and, above all, Tintoretto (1518–1594). Exceptionally, in his largest sketchbook, he produced a series of luminous watercolours (departing from his usual practice to colour them on the spot), barely fixing the topographical essentials on the page, except as they are shaped by light (pp.8, 43, 50, 64).

Remarkably, despite this revelatory beginning, Turner largely ignored his Venetian material once he was back in London, although his experience of Venice enriched the popular book designs he created for a

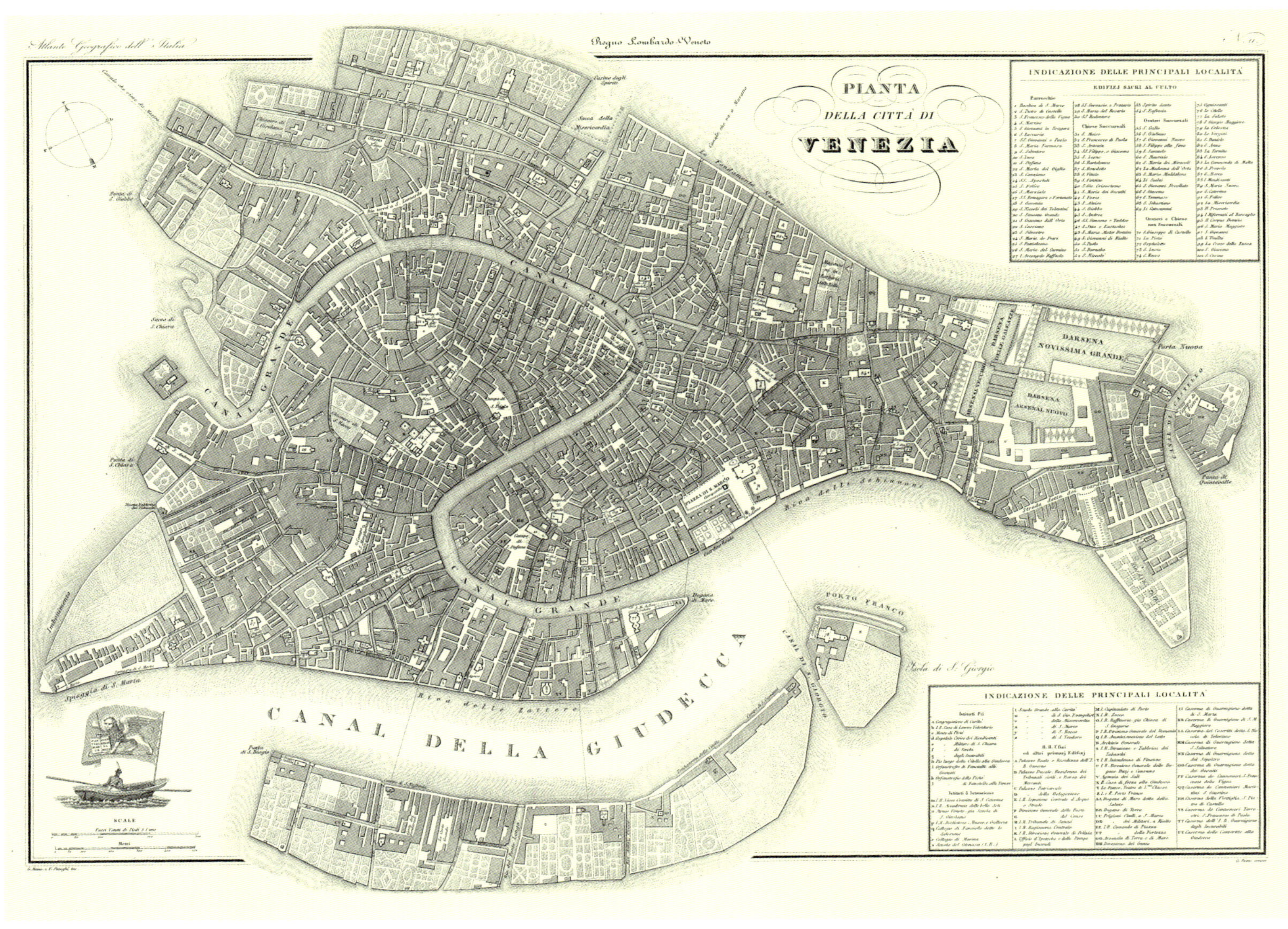

Map of Venice by Attilio Zuccagni-Orlandini, published by G. Maina and V. Stanghi, 1844–5

lavish edition of the poetry of Samuel Rogers (*Italy*, 1830). However, it was not until 1833 that he first exhibited pictures of Venice at the Royal Academy's annual show, which was coincidentally the year he decided to return to the city, arriving there on 9 September.

His outward route that year included a long detour to Vienna, where he acquired additional sketchbooks. It was probably also on this occasion that Turner obtained paper that purported to be made by James Whatman, the British brand he most often favoured.[5] However, these sheets were actually created in Austria as a means of overcoming export duty, and proved to be inferior in quality. While most of Turner's sketching in Venice in 1833 again took the form of hurried, compact spidery pencil notations, the fake Whatman sheets seem to have provided him with an outlet for more expansive image-making, and include the well-known depiction he made of his room in the Hotel Europa (p.30).

In 1840, when he returned for his third and final visit, he again secured a room in this well-placed hotel. He arrived slightly earlier that year, on 20 August, while the weather was sultry and stormy, a factor that perhaps induced him to stay a fortnight, double the length of his previous Venetian sojourns. The result was a flowering of creativity in watercolour, as he reacted afresh to the distinctive watery character of Venice. His choice of subjects was also frequently novel, taking advantage of his lofty vantage point in the Hotel Europa, or escaping from the narrow central thoroughfares to characterise the city as a mirage-like marvel, hovering above the Lagoon.

The same impulse for openness, coupled with a fascination for the inherent flux of Venetian life permeates the long series of oil paintings Turner produced following his 1840 visit, and is manifest as much in the vulnerable lives of its fishermen as the transient party-goers he included. Seventeen pictures were publicly exhibited, with more than half selling at the Royal Academy show, or soon afterwards. This unusual commercial success was in spite of the satirical mockery adopted by many critics, who described these 'atmospheric' late works as merely splashed palettes, made up of blots and handfuls of smeared paint, and only intelligible from a distance.

Unphased, Turner responded by developing further Venetian scenes, advancing them only as simple, blocked-out compositions, built up in thin layers of oil paint (pp.17, 73). Evidently interrupted while the images remained still indistinct, the idea was that more detail could be added should future commissions come in. These 'unfinished' works were not discovered and displayed until the early twentieth century, but have now been completely absorbed into our appreciation of Turner's achievement. Implicitly, they provide a useful metaphor. For we know that as late as 1845 he cherished hopes of returning once again to Venice. Taking this into account, the paintings constitute a physical expression of Turner's ongoing and ultimately unresolved relationship with Venice. And this unquenched yearning is one reason why so many people have come back repeatedly to his pictures for inspiration.

1. For detailed discussion of these works, see Butlin, Martin, and Evelyn Joll, *The Paintings of J.M.W. Turner*, New Haven and London 1984.

2. Turner's views of Venice have been discussed in the following detailed studies: A.J. Finberg, *In Venice with Turner*, London 1930; Lindsay Stainton, *Turner's Venice*, London 1985; Andrew Wilton, *Venise: Aquarelles de Turner*, Paris 1995, and most recently Ian Warrell (ed.), *Turner and Venice*, London 2003.

3. A.J. Finberg located a reference to the arrival of 'Turner' on 8 September (one of several British travellers of this name in the records for the month), which he plausibly associated with the artist. However, since 2003, both James Hamilton and Federico Crimi have made the case for identifying J.M.W. Turner with the person listed in records as 'Curner', who arrived around a week earlier (see James Hamilton (ed.), *Turner & Italy*, Edinburgh 2009, and Federico Crimi, *J.M.W. Turner a Milano*, Milan 2017). The mistake perhaps arose from the florid curl of the first letter in Turner's signature.

4. See Cecilia Powell in Warrell 2003, pp.30–3.

5. The paper types were identified and discussed by Peter Bower (see Appendix, pp.258–9, in Warrell 2003). However, there was not time in advance of that exhibition catalogue deadline to assimilate fully the ramifications of the paper coming from Austria.

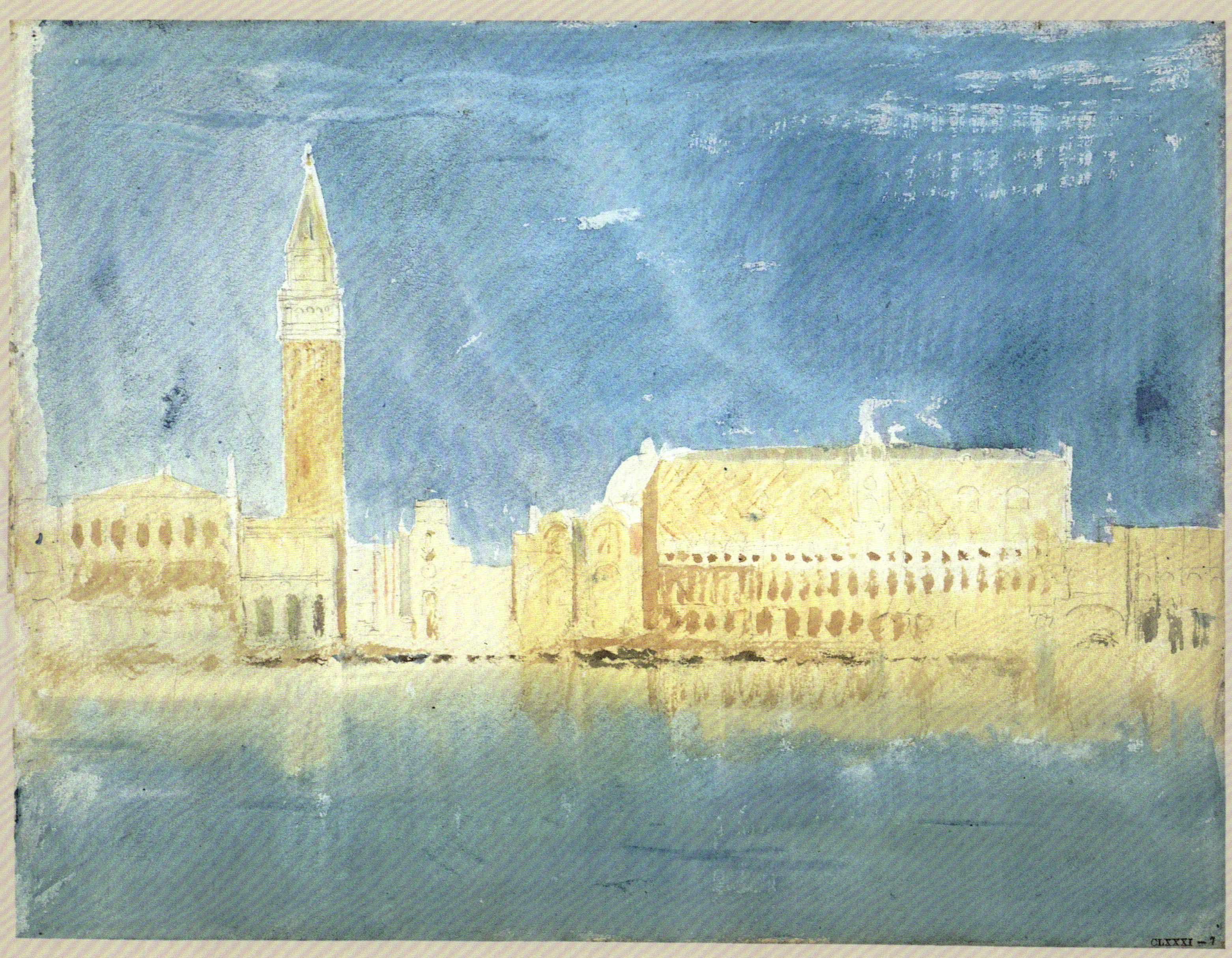

8

Piazza San Marco and the Doge's Palace

Today the image of Venice is inescapable, offering a fantasy for every budget, whoever you are and wherever you come from. Long before international tourism on this scale, Turner would also have set off to Venice with a clear idea of what to expect, having seen countless pictures and prints of the city's most celebrated landmarks. Indeed, as one of his contemporaries claimed, 'No one enters Venice as a stranger'. The chief magnet, then as now, was the Piazza San Marco, the greatest of the city's public places, presided over by the exotically encrusted façade of the Basilica San Marco, dedicated to Venice's patron saint, beside which stands the Doge's Palace (Palazzo Ducale), from which the 'Most Serene Republic' and its various dominions were governed. Both buildings have long histories testifying to the riches of Venice and its immense civic pride.

Turner's generation found the appearance of the basilica curious, and were often dismissive of the unfamiliar forms of Byzantine architecture. Just as extraordinary to them was the accumulation of 'trophies' throughout the building, the most notable of which were four gilded bronze horses installed on the balcony over the central entrance. These had been captured in Constantinople after 1204. But following the fall of Venice to Napoleon's French troops in May 1797, they had been shipped to Paris, along with some of the greatest paintings from churches and palaces throughout the city. Consequently, when Turner sketched the horses back in place in 1819, four years after the Battle of Waterloo brought an end to Napoleon's mastery over Europe, he was preserving evidence of dramatic recent history. Similarly, in some of his other drawings and watercolours, he noted that iconic representations of the Lion of St Mark (the symbolic guardian of the city) had been removed as part of the subjugation of the former republic; see, for example, the striking blank plaque above the doorway into the Doge's Palace (p.25). Of course, the ultimate fate of Venice remained in play throughout the time Turner knew it, and he brings this to the fore by including representatives of the latest occupying troops – the Austrians – stationed by the Doge's Palace and around the city (see p.21).

Musing on Venice's former glories naturally summoned up the festive images of Canaletto, especially his representations of the Doge's Palace and other prestigious buildings along the Molo, the main water front and principal 'face' of the city. Turner's first depictions of Venice, therefore, inevitably made specific references to his predecessor, even featuring Canaletto at work *en plein air* (p.11, see also p.102). And in a small book illustration (p.10), featuring the state barge – the Bucintoro – he skilfully reduced one of Canaletto's most well-known paintings (*The Bacino di San Marco on Ascension Day*, c.1733–4, then and now in the Royal Collection, London). Having digested this powerful influence, he attempted to produce his own conception of the Ascension Day festivities, one of the great ceremonial and symbolic events in the Venetian calendar – the Sposalizio del Mare – when the Doge set out to marry the sea (p.13). Curiously, however, Turner abandoned the composition before he had fully defined the height and detail of the Campanile di San Marco, and at some stage the upper areas of the Doge's Palace were accidentally smeared with brown paint.

Turner's finest representations of the Doge's Palace are actually the watercolours he made on his final visit, whether in fluid, schematic renderings, or the more detailed images he possibly created to sell to dedicated collectors. By then, thoroughly familiar with the elements of the city's urban vistas, he distorted the relationships between the constituent elements and their natural perspective to create bold compositions; none more so than the dramatic scene illuminated by a flash of lightning (created by scratching the paper surface) that explodes behind and silhouettes the column of St Theodore at the entrance to the Piazzetta (p.18).

The Campanile of San Marco (St Mark's) and the Palazzo Ducale (Doge's Palace) – Morning
from the Como and Venice sketchbook 1819
Graphite and watercolour on paper, 22.3 × 28.7

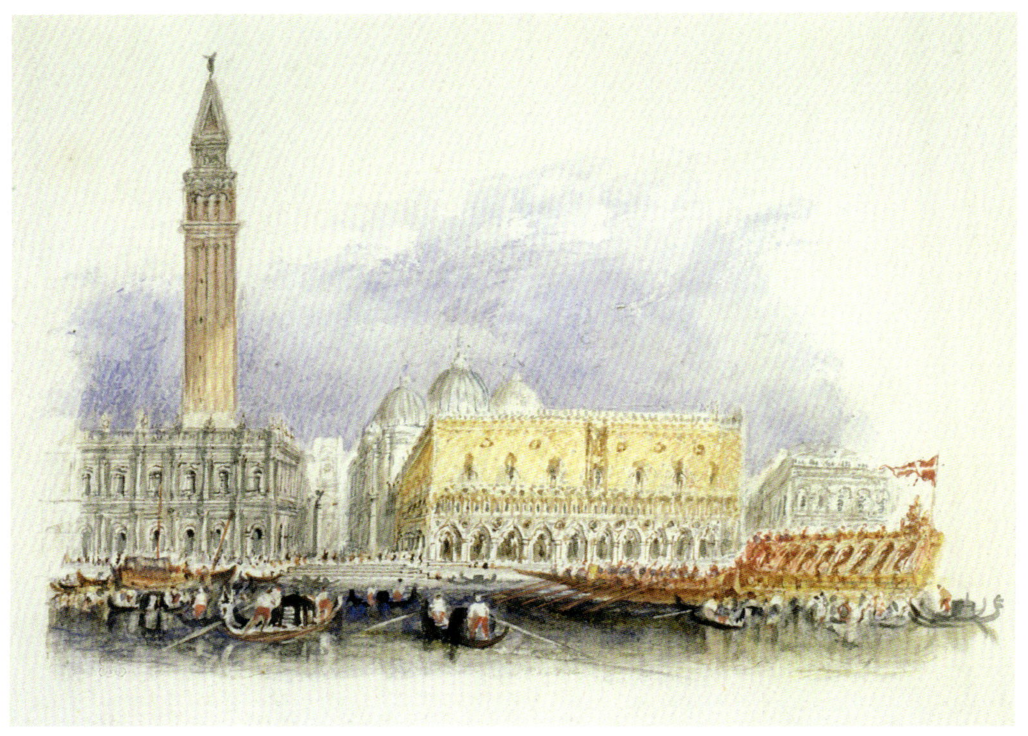

*Venice: The Ducal Palace (for
Samuel Rogers's 'Italy')* c.1826–7
Watercolour on paper, 24 × 30.6

*The Punta della Dogana, with the Campanile
and Domes of San Marco, the Zecca, the
Piazzetta, and the Doge's Palace* from the
Venice Sketchbook 1833
Graphite on paper, 10.9 × 20.3

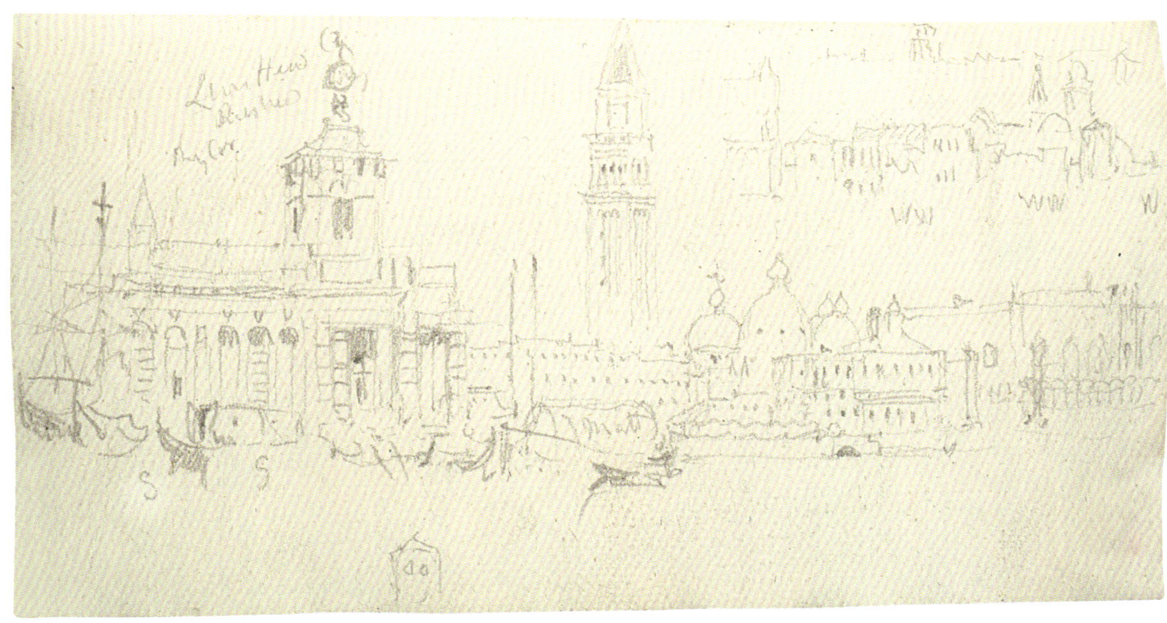

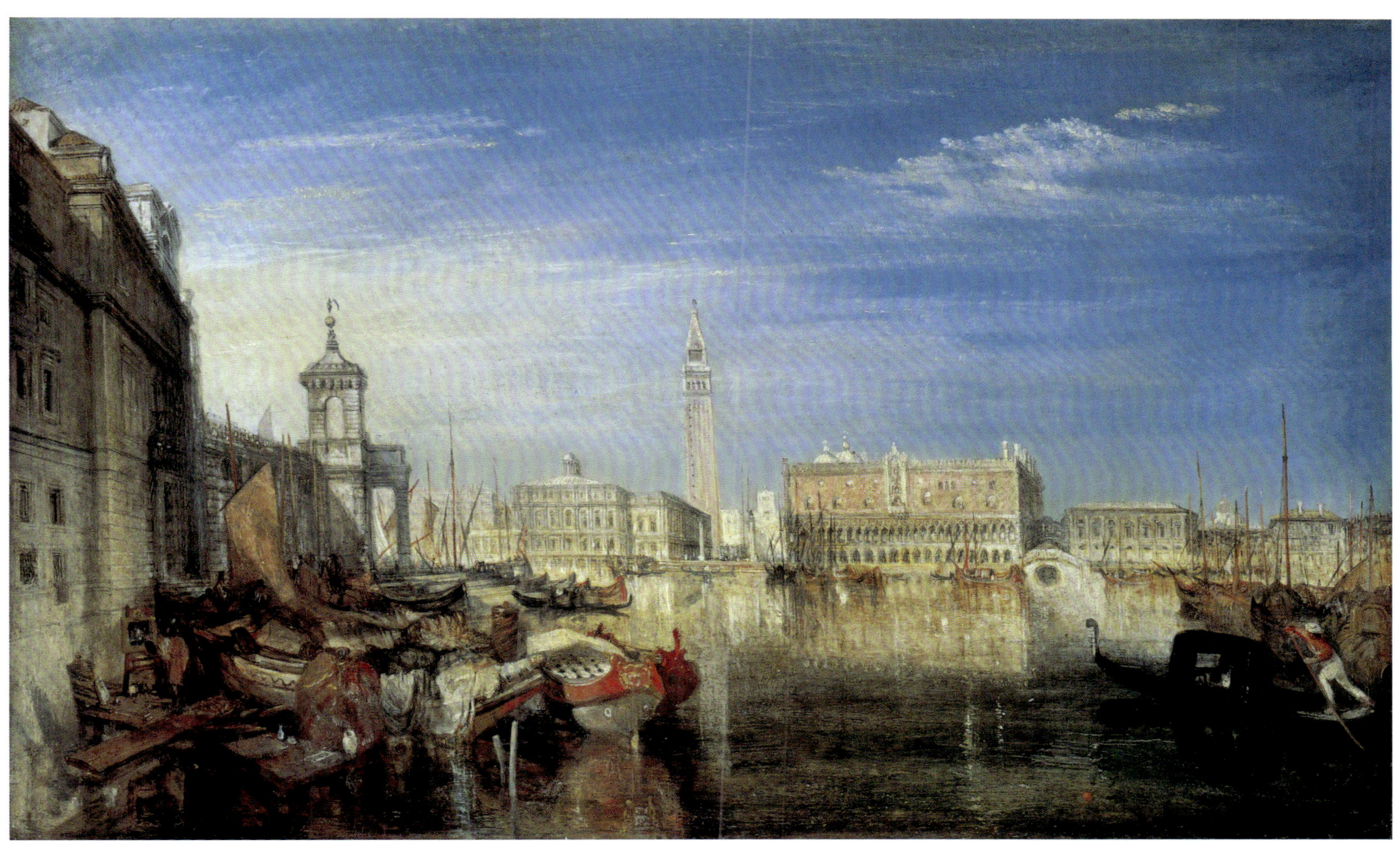

Bridge of Sighs, Ducal Palace and Custom-House, Venice:
Canaletti Painting, exhibited 1833
Oil paint on mahogany, 51.1 × 81.6

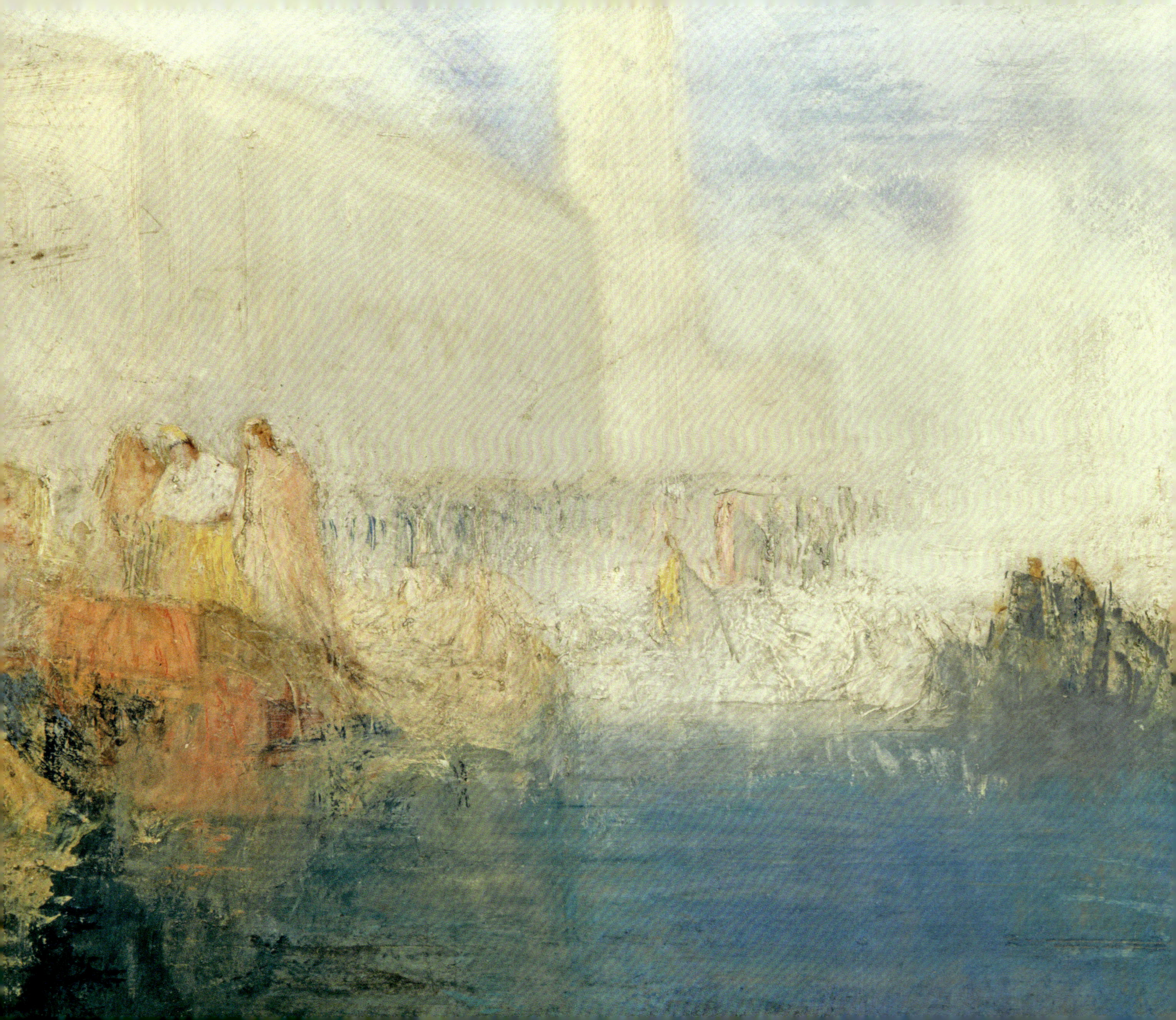

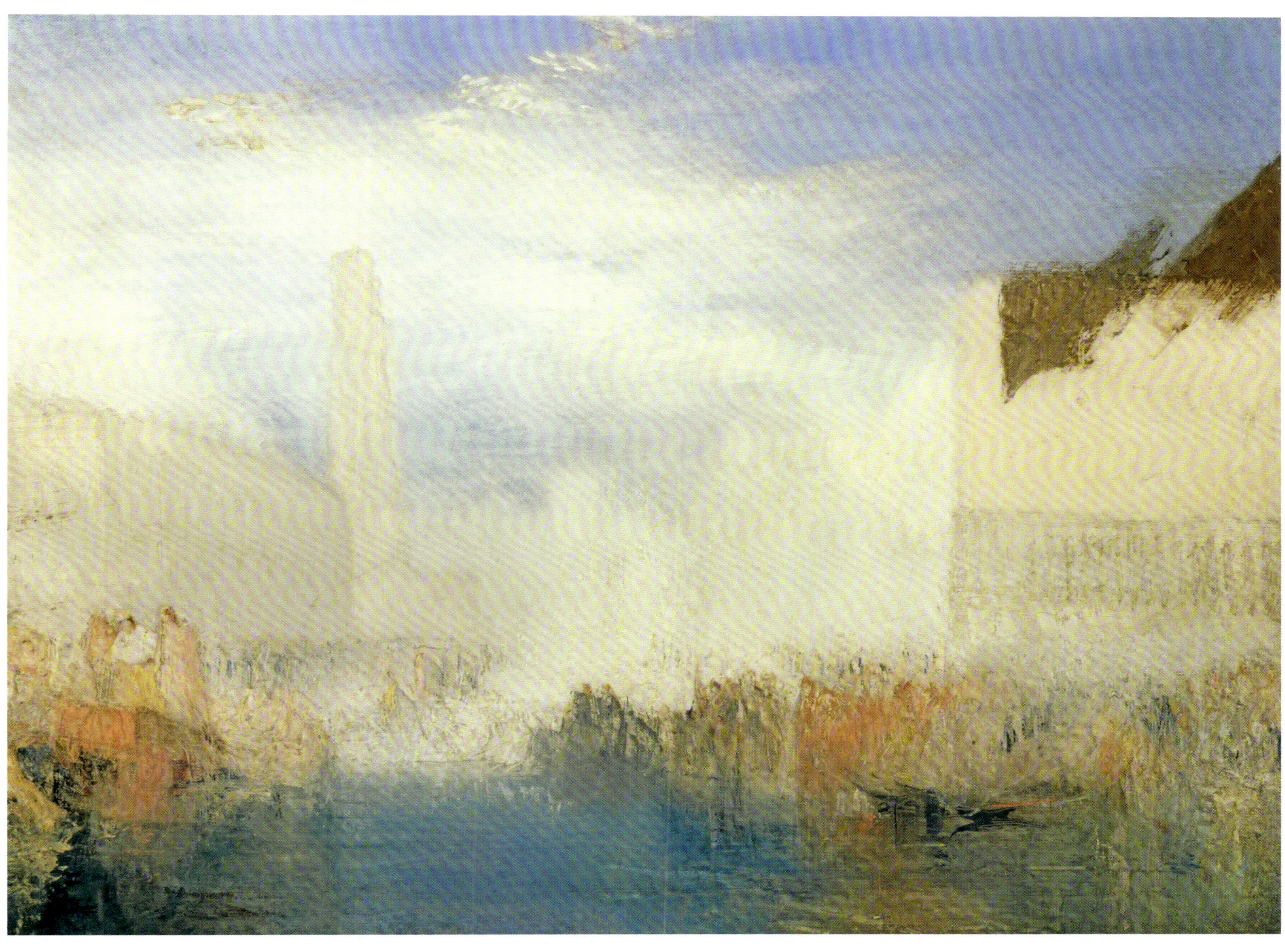

The Piazzetta, with the Ceremony of the Doge Marrying the Sea c.1835
Oil paint on canvas, 91.4 × 121.9 (detail, opposite)

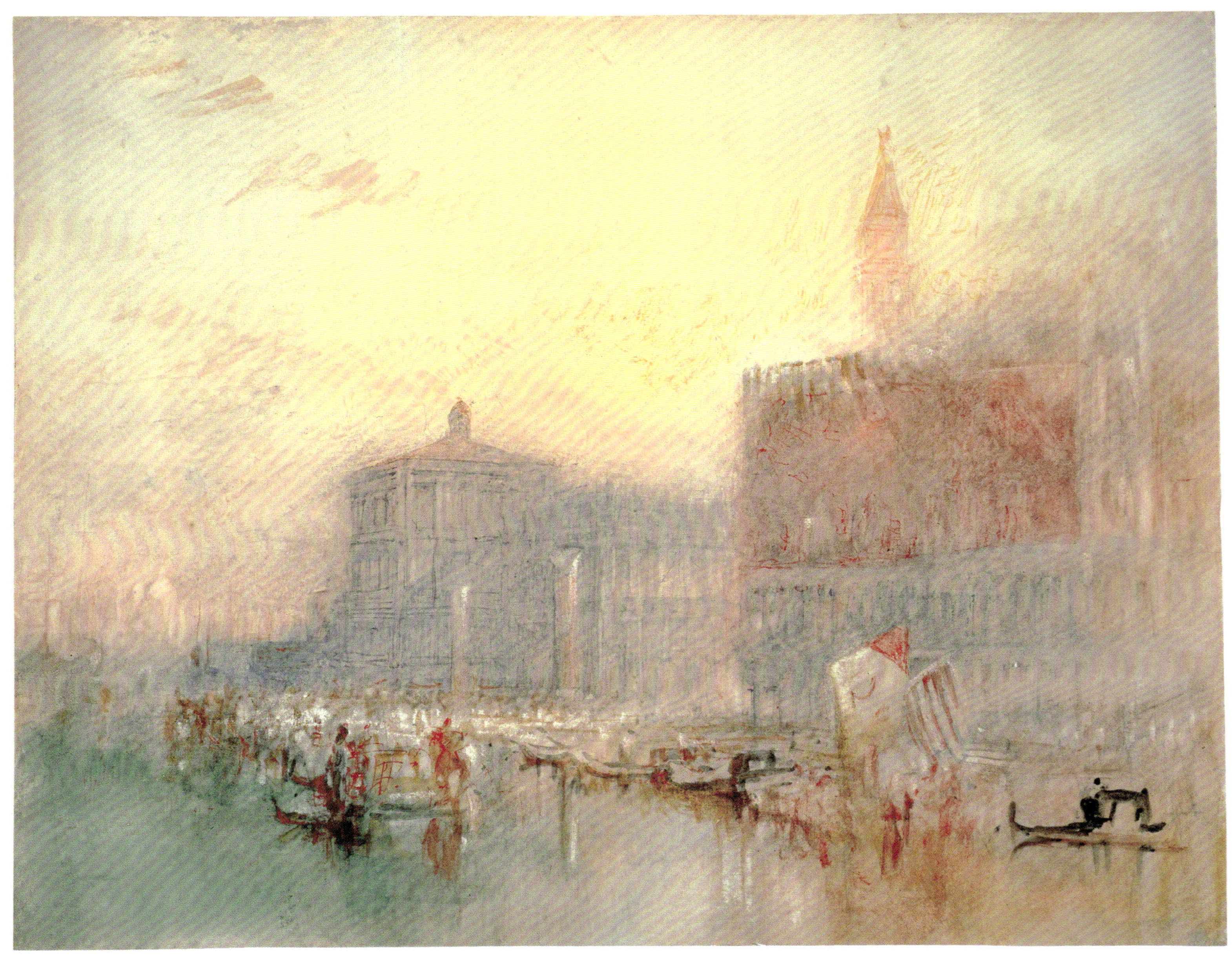

The Doge's Palace and Piazzetta c.1840
Watercolour, gouache and scraping-out on off-white paper, 24 × 30.3
National Gallery of Ireland, Dublin

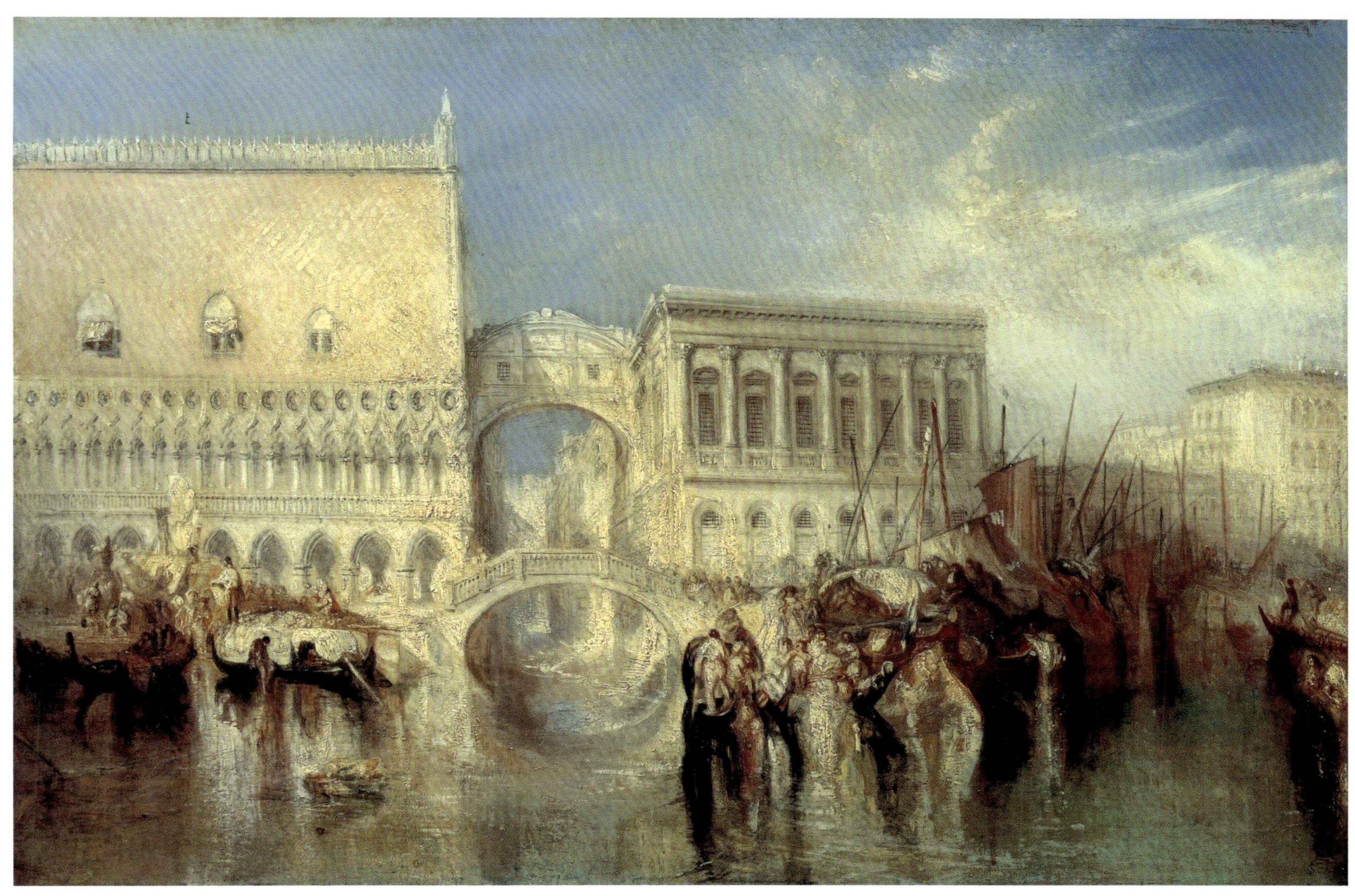

Venice, The Bridge of Sighs exhibited 1840
Oil paint on canvas, 68.6 × 91.4

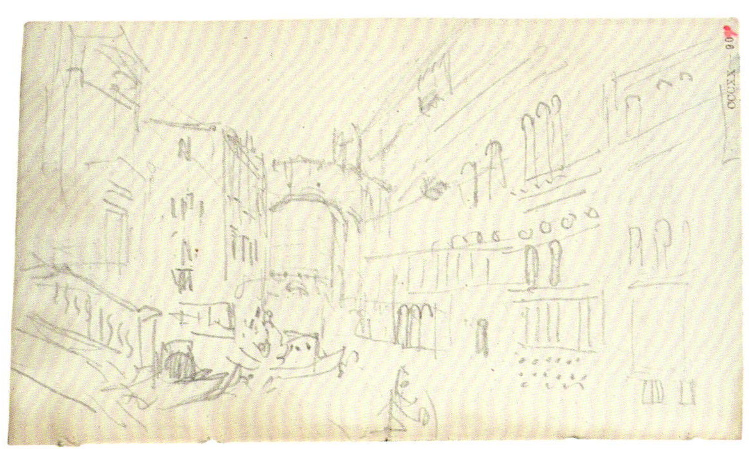

*The Bridge of Sighs from the Rio de Palazzo, with the Doge's Palace
to the right, and the Fondamenta Sant'Apolonia on the left*
from the Rotterdam to Venice Sketchbook 1840
Graphite on paper, 8.9 × 14.9

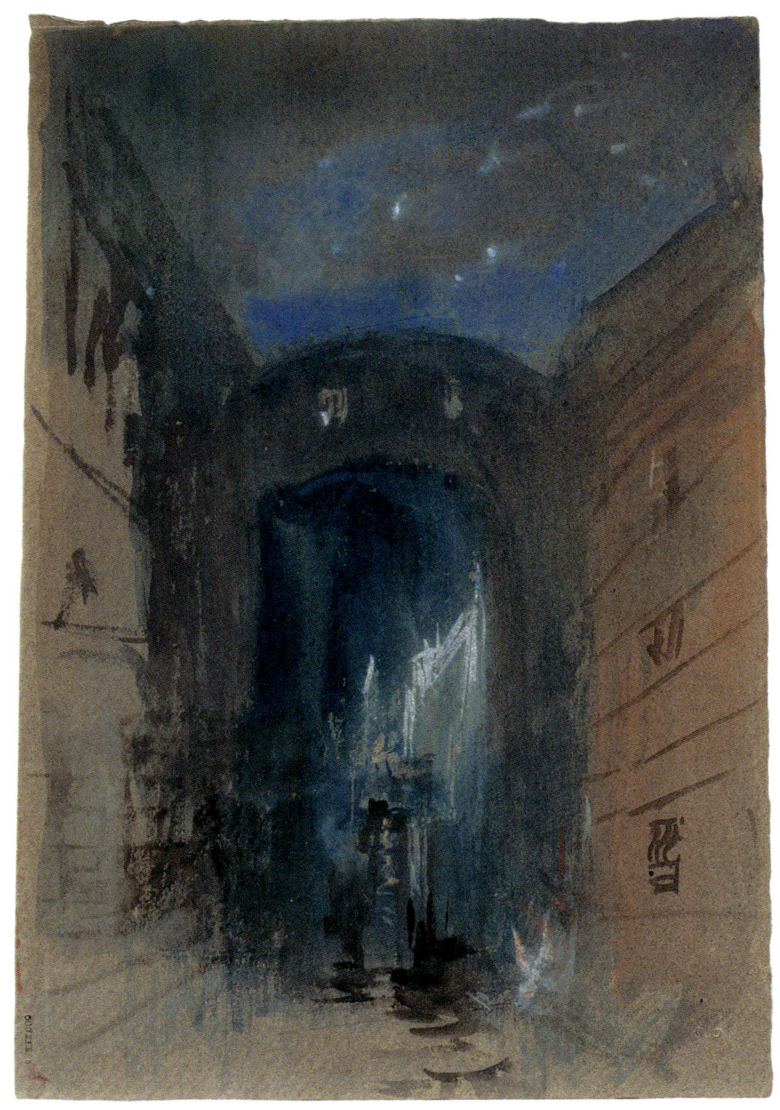

The Bridge of Sighs, Night 1840
Watercolour and gouache on grey-brown paper, 22.7 × 15.4

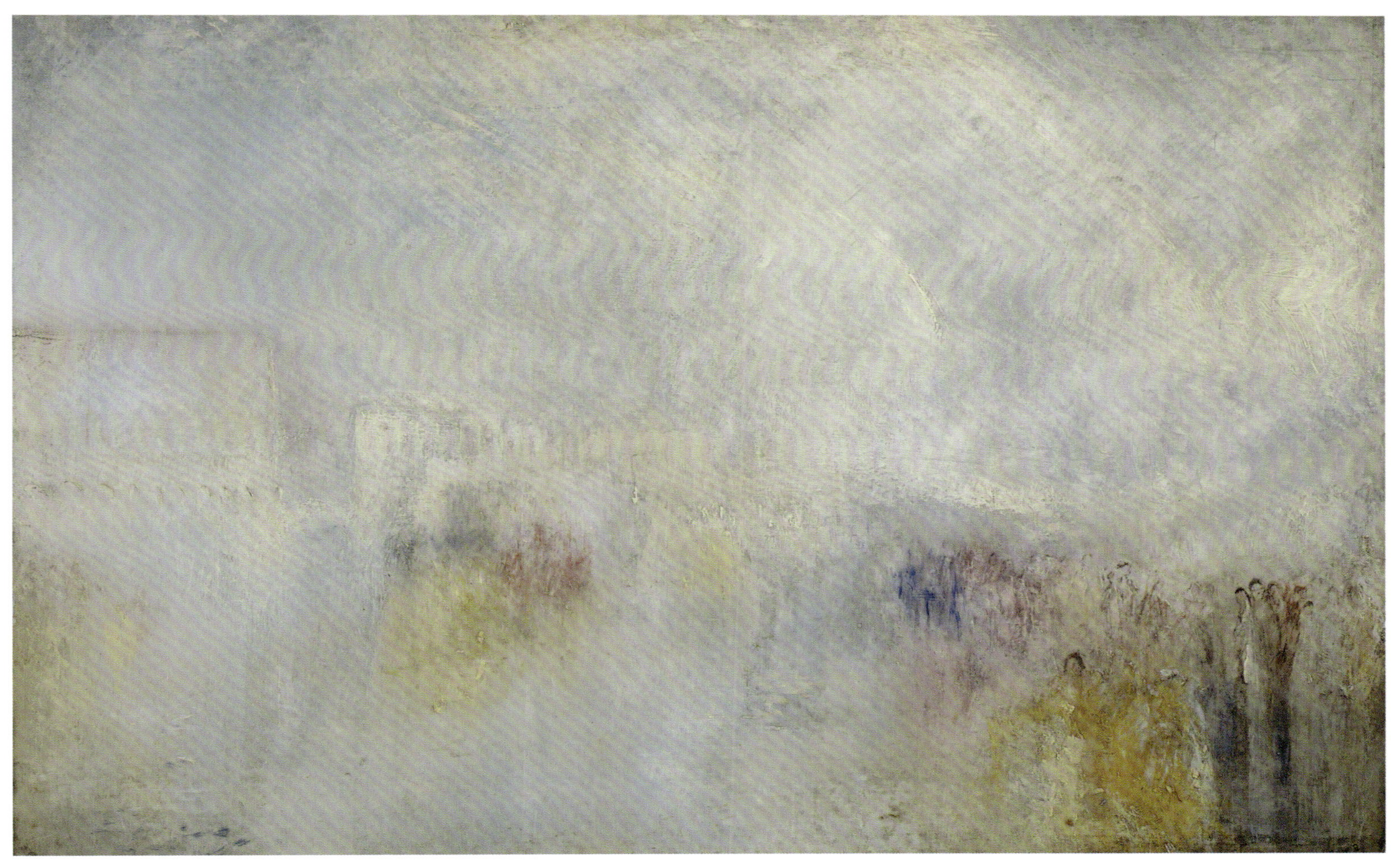

Riva degli Schiavone, Water Fête c.1845
Oil paint on canvas, 72.4 × 113

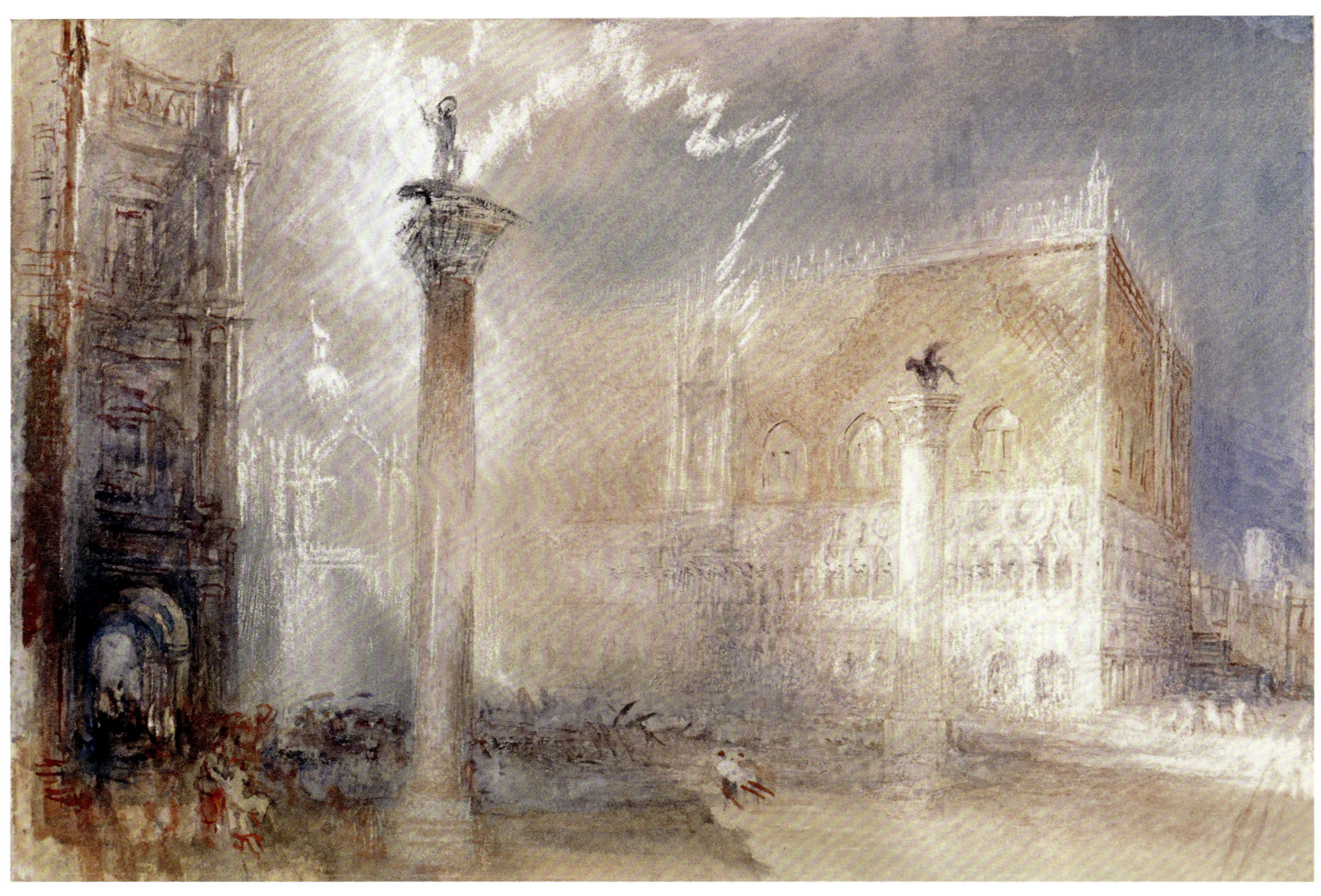

Lightning in the Piazzetta 1840
Watercolour and gouache with pen and scraping out on paper, 22.1 × 32.1
National Galleries Scotland, Edinburgh (detail, opposite)

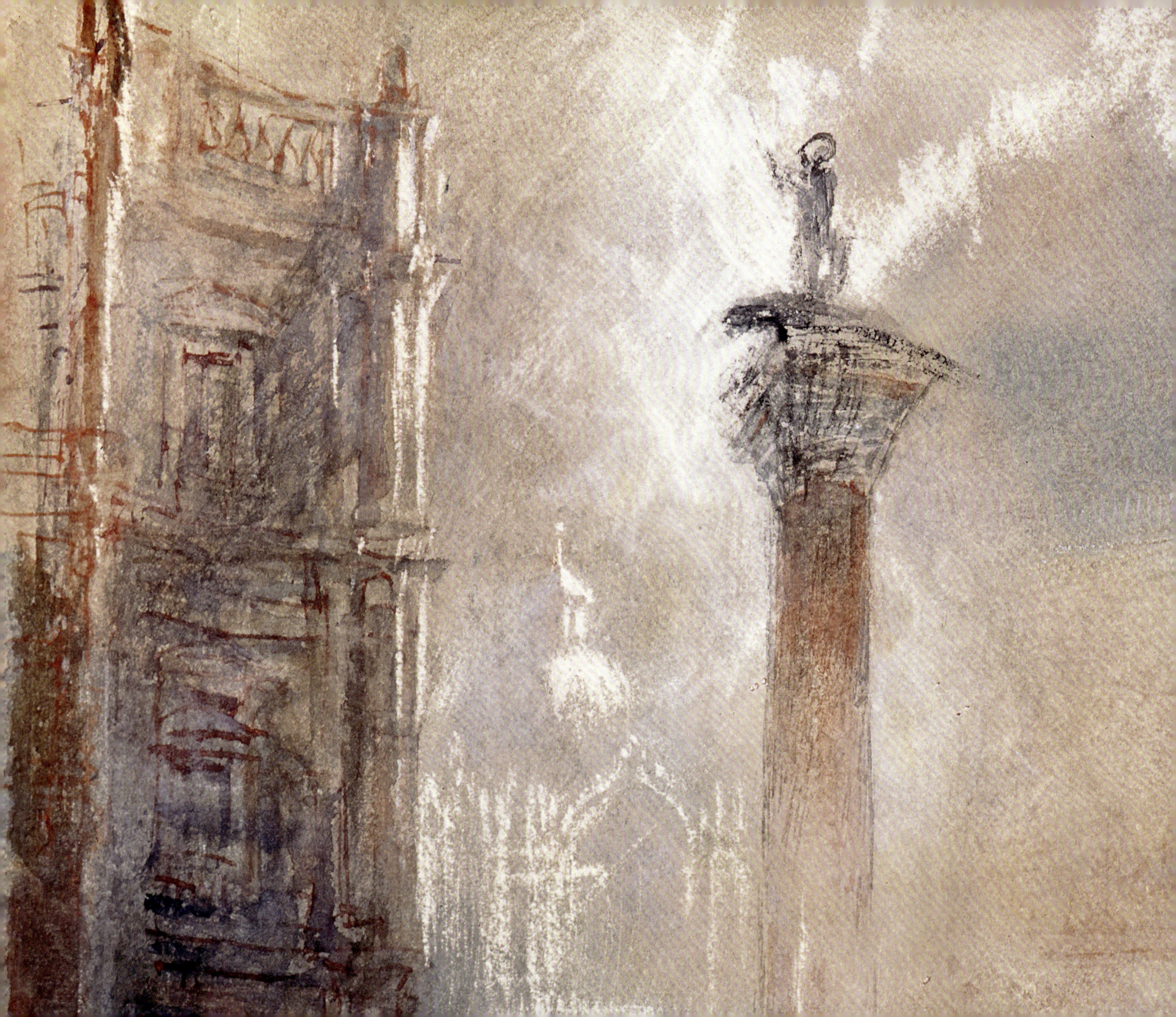

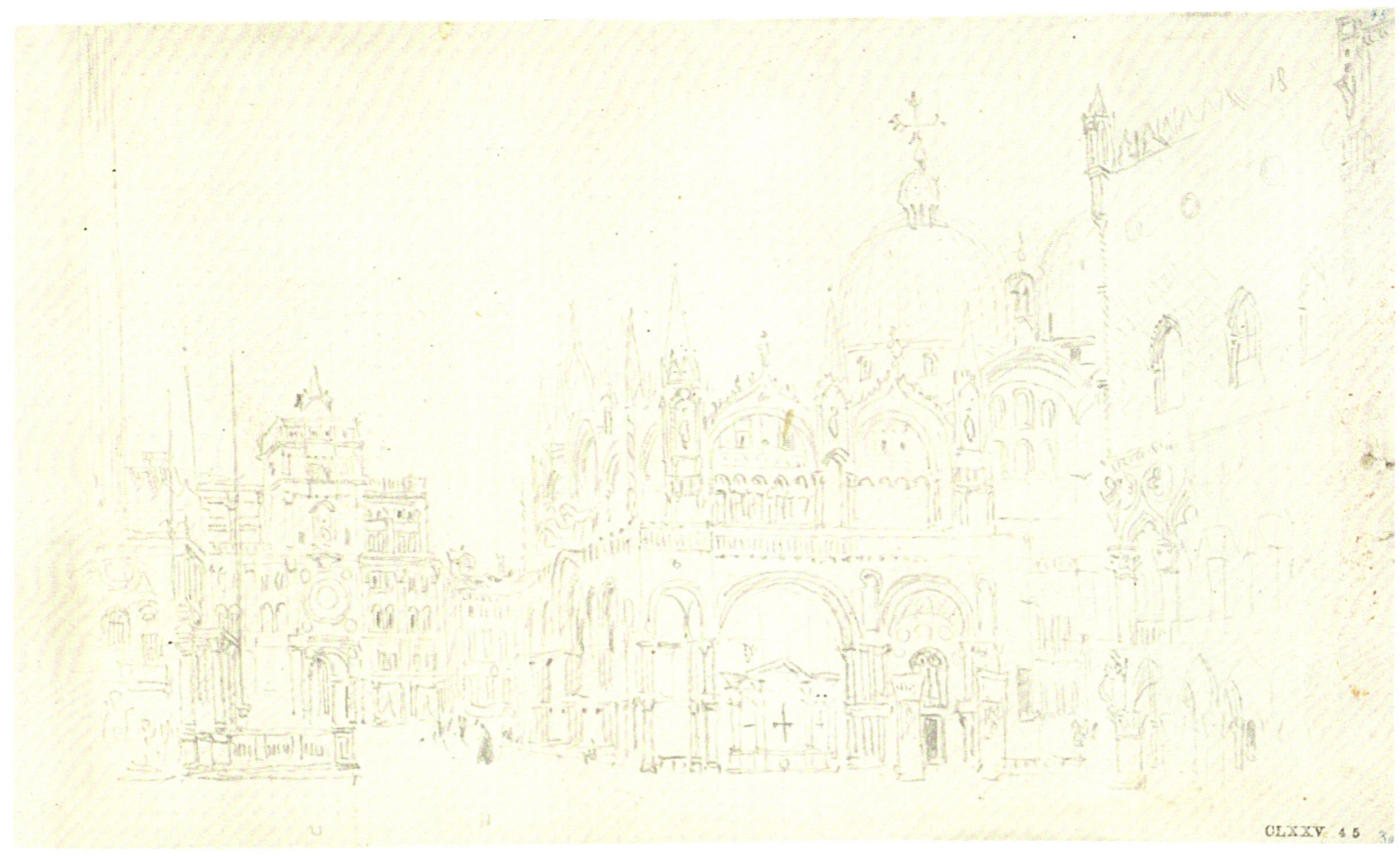

View from the Piazzetta, looking towards the Doge's Palace, the Basilica of San Marco and Torre d'Orologio, with the Flag Poles of the Piazza beyond the Loggetta of the Campanile from the Milan to Venice Sketchbook 1819
Graphite on paper, 11.2 × 18.5

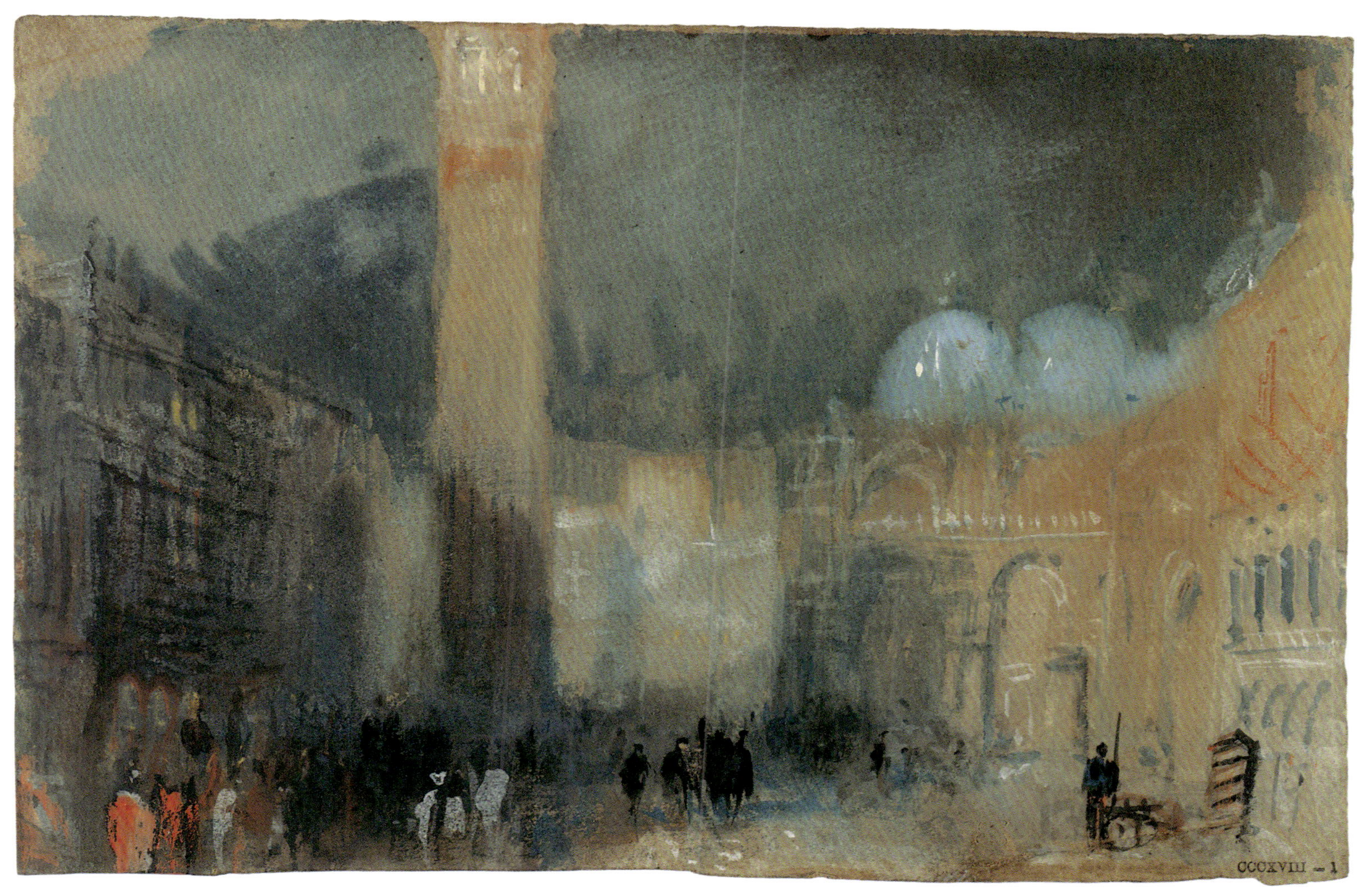

*The Piazzetta, with the Doge's Palace, looking towards San Marco
and its Campanile; Night* 1840
Watercolour and gouache on grey-brown paper, 15 × 22.8

*The Basilica of San Marco, with the
Piazzetta and the Campanile* from the
Milan to Venice Sketchbook 1819
Graphite on paper, 11.2 × 18.5

*The Loggetta of the Campanile, from
in front of the Basilica, looking into the
Piazzetta, with the Columns of San Marco
and Theodoric* from the Milan to Venice
Sketchbook 1819
Graphite on paper, 11.2 × 18.5

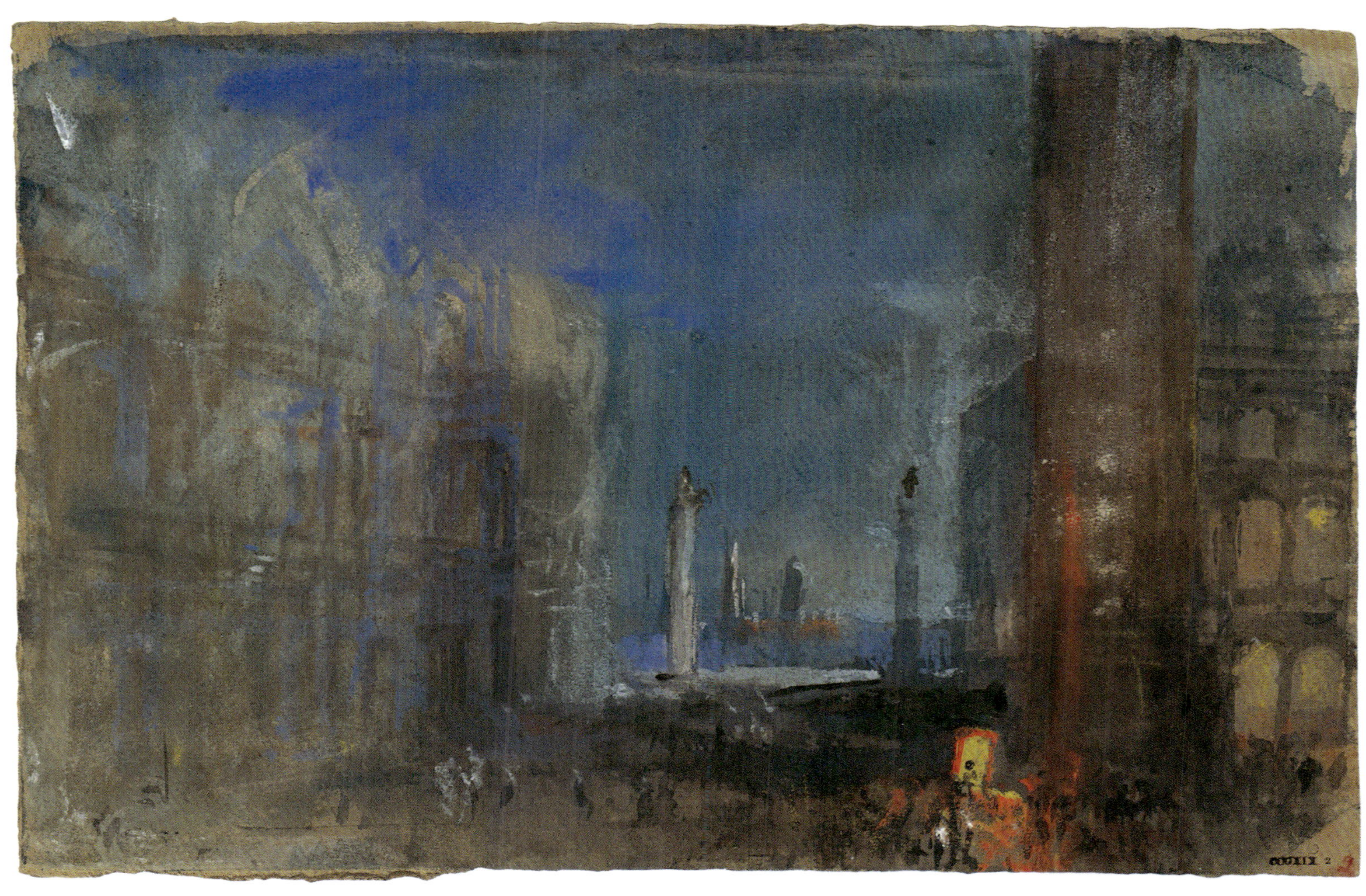

San Marco and the Piazzetta, with San Giorgio Maggiore, Night c.1840
Watercolour and gouache on grey-brown paper, 14.9 × 22.7

The Statues of Neptune and Mars at
the top of the Giants' Staircase in the
Courtyard of the Doge's Palace from the
Venice and Botzen Sketchbook 1840
Graphite on paper, 12.3 × 17.3

The Northern End of the Courtyard
of the Doge's Palace, with the Arco
Foscari, the Giants' Staircase, and the
Domes of San Marco from the Venice
Sketchbook 1833
Graphite on paper, 10.9 × 20.3

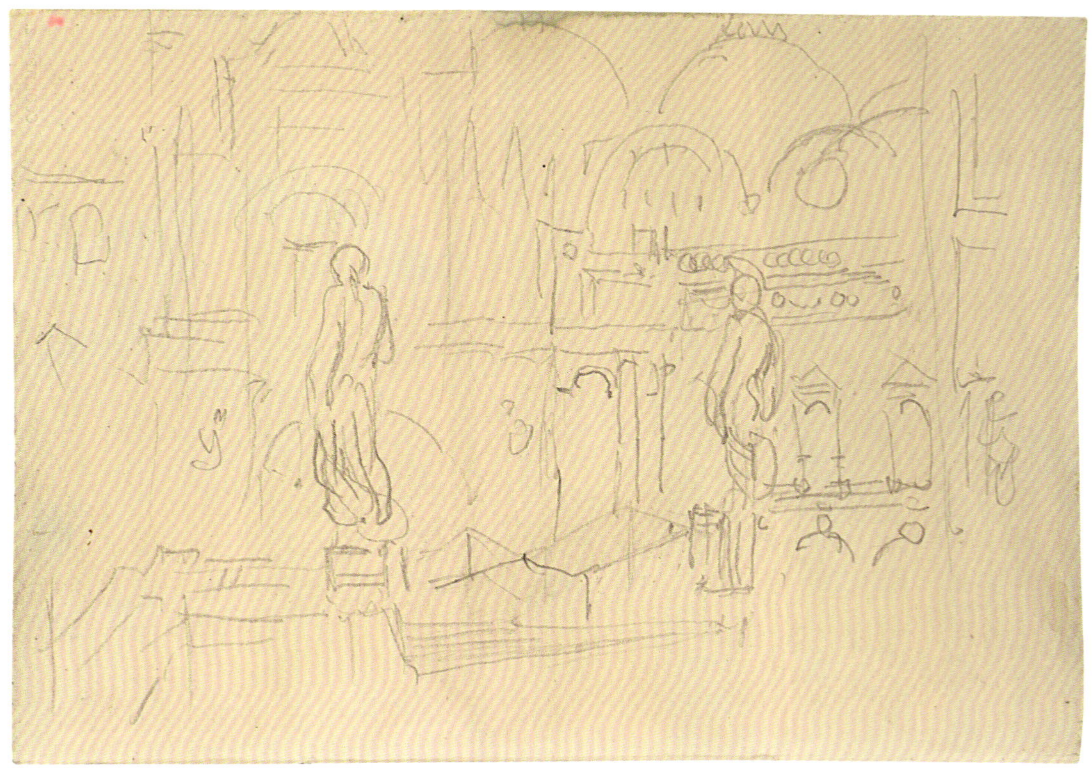

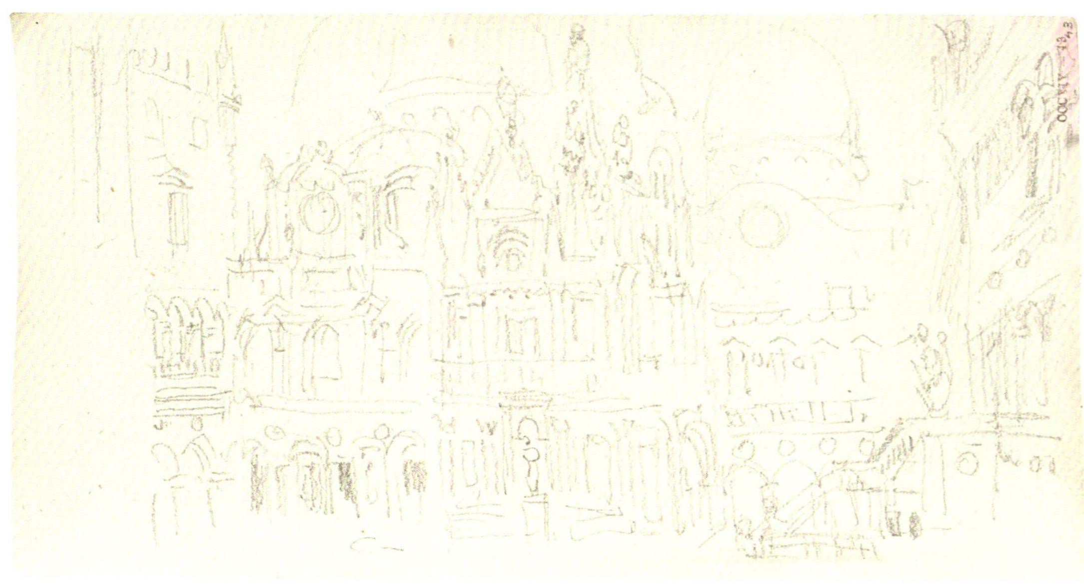

The Porta della Carta, Doge's Palace ?1833/1840
Graphite, watercolour and gouache
on buff paper, 30.5 × 23.4

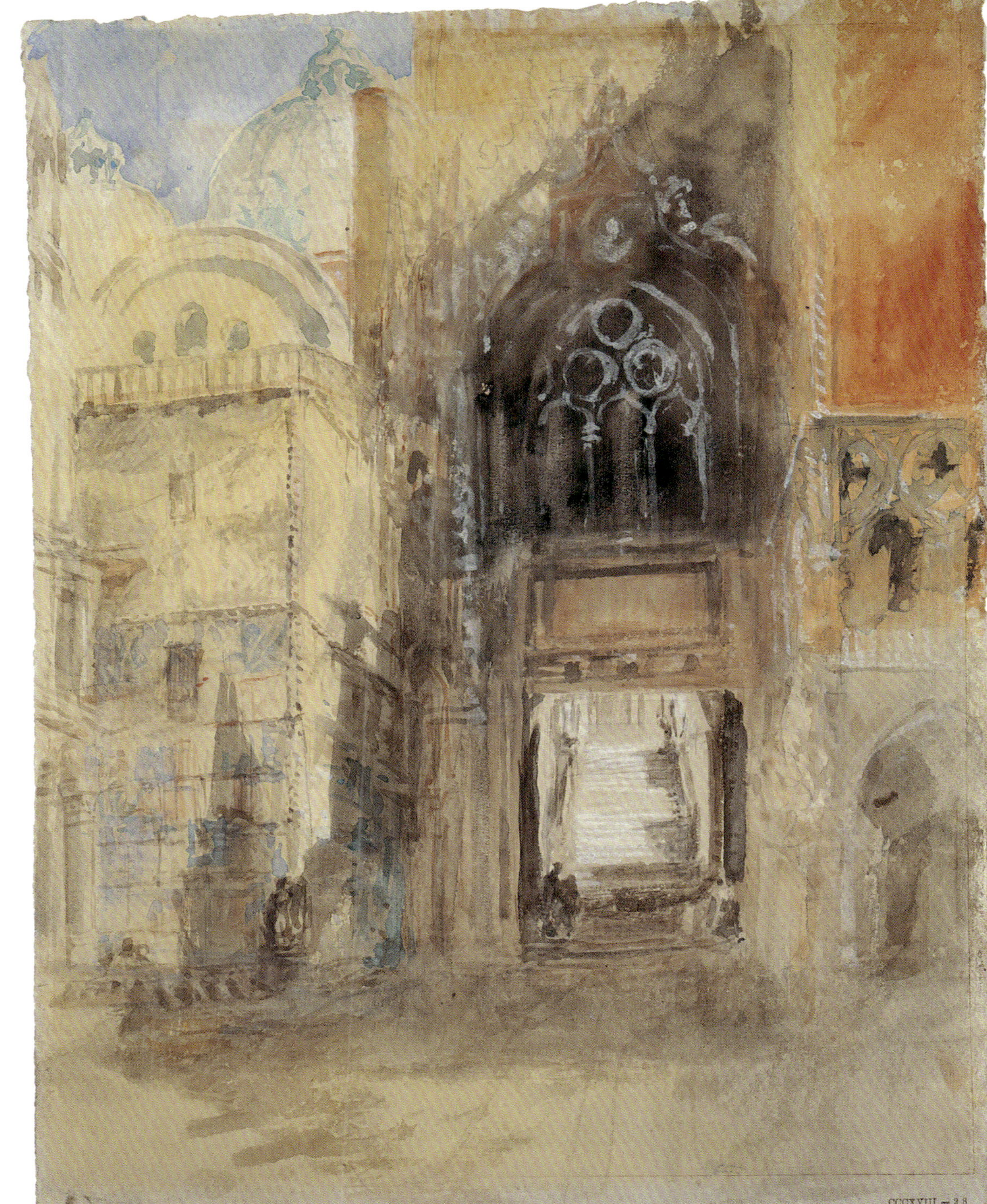

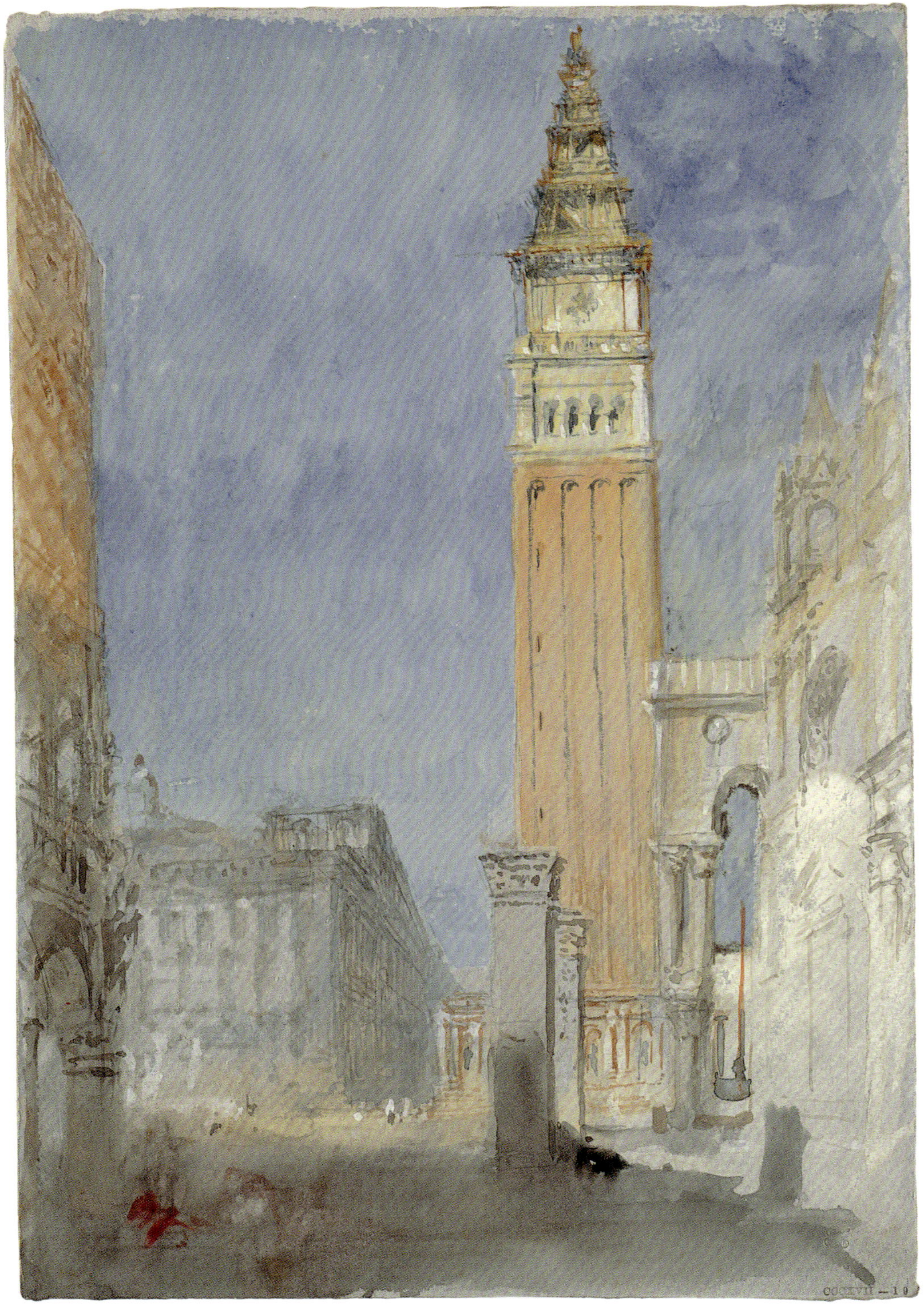

*The Campanile of San Marco, with the Pilastri
Acritani, from the Porta della Carta* 1840
Graphite, watercolour and gouache on grey paper,
28.2 × 19.1

*The Campanile of San Marco framed by the
Arches of a Palace* c.1840
Watercolour and gouache on grey-brown paper,
14.8 × 22.6

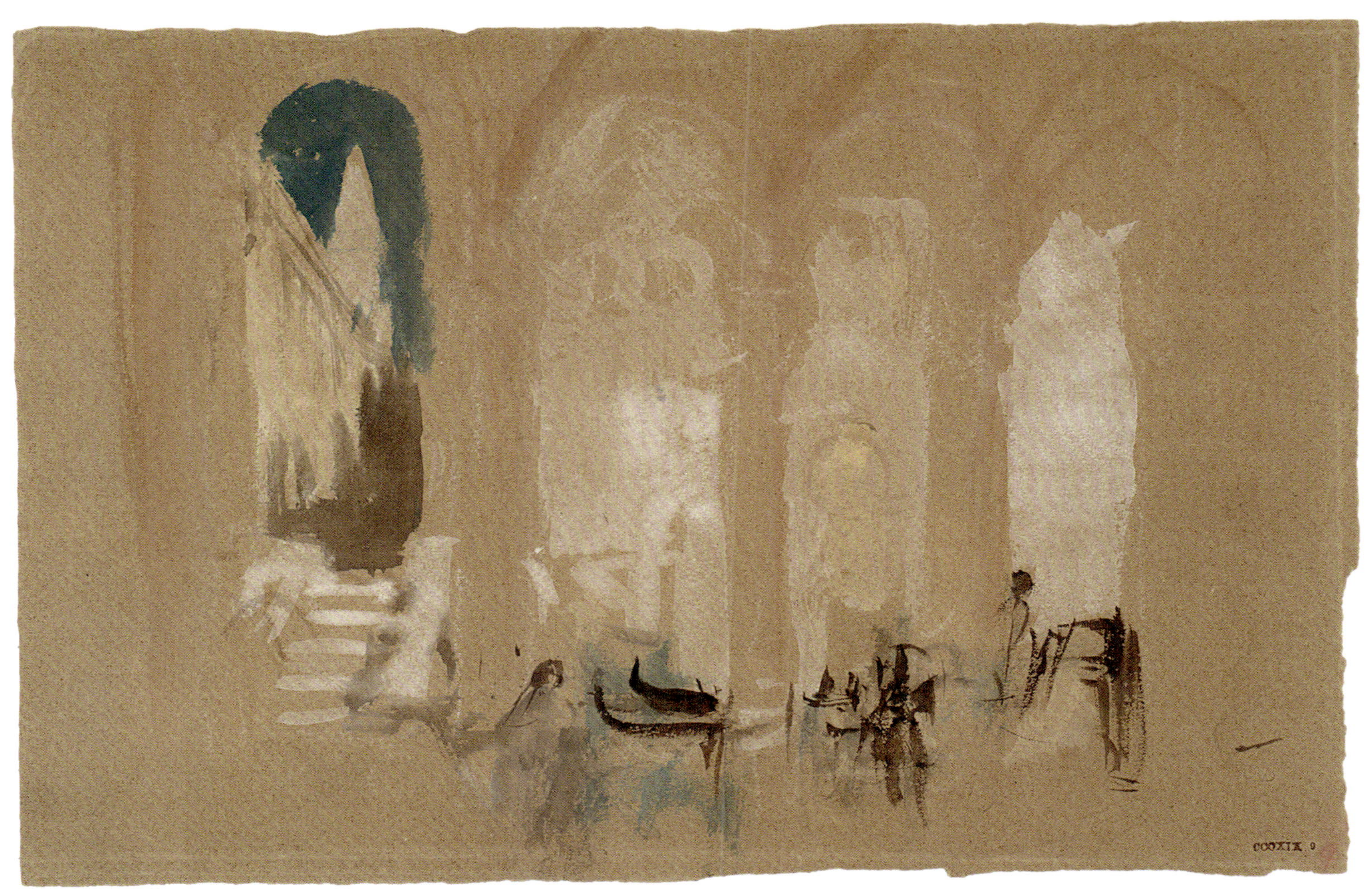

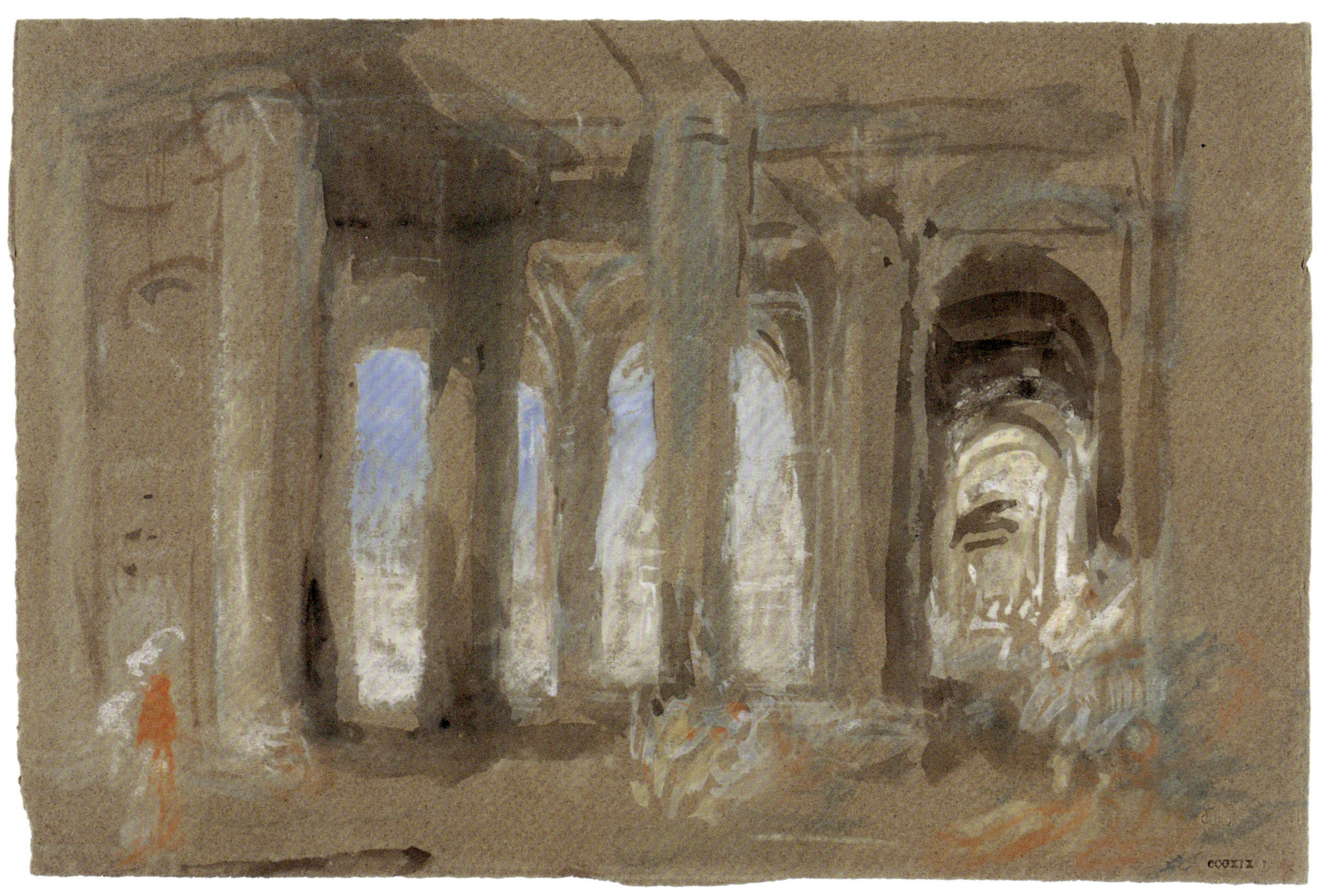

The Arcades of the Procuratie Nuove and the Palazzo Reale,
with the Piazza beyond c.1840
Watercolour and gouache on grey-brown paper, 15.5 × 22.4

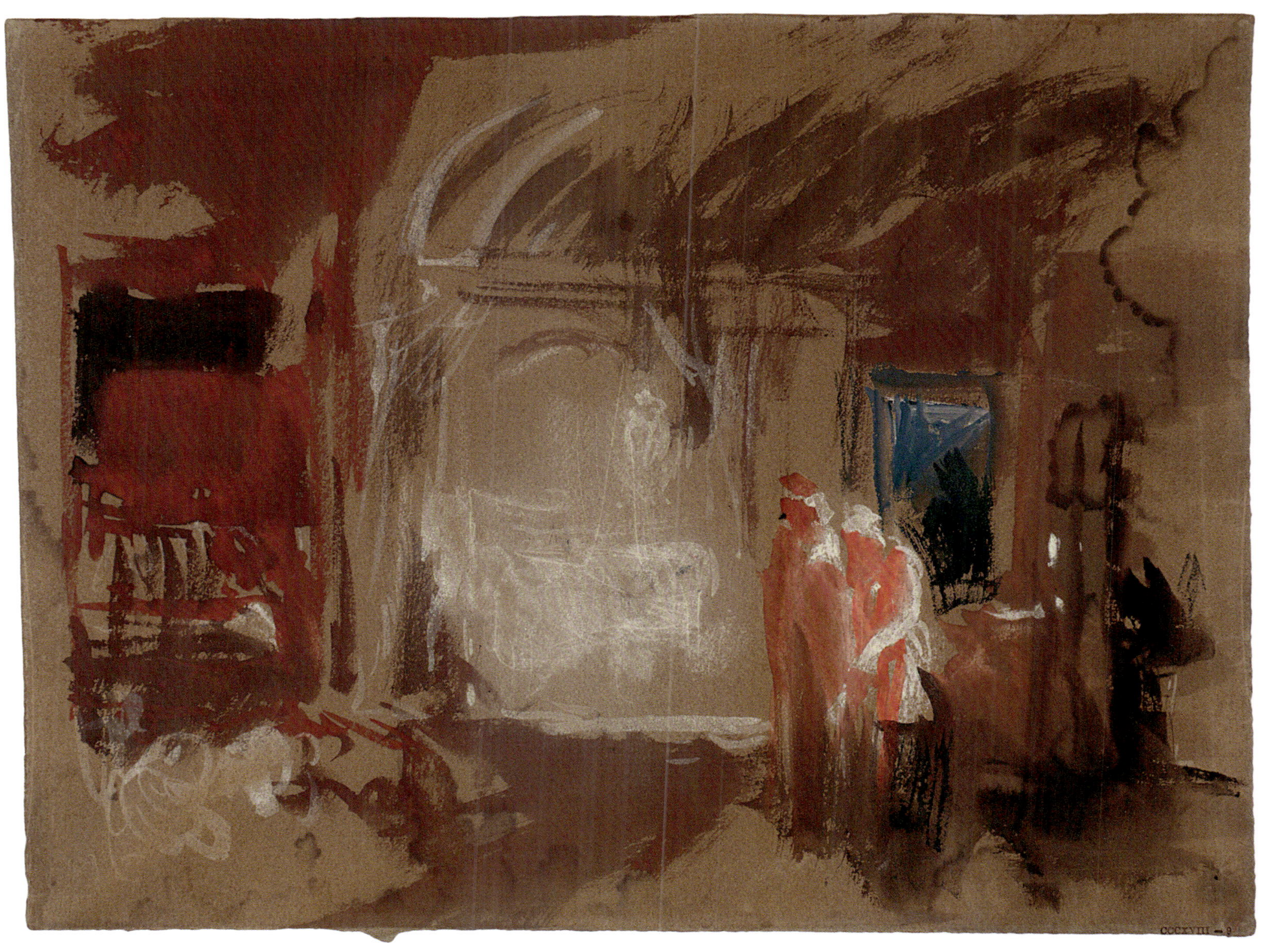

An Interior with Figures 1840
Watercolour and gouache on brown paper, 22.6 × 29.5

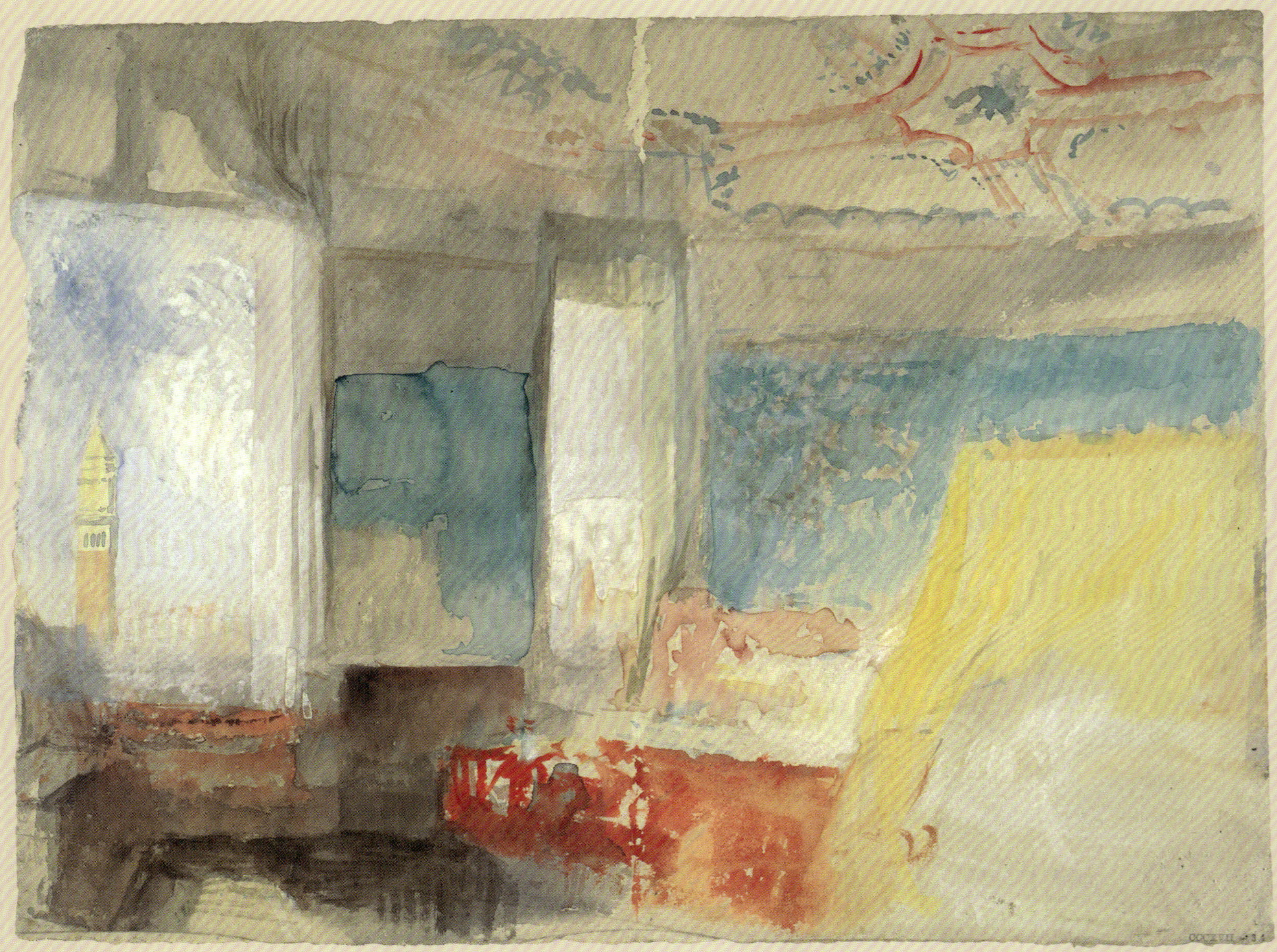

30

From the Hotel Europa

Location is crucial in any city. But in Venice where you stay can sometimes determine whether the city fully enchants you. Assuming Turner followed the advice he had absorbed from James Hakewill, he seems likely to have resided on his first trip at the Albergo Leon Bianco (the 'White Lion'), near the Rialto. The hotel's proximity to the markets at the heart of the city provided a colourful outlook, with an endless variety of vessels unloading diverse, often unfamiliar, produce from all over the Mediterranean and beyond.

Could the Rialto area perhaps have been too dynamic for Turner; too reminiscent of his childhood home in bustling Covent Garden? Judging by the extent of what he produced on his two later visits, he appears to have been more temperamentally suited to the lodgings he secured at the Hotel Europa (Grande Albergo l'Europa, then established in the palace known as Ca' Giustinian), facing the customs house, the Dogana da Mare, at the mouth of the Grand Canal. (Until recently, a later Hotel Europa operated in the Palazzo Tiepolo opposite Santa Maria della Salute; it was relaunched in 2019 as the St Regis.) The Europa was obviously a prestigious type of accommodation; in fact, during Turner's 1833 visit François-René, Vicomte de Chateaubriand also resided there. Putting considerations of comfort and status aside, Turner was no doubt principally drawn to the hotel by its wonderful location, looking across the Bacino towards the islands of San Giorgio Maggiore and Giudecca. He had actually discovered and sketched the enticing prospect during his first visit in 1819 (pp.50, 64). You can reach this view via the Calle del Ridotto, behind the church of San Moisè.

Turner's childlike sense of wonder and excitement about his new lodgings is vividly preserved in the panoramic watercolour he made of his very grand bedroom, with its billowing bed curtains and flamboyant stucco ceiling decoration. Located high in the Ca' Giustinian, he was – just possibly – able to glimpse simultaneously the bell-towers of San Marco and San Giorgio Maggiore through the tall eastward-facing windows (perhaps with the assistance of a little artistic license). On a practical note, an airy room of this kind was an ideal space in which to work up his sketches in watercolour.

Just as significantly, the elevated viewpoint delivered an unfamiliar and privileged vantage point across the rooftops of the city – a fantastical chimney-scape. Turner could also peer into the adjacent buildings and witness everyday life. As well as watching the playful peek-a-boo games of the neighbouring children, he observed women relaxing in the privacy of their homes. The romance of this insight into Venetian life was coupled for Turner with the enduring appeal of traditional nocturnal revelry, most notably the city's carnival (which had been outlawed from 1797, once Venice fell under Austrian rule). These highly charged ideas stimulated his well-known view of the Piazza, exhibited in 1836 as *Juliet and her Nurse*, which features festive crowds milling around and watching open-air entertainments, during a celebratory firework display (p.35). Improbably, however, he added to the foreground Shakespeare's heroine Juliet, along with her nurse, transporting them from their native Verona. This was just one aspect of the atmospheric image that led critics to mock the painting.

Turner's Bedroom in the Ca' Giustinian (The Hotel Europa) ?1833/1840
Watercolour and gouache on buff paper, 23 × 30.2

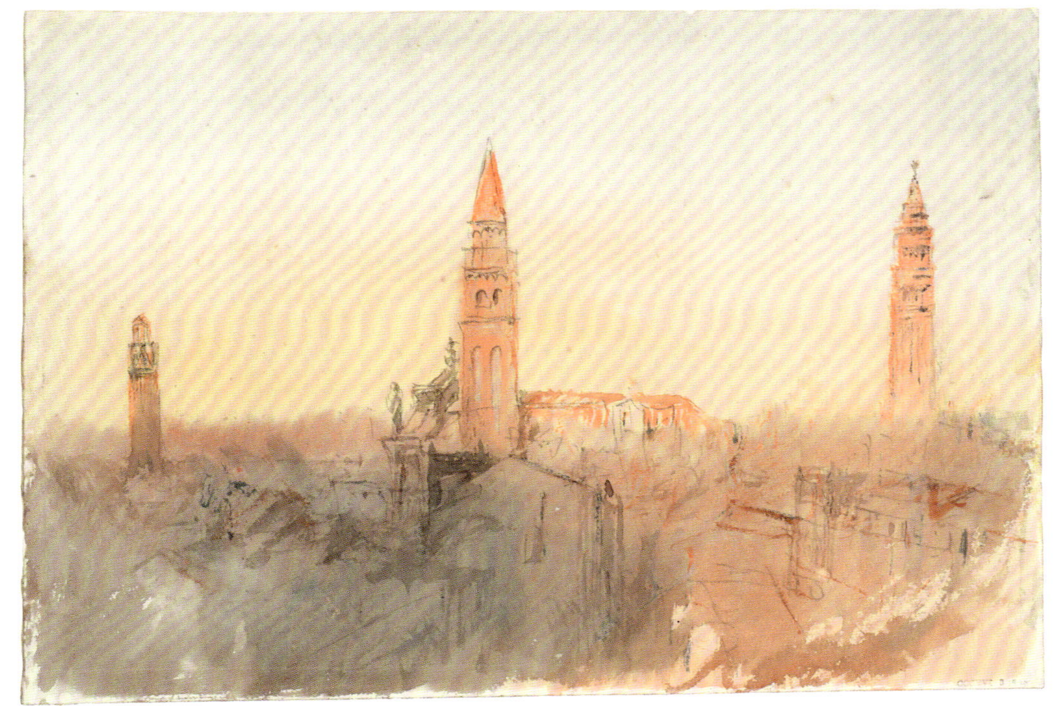

*The Campanili of Santo Stefano, San Moisè
and San Marco (St Mark's), Venice, from the
Hotel Europa (Palazzo Giustinian)* 1840
Graphite, watercolour and gouache on paper,
19.8 × 28.2

*The Ca' Giustinian (the Hotel Europa) and
other palaces on the Grand Canal, with the
Campanile of San Moisè* from the Venice
Sketchbook 1833
Graphite on paper, 10.9 × 20.3

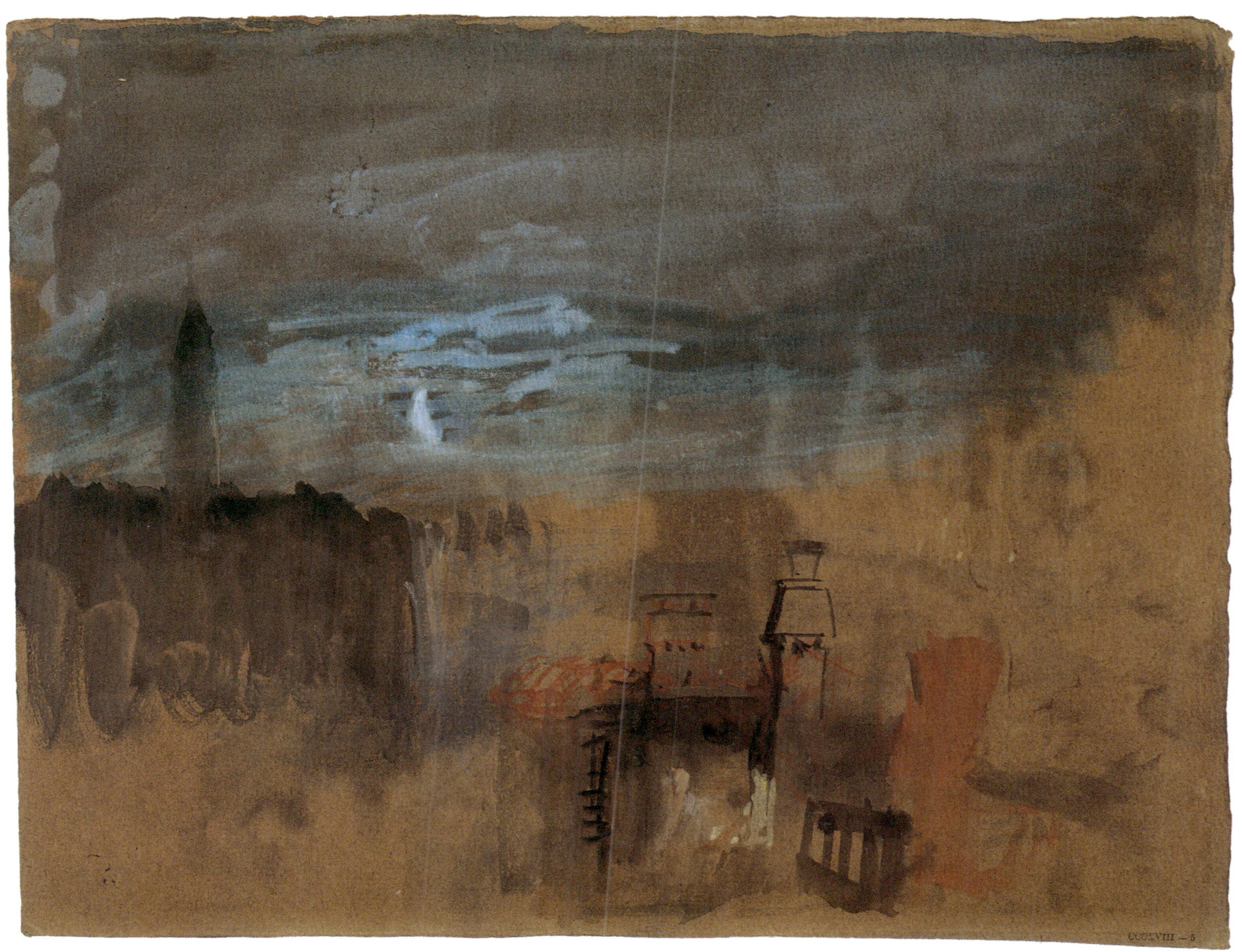

*The Campanile of San Marco from the Roof of the
Hotel Europa: Moonlight* c.1840
Watercolour and gouache on brown paper, 24.2 × 30.7

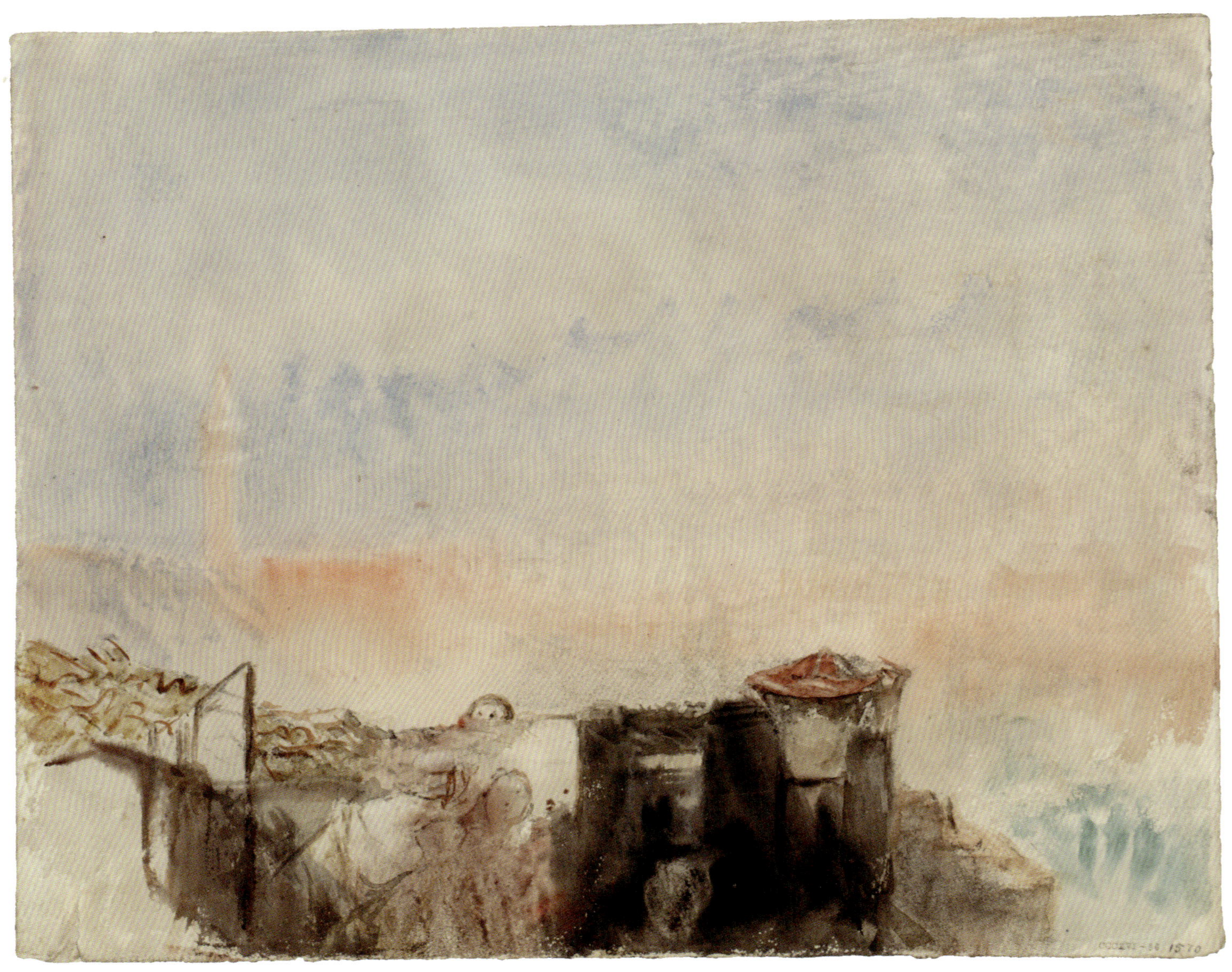

*Among the Chimney-pots above Venice; the Roof of the Hotel Europa
with the Campanile of San Marco* 1840
Graphite, watercolour and gouache on paper, 24.5 × 30.6

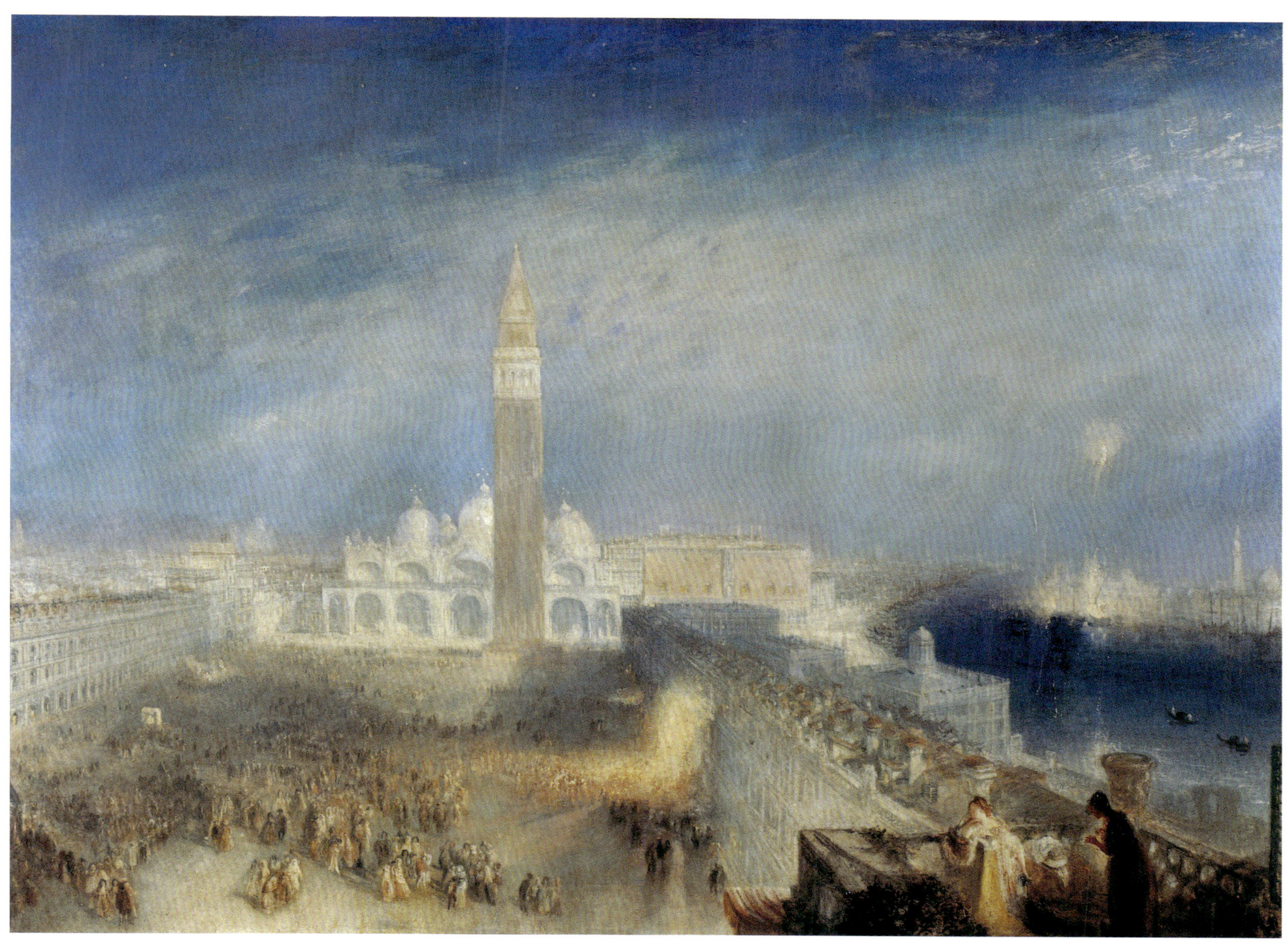

Juliet and her Nurse exhibited 1836
Oil paint on canvas, 88 × 121
Colección de Arte Amalia Lacroze de Fortabat, Buenos Aires

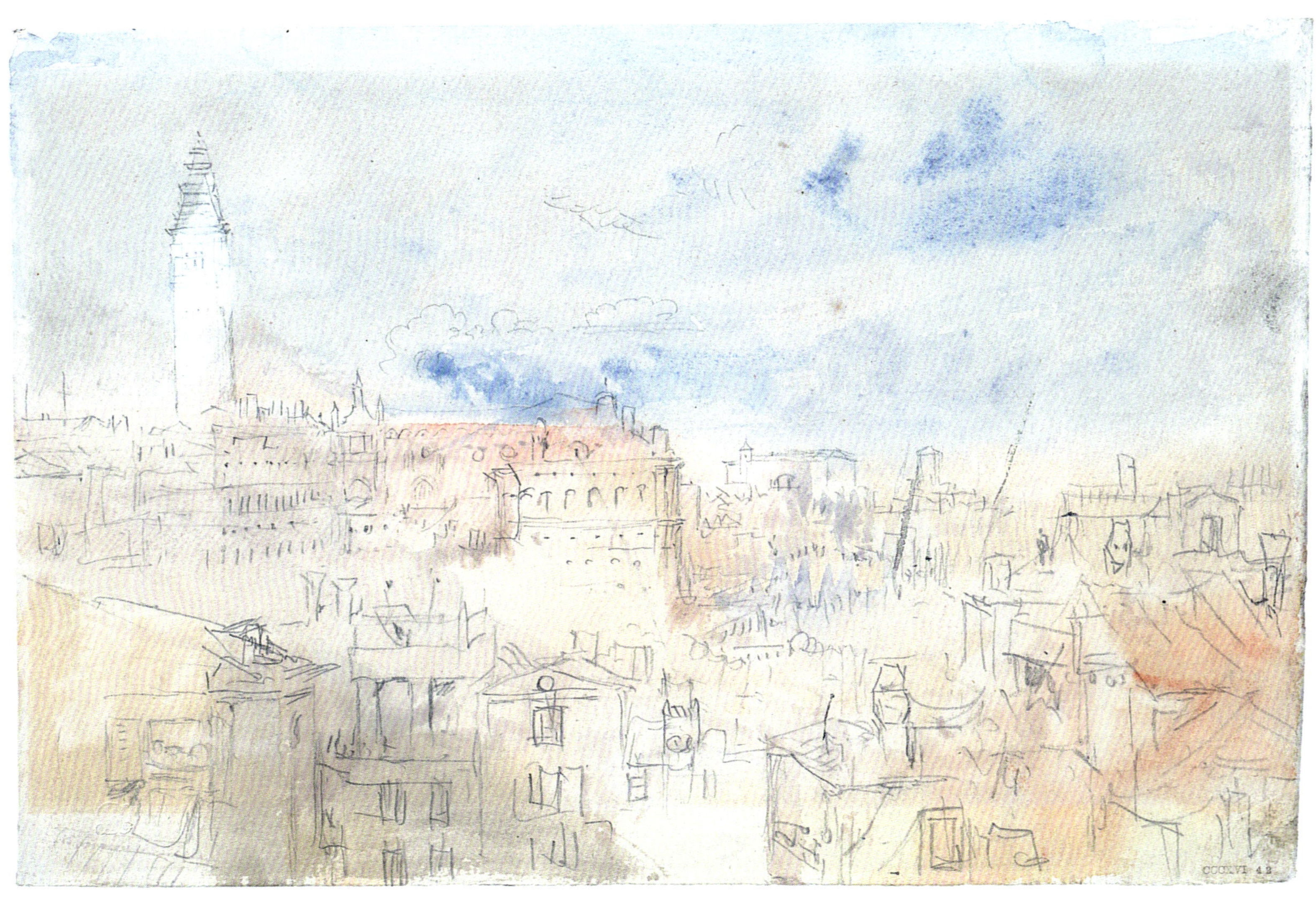

View over the Rooftops towards the Giardini Reali and the Campanile of San Marco 1840
Graphite, watercolour and gouache on paper, 19.3 × 28

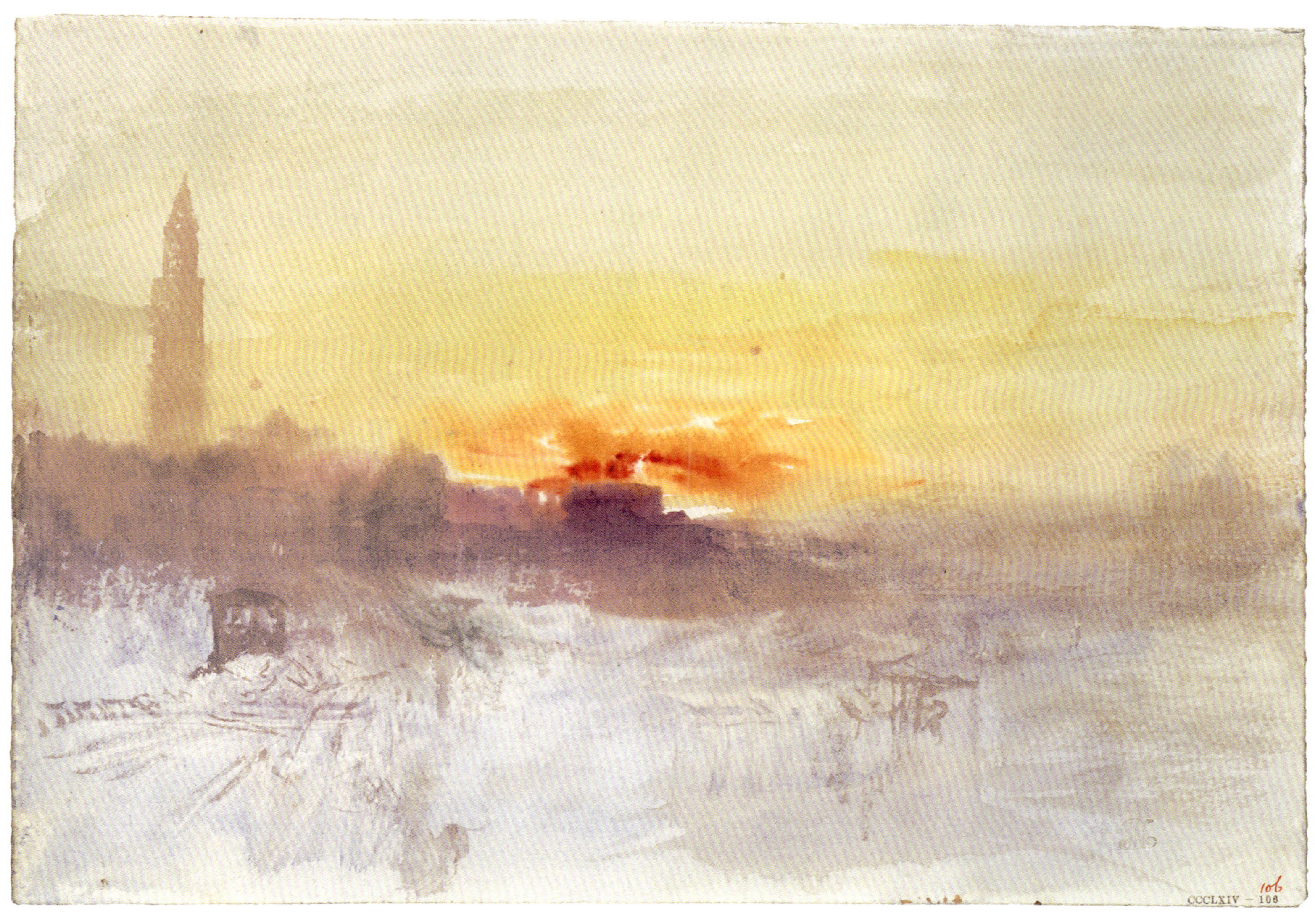

Venice at Sunrise, from the Hotel Europa, with Campanile of San Marco 1840
Watercolour on paper, 19.8 × 28

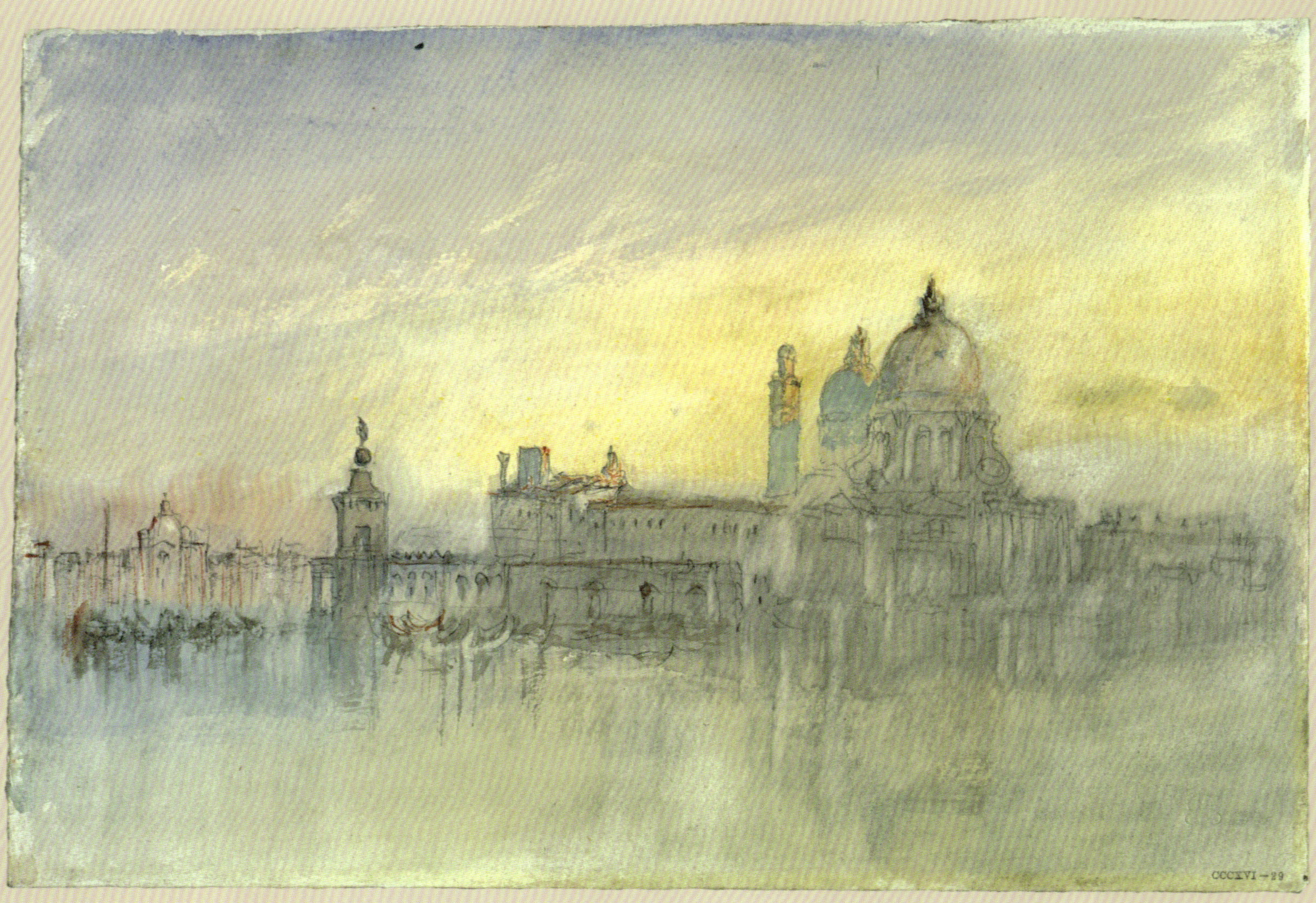

CCCXVI — 29

The Bacino and San Giorgio Maggiore

Without even having to leave the steps of the Hotel Europa, Turner had one of the finest views of Venice, looking out over the wide, deep anchorage of the Bacino di San Marco. Here visiting schooners and brigs had to register on arrival, while not far away, on the long quayside known as the Riva degli Schiavoni, the local fishing fleet secured their *bragozzi* and *sandolos*, both typical vessels of the Venetian Lagoon. Whereas this watery arena had been the focus of grand pageantry in the eighteenth century, for Turner the spectacle of the Bacino was all about light.

Turner's dazzling vista was framed on the right by the Dogana da Mar directly opposite, with the church of Santa Maria della Salute a short distance up the Grand Canal. To the left Turner could see the waterfront bordering the gardens running along to the Molo and the Doge's Palace; and behind all that the Riva degli Schiavoni tapered off into the Castello district. Across the waters, beyond the Dogana, he could see the dome of the Zitelle (part of a suppressed convent) on the Giudecca. However, all eyes are inevitably pulled towards the southern edge of the Bacino, where the great monastery church of San Giorgio Maggiore, designed by Andrea Palladio (1508–1580), miraculously emerges from its own reflection, to perfectly crown the setting.

From the Europa outlook, San Giorgio's elegant campanile stands to the left, slightly separate from the main church, with its pearly dome and grand marble façade. The interaction of these elements of the church captivated Turner as he wandered sketching along the city's waterfront, or as he was ferried back and forth over the Bacino. In his sketchbooks, the positions of dome, tower and façade shift around, as though they have danced across the pages. Despite having scrutinised these motifs intensely in 1819, he continued to study them on two subsequent visits, fixing in his mind's eye the relationships between the parts and charting the daily transformation of the stone and bricks as the sun made its passage above. In one anecdote, as the sinking sun illuminated the façade of San Giorgio with a warm coral glow, another British painter called William Callow spied Turner still hard at work sketching. Ashamed at having himself already given up for the day, despite being considerably less than half Turner's age, Callow could only marvel at such dedication.

During Turner's first experience of Venice, he evidently struggled to make sense of the incomparable panoramic spectacle seen from the Bacino. His sketchbooks frequently contain compositions that jump from page to page (and sometimes extend to further sheets) in order to encompass the great landmarks surrounding the ceremonial heart of the city. In much the same way that he stalked San Giorgio from all angles, it was one thing to recognise from earlier depictions the most celebrated individual architectural features; but it was much more complicated to understand how they worked in ensembles seen from a variety of viewpoints. A further influence on Turner's panoramic approach was the popularity of large painted presentations that immersed viewers in a 360-degree experience of a significant setting. Prior to leaving London for Venice, Turner may have seen the latest of these, showing the Piazza San Marco, by Messrs Barker and Burford.

The Punta della Dogana and Santa Maria della Salute at Twilight, from the Hotel Europa 1840
Graphite, watercolour and pen and ink on paper, 19.4 × 28

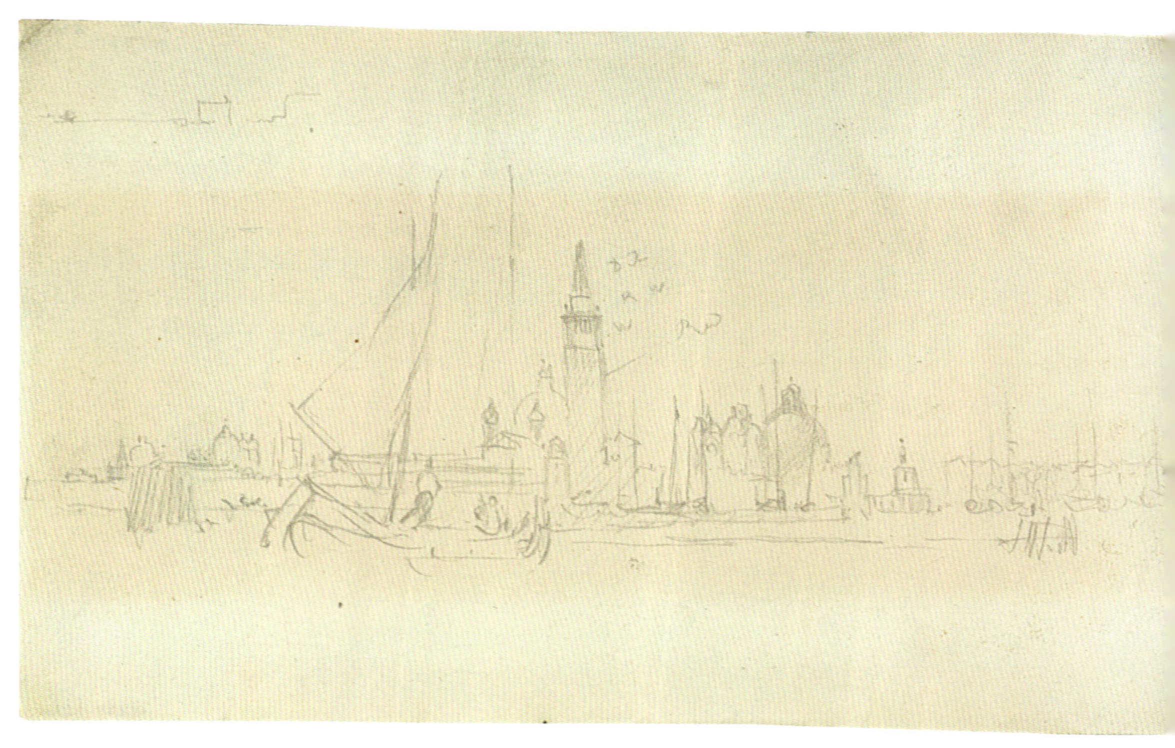

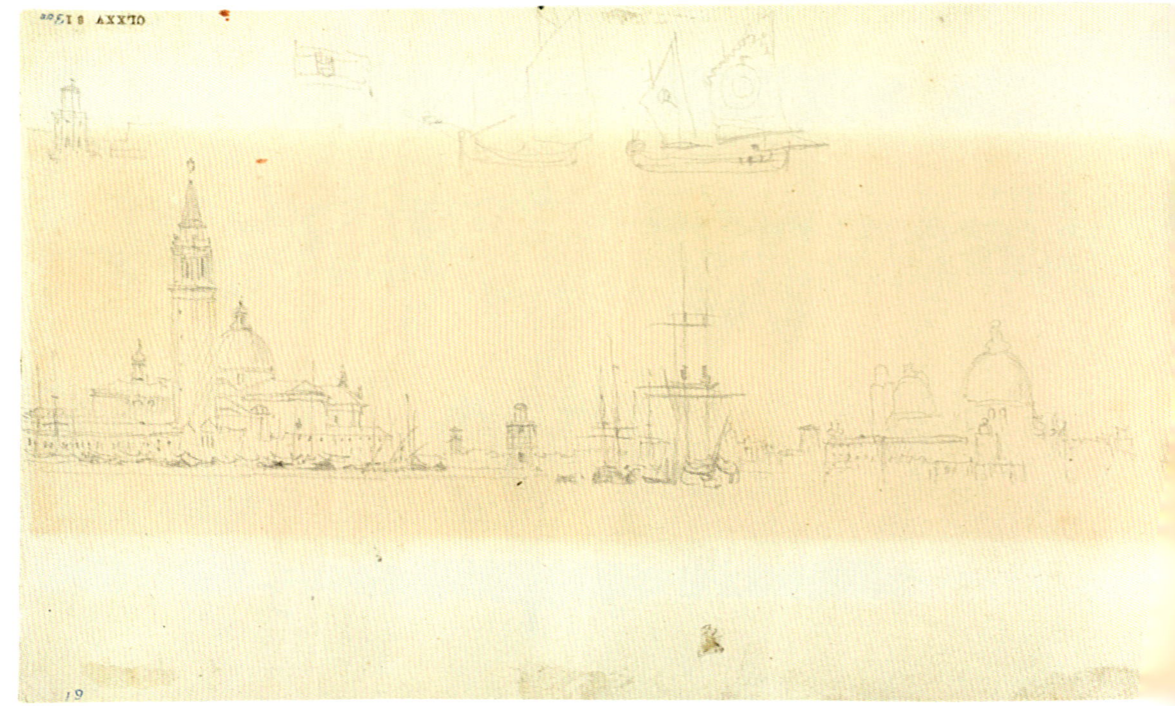

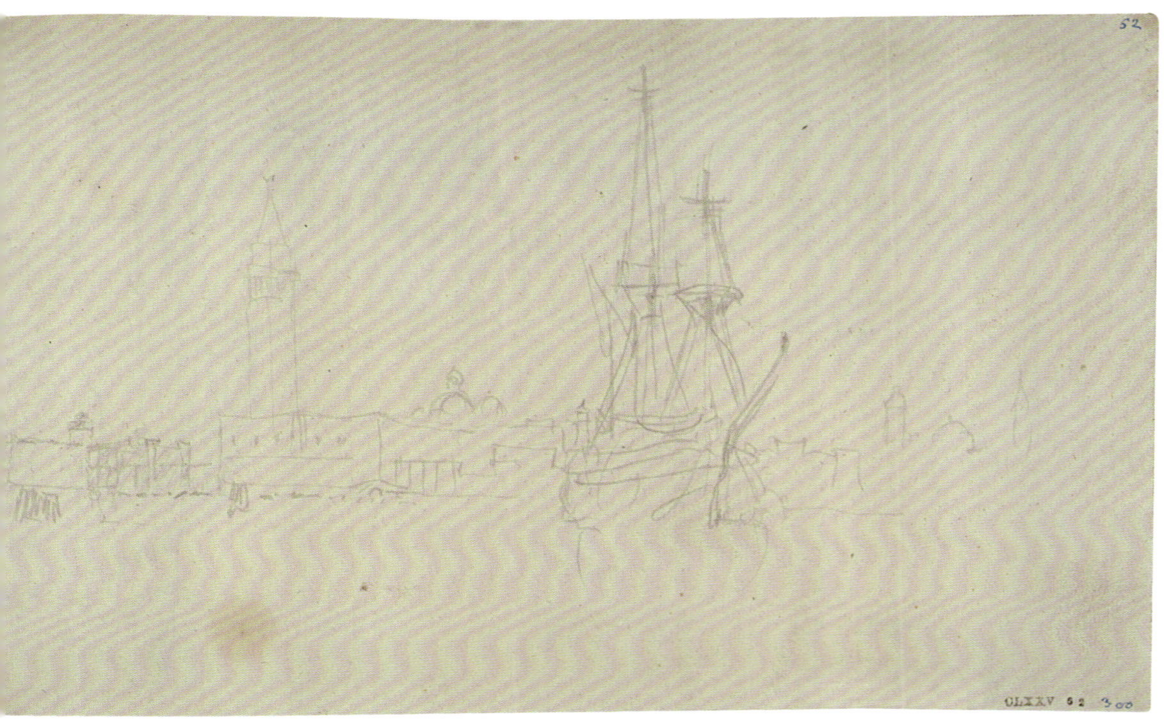

*A Panoramic View of the Bacino from the
Canale di San Marco, with San Giorgio Maggiore,
Santa Maria della Salute, the Doge's Palace
and the Campanile and Domes of San Marco*
from the Milan to Venice Sketchbook 1819
Graphite on paper, 11.2 × 18.5

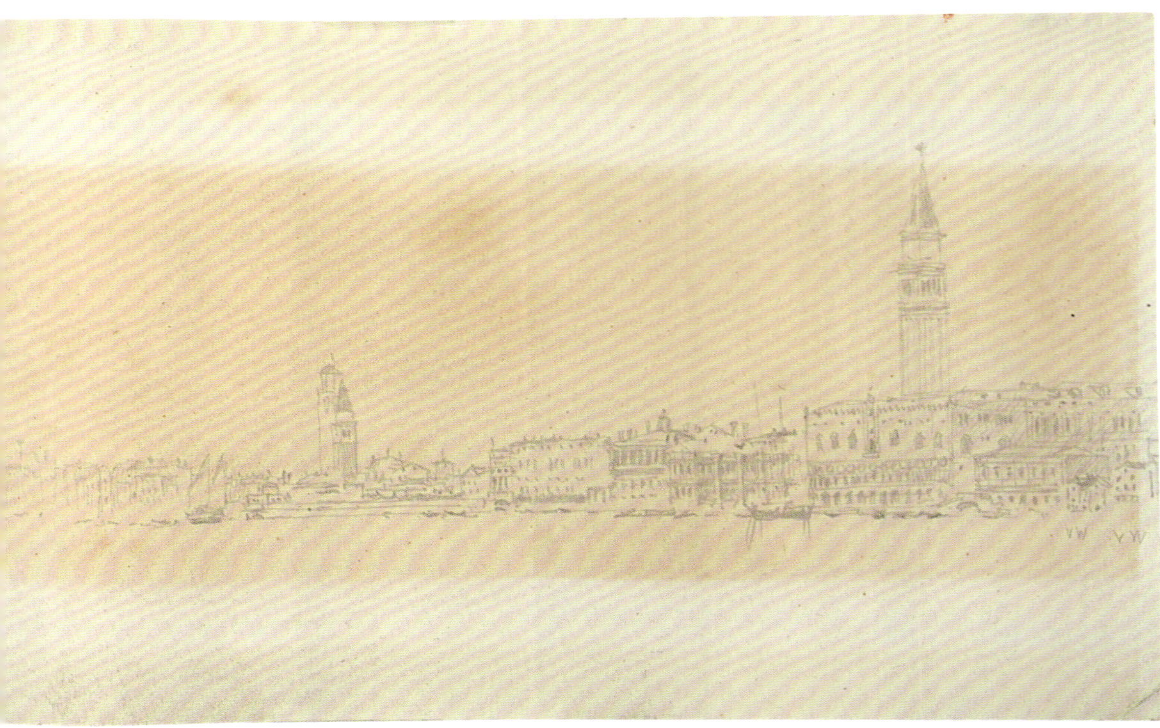

*A Panoramic View from the Bacino, with San Giorgio
Maggiore and its Harbour, the Punta della Dogana
and Santa Maria della Salute, the bell-towers of Santo
Stefano and San Moise, the Molo waterfront, including
the Zecca, the Doge's Palace and the Campanile of San
Marco* from the Milan to Venice Sketchbook 1819
Graphite on paper, 11.2 × 18.5

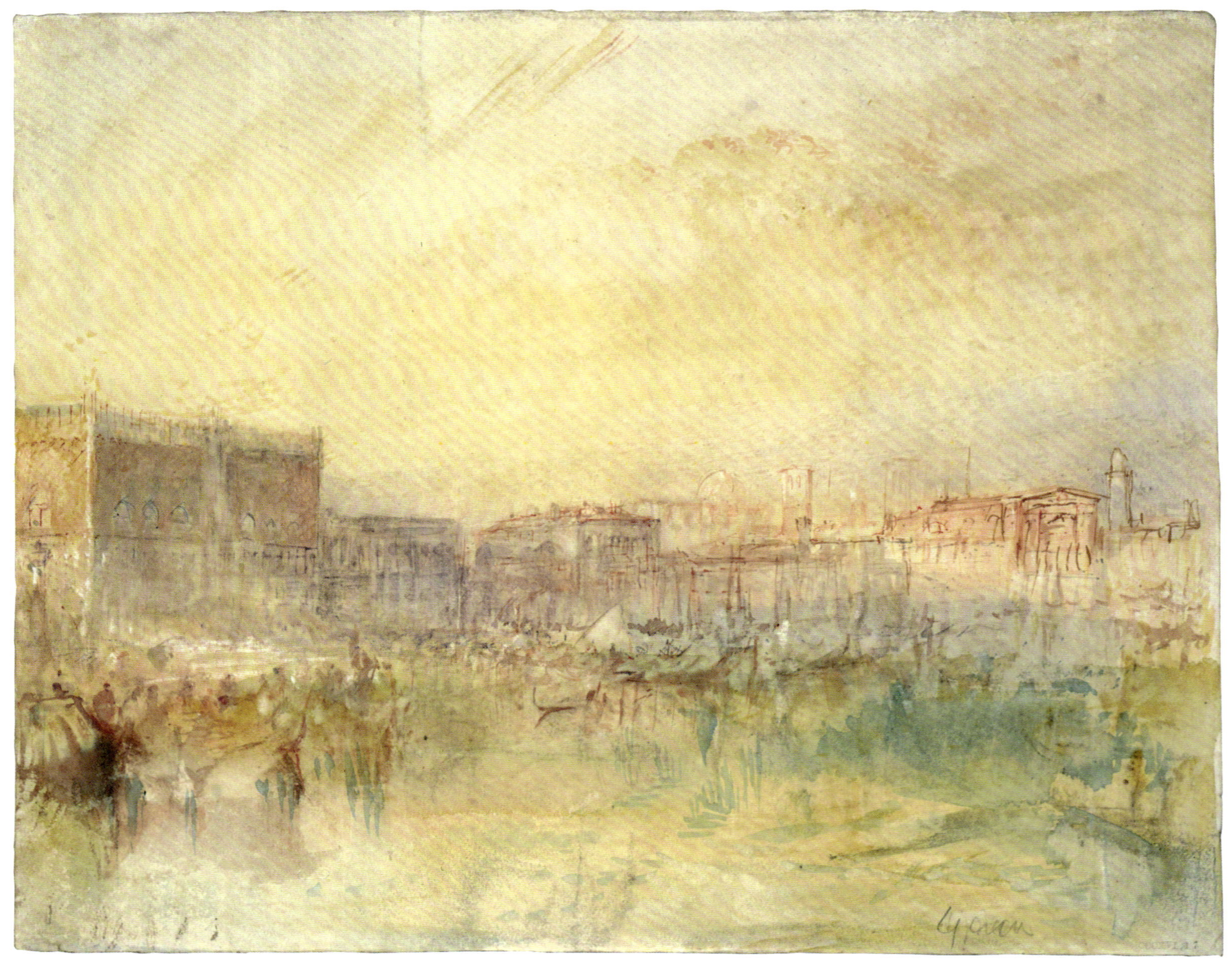

The Doge's Palace and the Riva degli Schiavoni from the Bacino 1840
Graphite, watercolour, gouache and pen on paper, 24.3 × 30.4

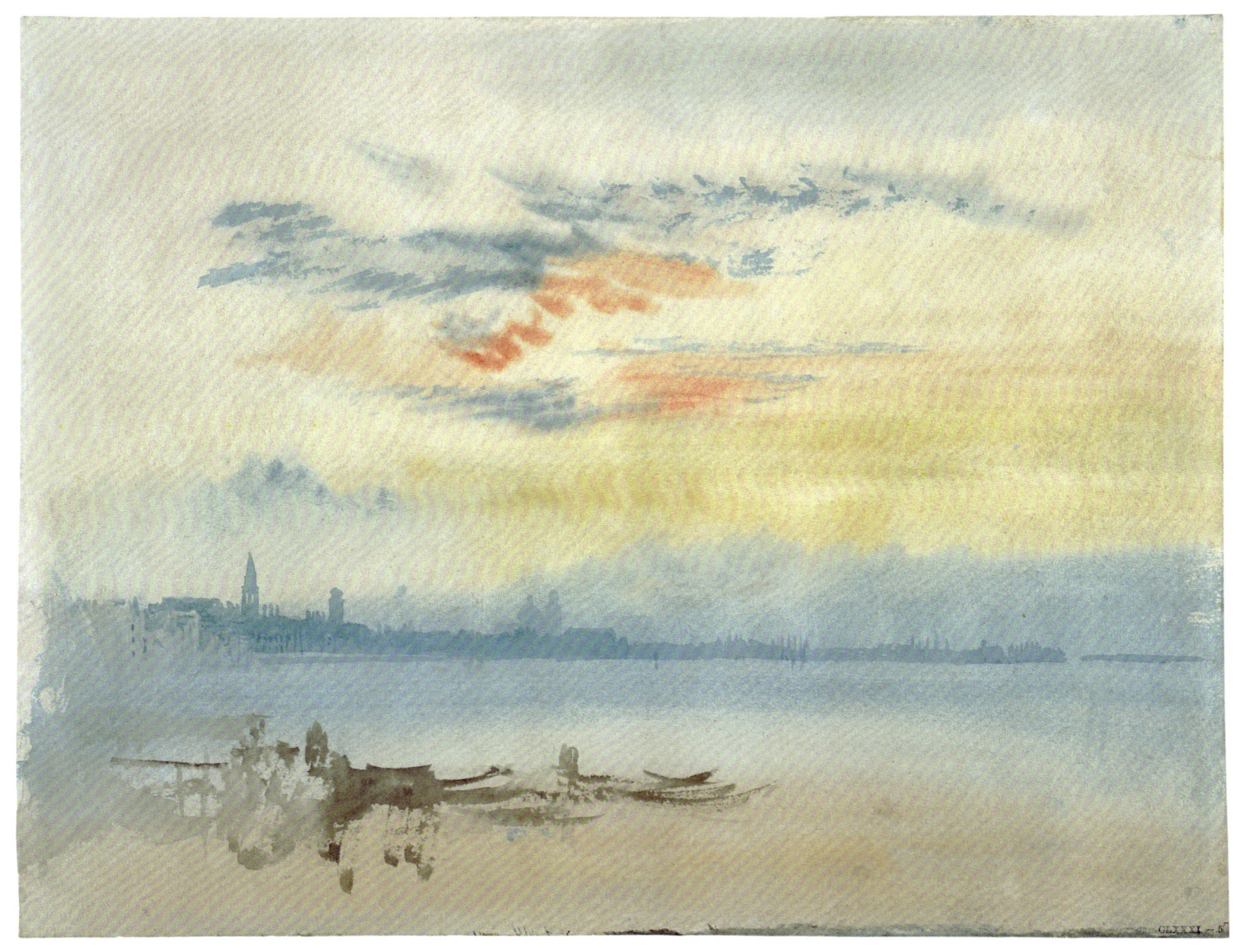

Venice: Looking East towards San Pietro di Castello – Early Morning
from the Como and Venice Sketchbook 1819
Watercolour on paper, 22.3 × 28.7

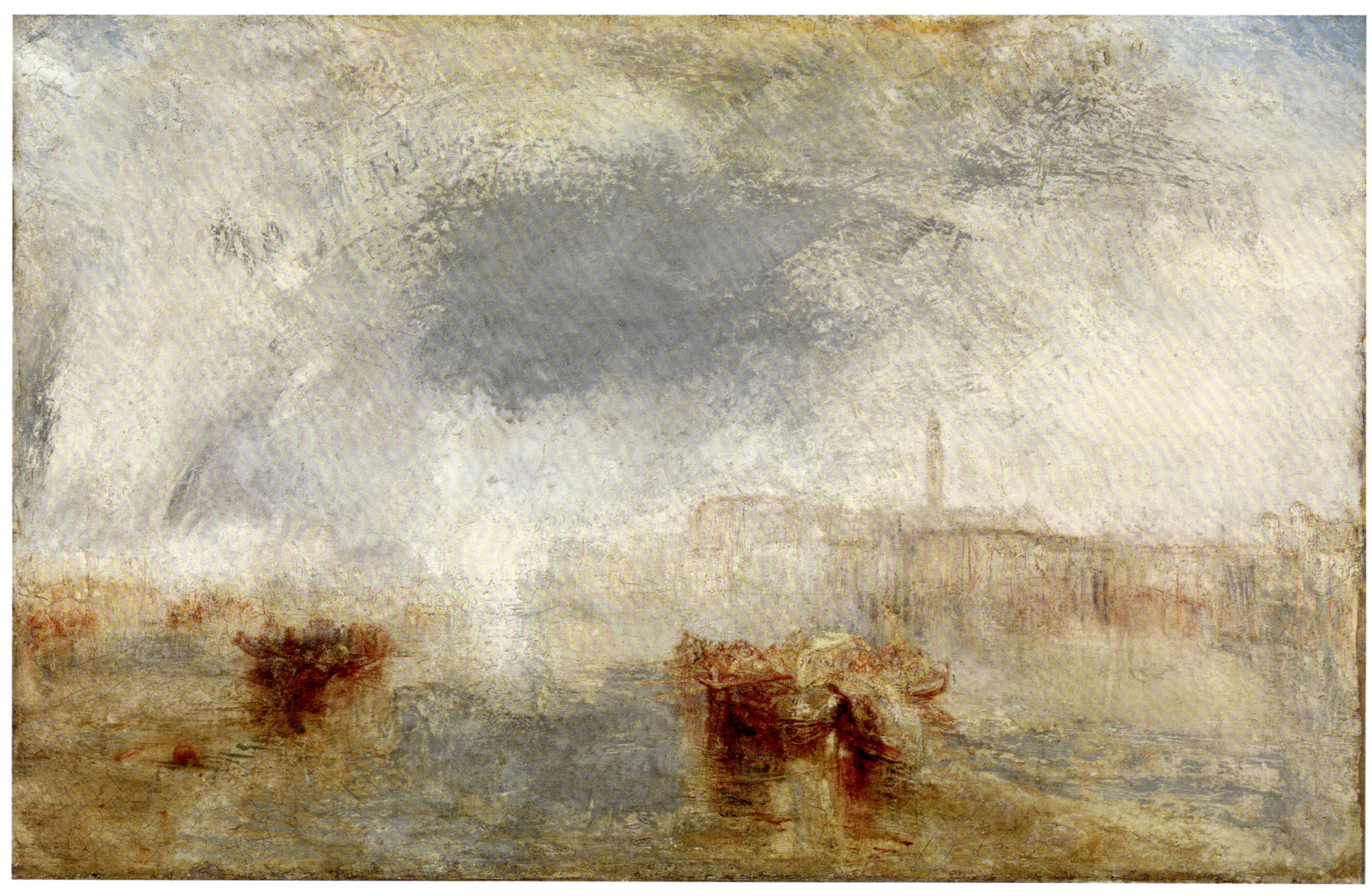

Venice – Noon exhibited 1845
Oil paint on canvas, 91.8 × 61

In 1845 Turner used materials that proved unstable, including thickly applied megilp in the sky. This resulted in changes to the appearance of the image soon afterwards. In this instance the picture sustained further damage and was removed from its original canvas in the 1920s. It and its pair (on.p.96) have only been fully conserved in the last few years.

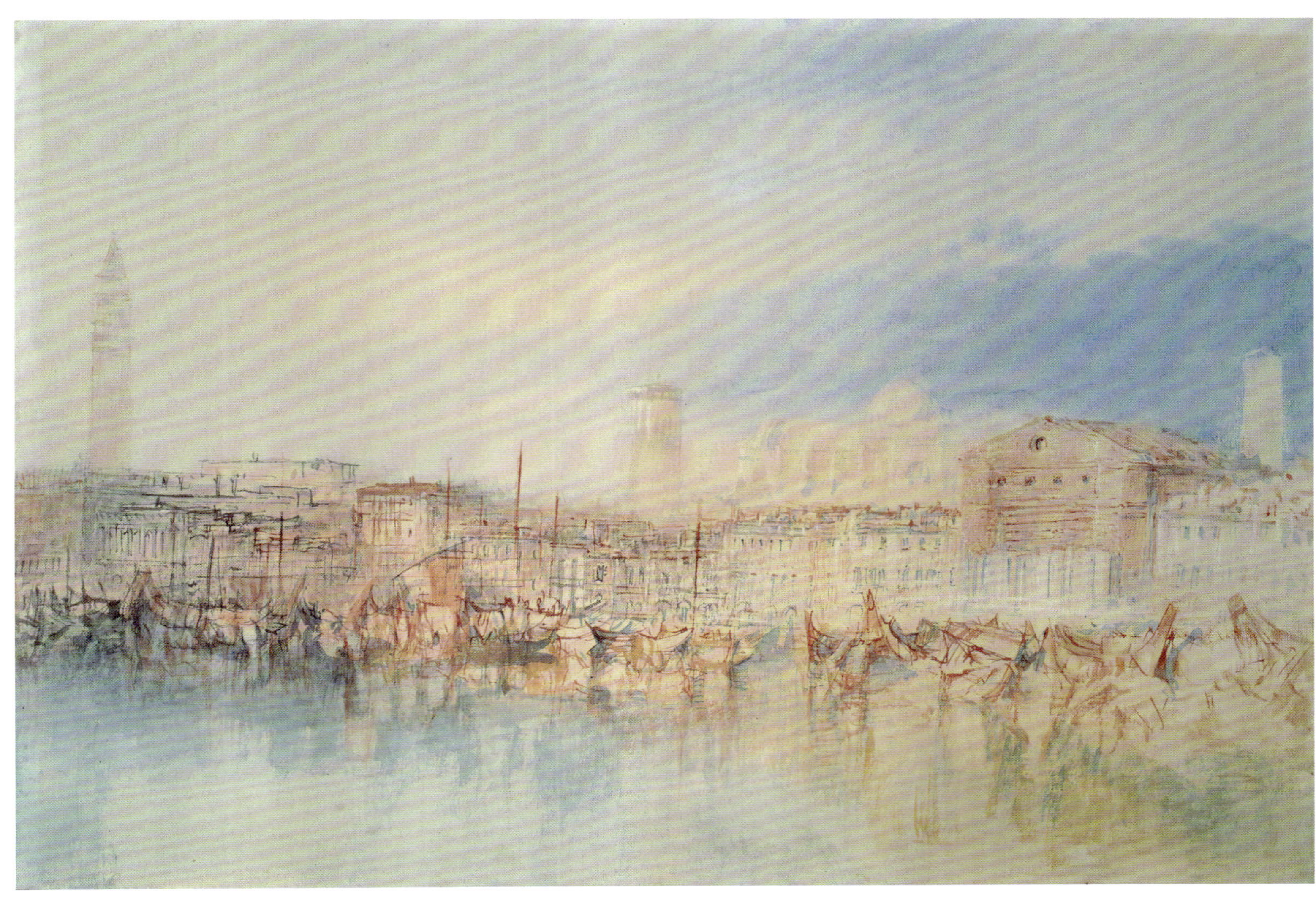

The Riva degli Schiavoni 1840
Watercolour with pen and red and brown ink, 21.7 × 31.8
Ashmolean Museum, Oxford

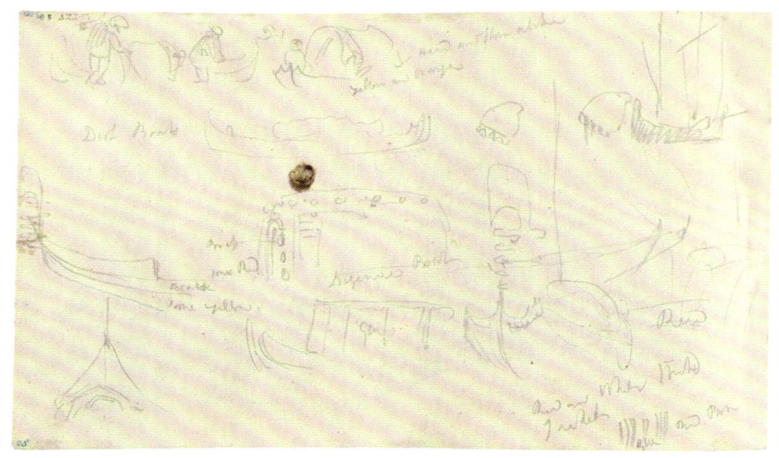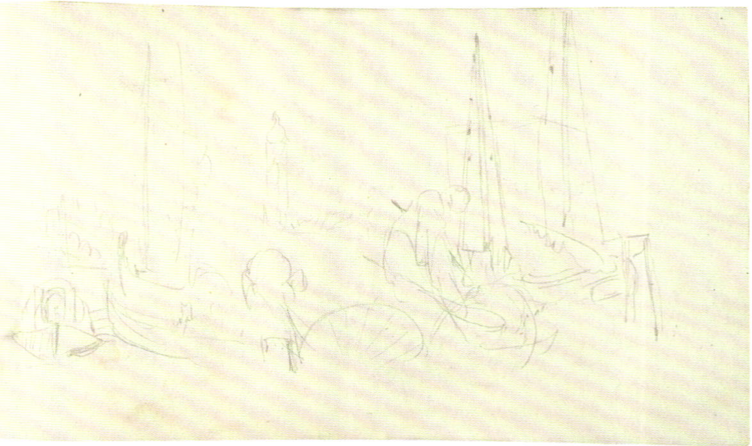

*Studies of Venetian Boats including a Gondola, on the Grand Canal near
the Rialto Bridge* from the Milan to Venice Sketchbook 1819
Graphite on paper, 11.2 × 18.5

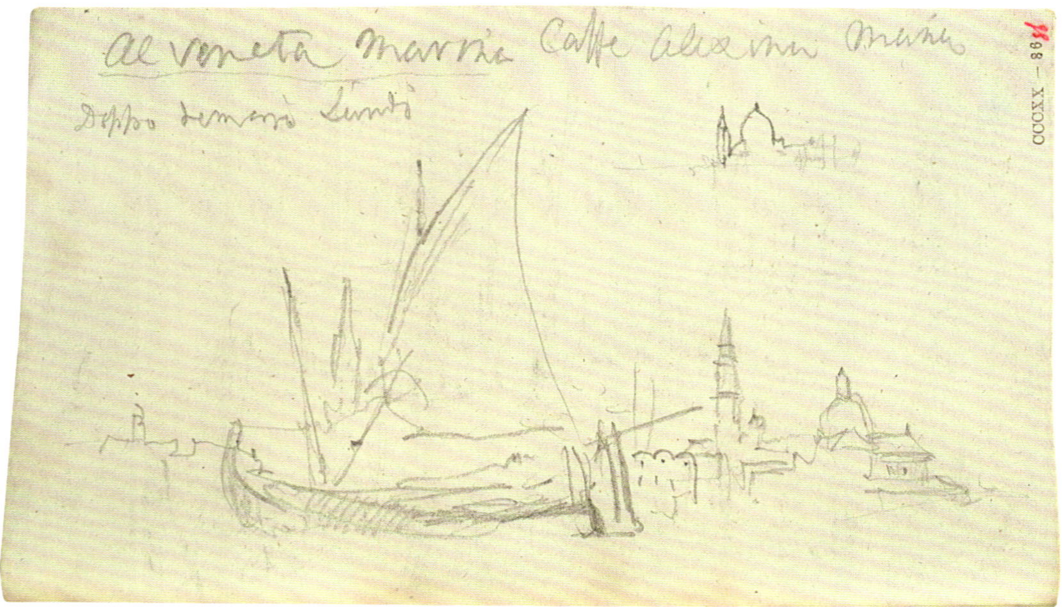

*A Venetian Fishing Boat (a Bragozzo), with
San Giorgio Maggiore, seen from the Ponte
Veneta Marina, near the Arsenale* from the
Rotterdam to Venice sketchbook 1840
Graphite on paper, 8.9 × 14.9

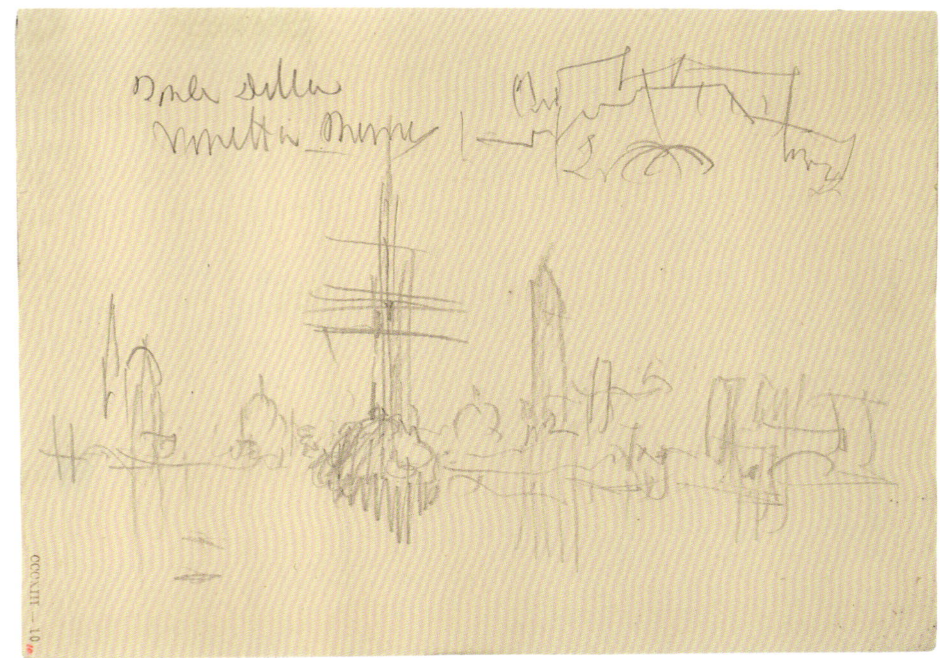

A Brigantine Moored near the Ponte de la Veneta Marina from the Venice and Botzen sketchbook 1840
Graphite on paper, 12.3 × 17.3

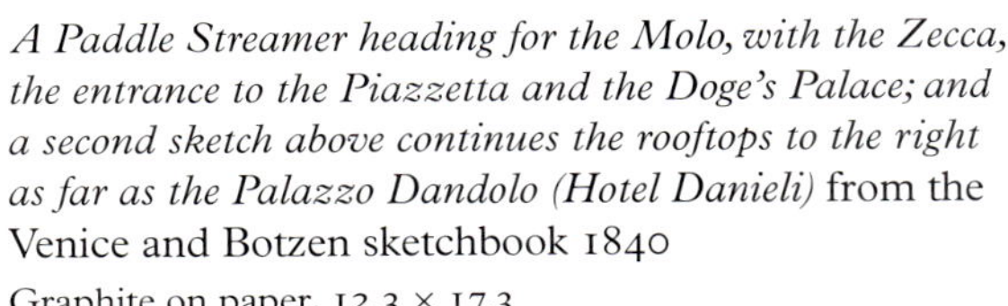

A Paddle Streamer heading for the Molo, with the Zecca, the entrance to the Piazzetta and the Doge's Palace; and a second sketch above continues the rooftops to the right as far as the Palazzo Dandolo (Hotel Danieli) from the Venice and Botzen sketchbook 1840
Graphite on paper, 12.3 × 17.3

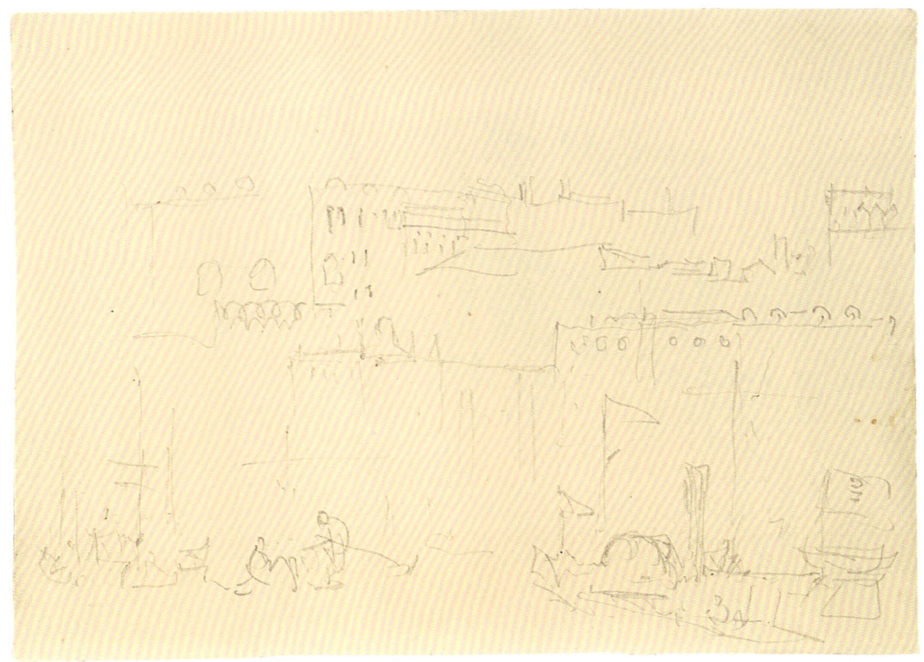

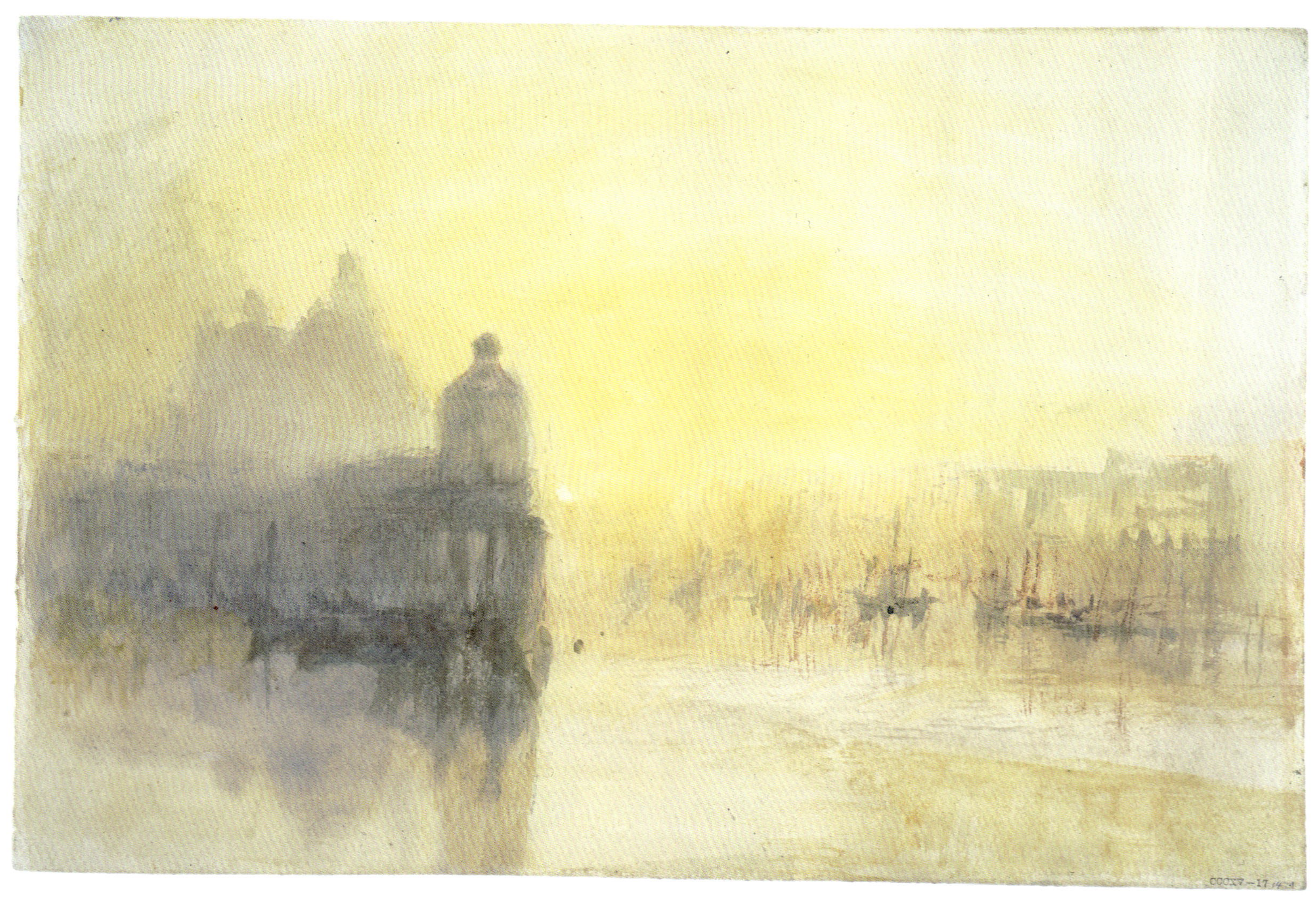

The Punta della Dogana at Sunset, with the Domes of Santa Maria della Salute from the Grand Canal and Giudecca Sketchbook 1840
Watercolour on paper, 22.1 × 32.2

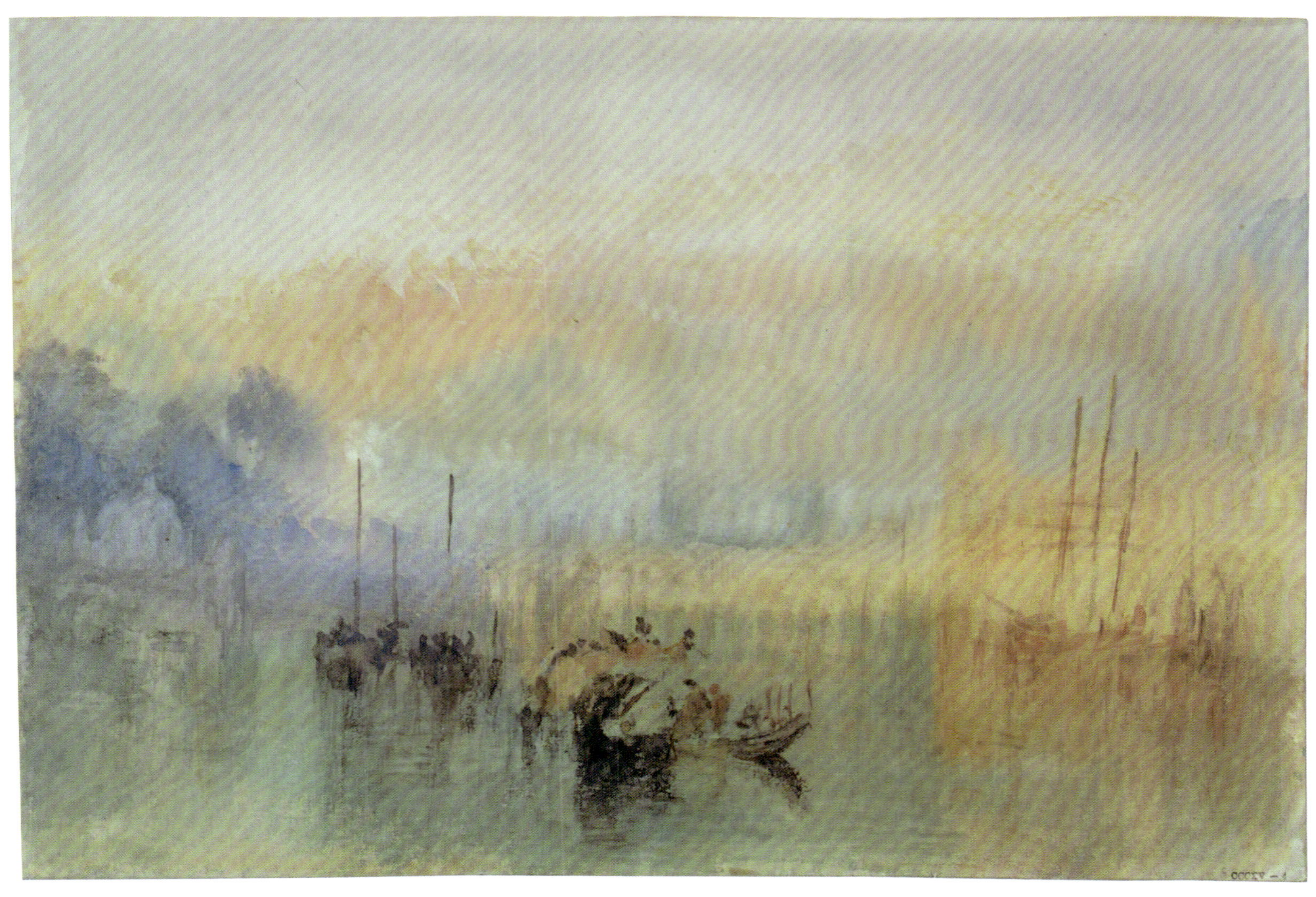

Shipping in the Bacino, with the Entrance to the Grand Canal from the
Grand Canal and Giudecca Sketchbook 1840
Watercolour on paper, 22.1 × 32.2

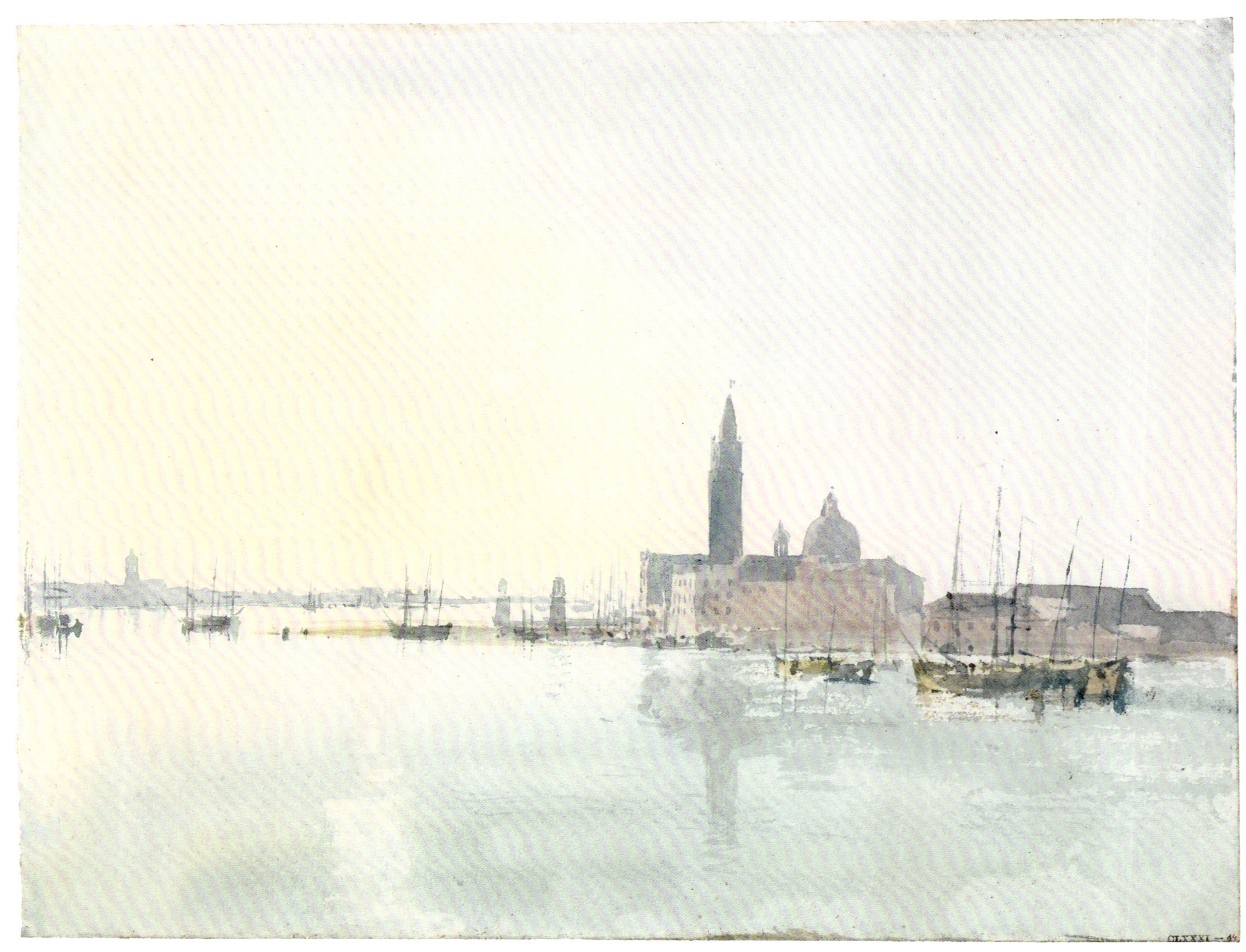

San Giorgio Maggiore – Early Morning
from the Como and Venice Sketchbook 1819
Watercolour on paper, 22.3 × 28.7

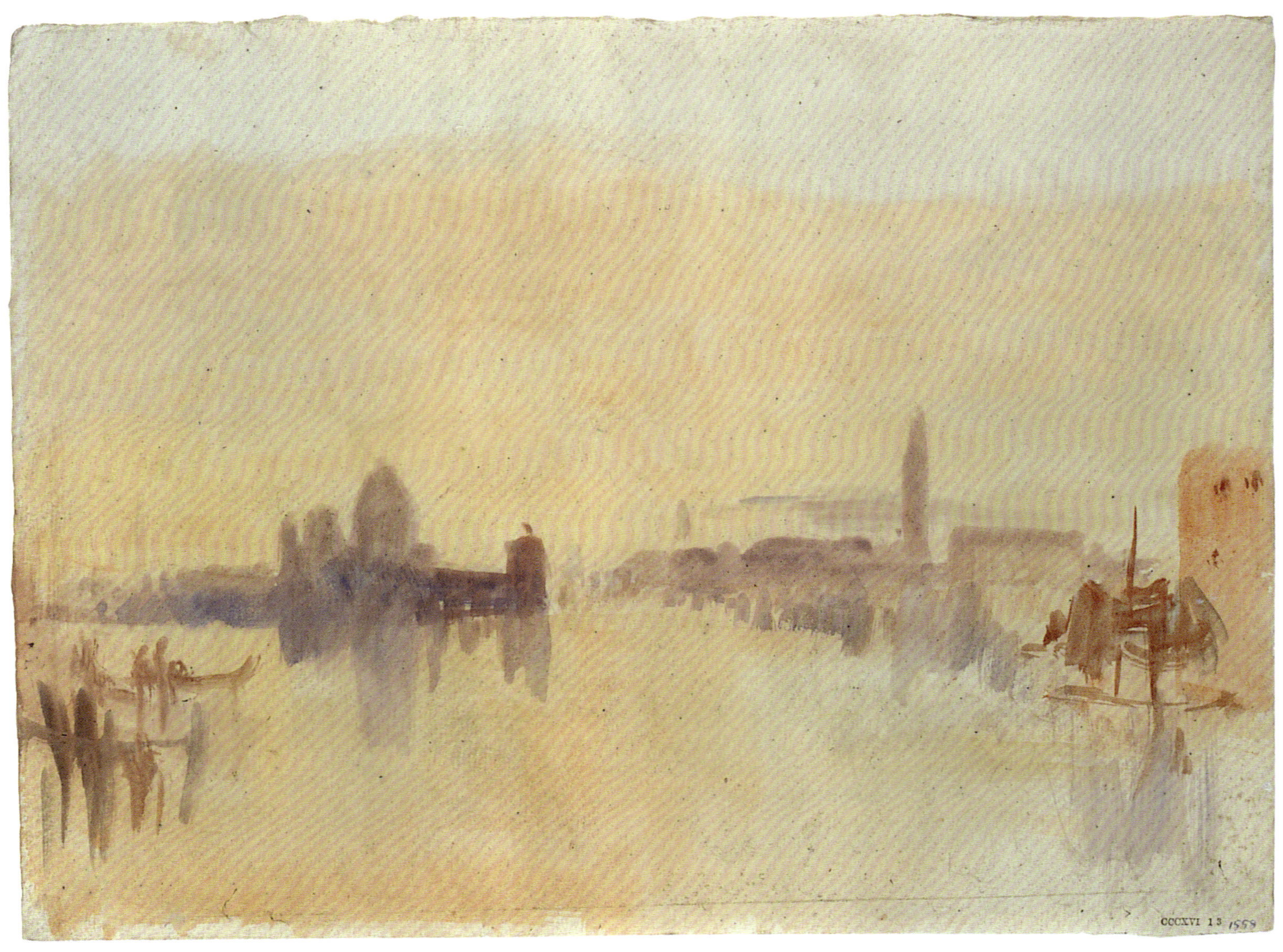

Distant View of the Entrance to the Grand Canal from the Bacino c.1840
Graphite and watercolour on paper, 23 × 30.5

San Giorgio Maggiore, with a Brigantine from the Venice Sketchbook 1833
Graphite on paper, 10.9 × 20.3

Two Sketches of San Giorgio Maggiore from the Venice and Botzen Sketchbook 1840
Graphite on paper, 12.3 × 17.3

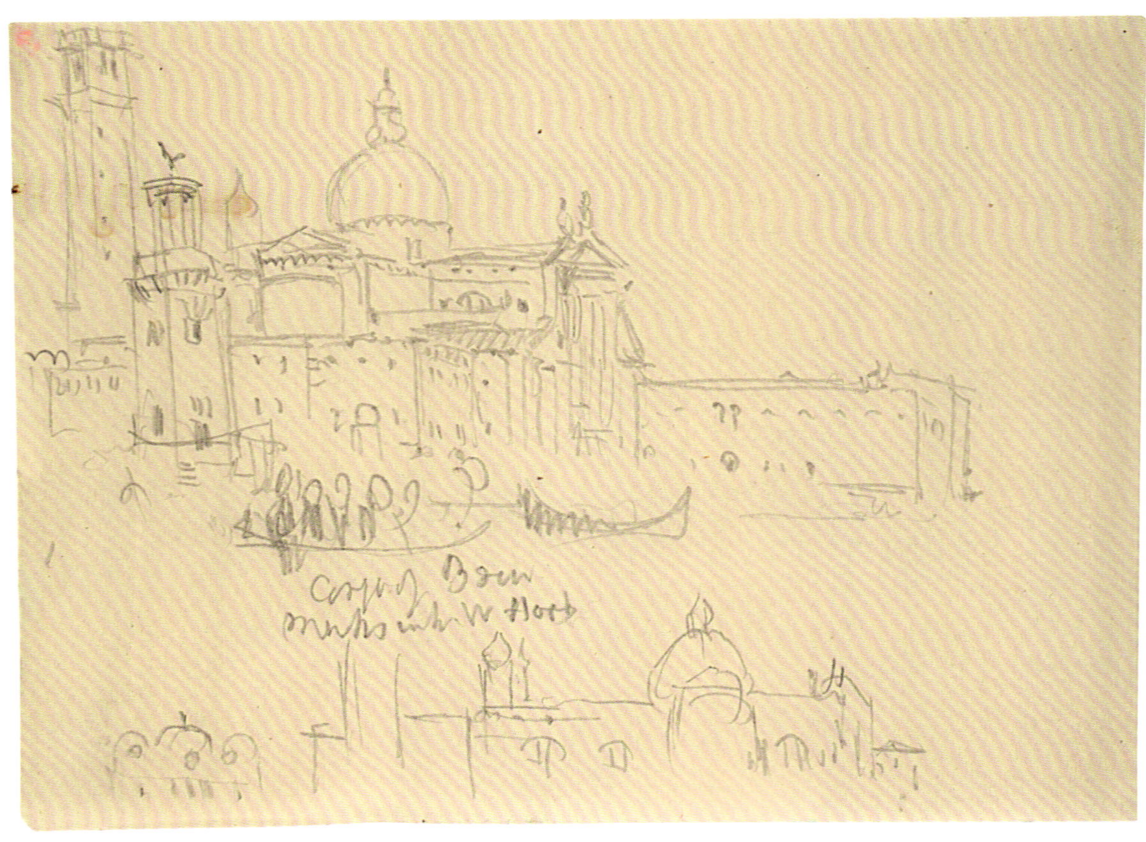

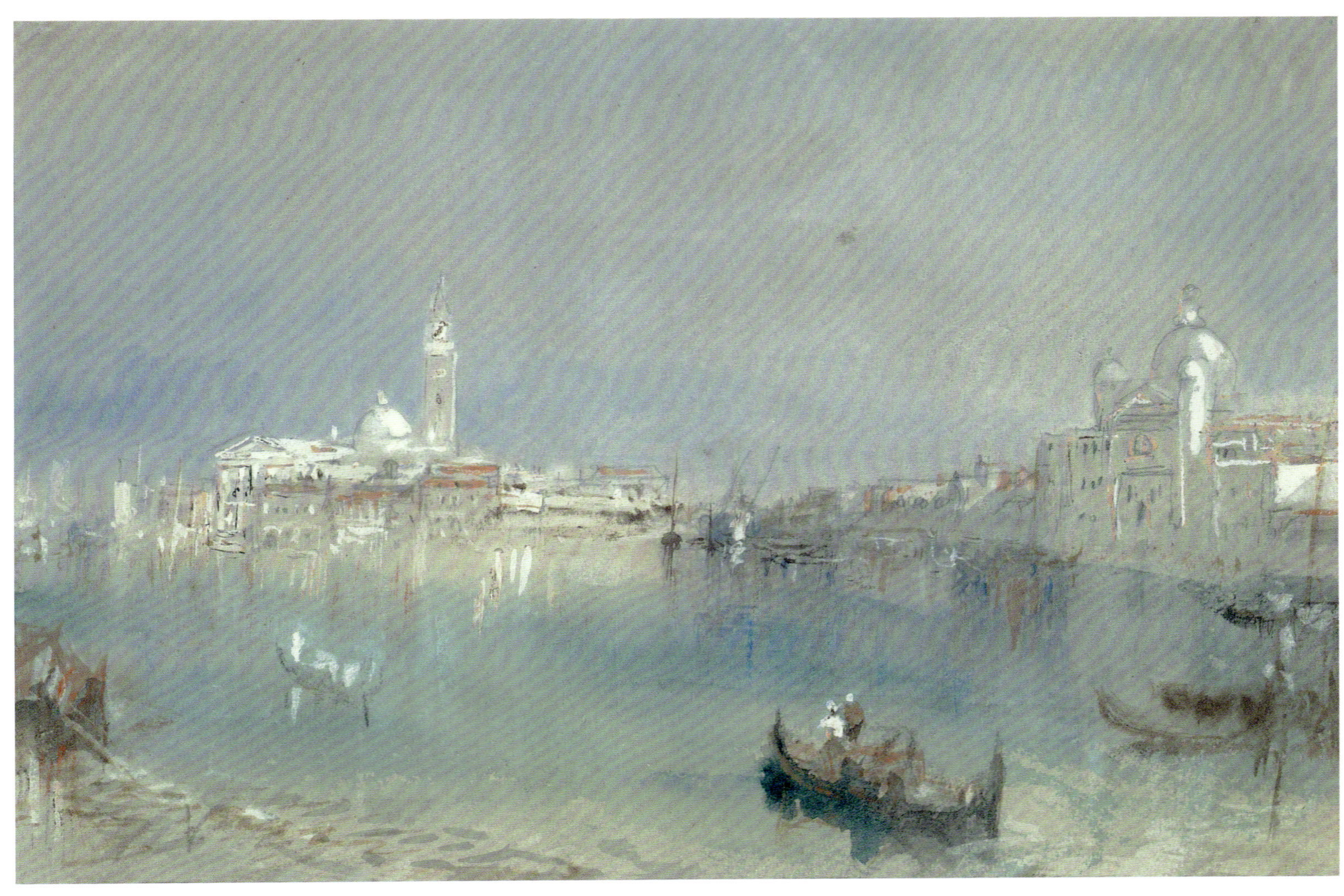

San Giorgio Maggiore and the Zitelle from the Giudecca Canal 1840
Graphite, watercolour and gouache on grey paper, 34.6 × 45.1
Whitworth Art Gallery, Manchester

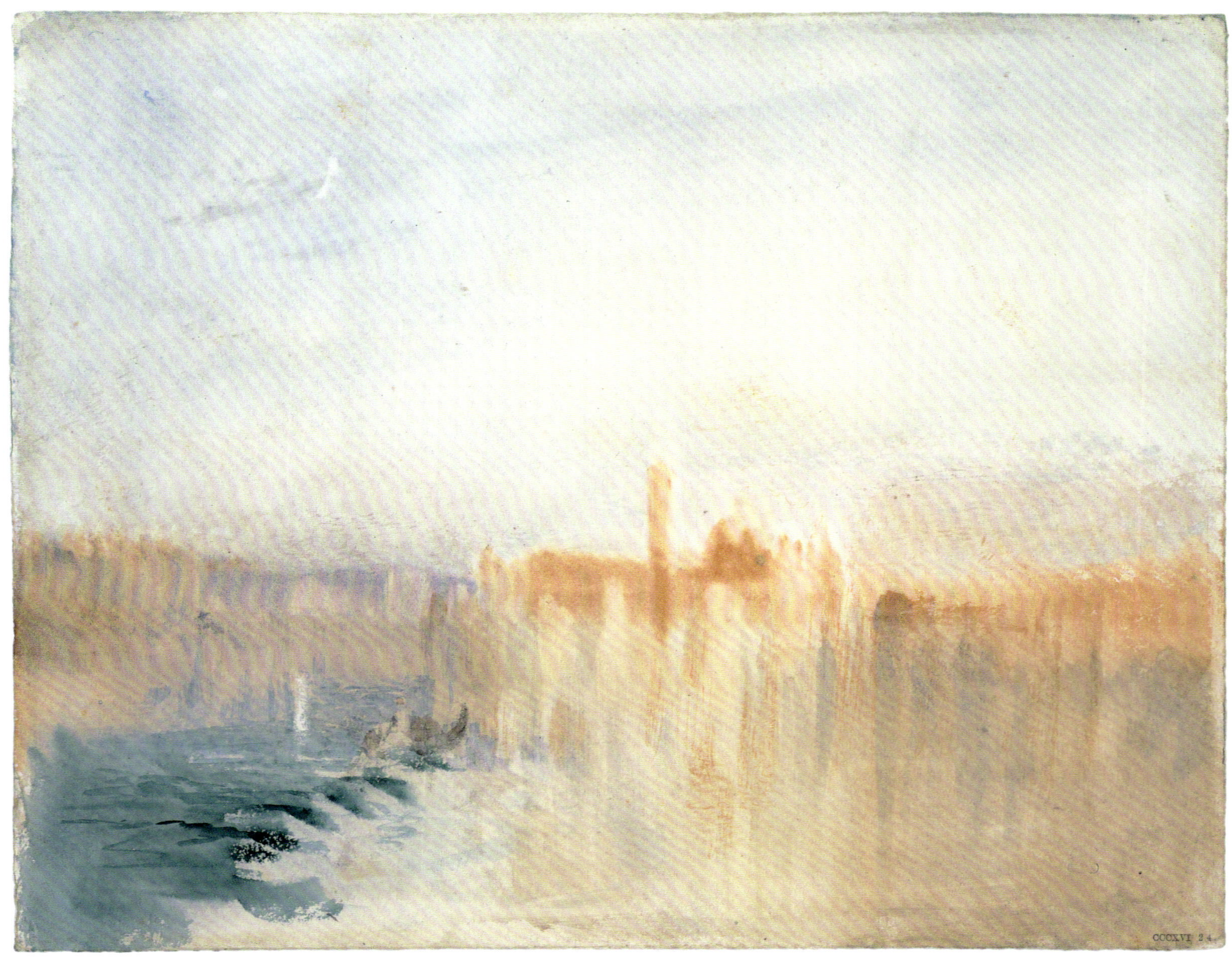

San Giorgio Maggiore at Sunset, from the Riva degli Schiavoni 1840
Watercolour on paper, 24.4 × 30.6

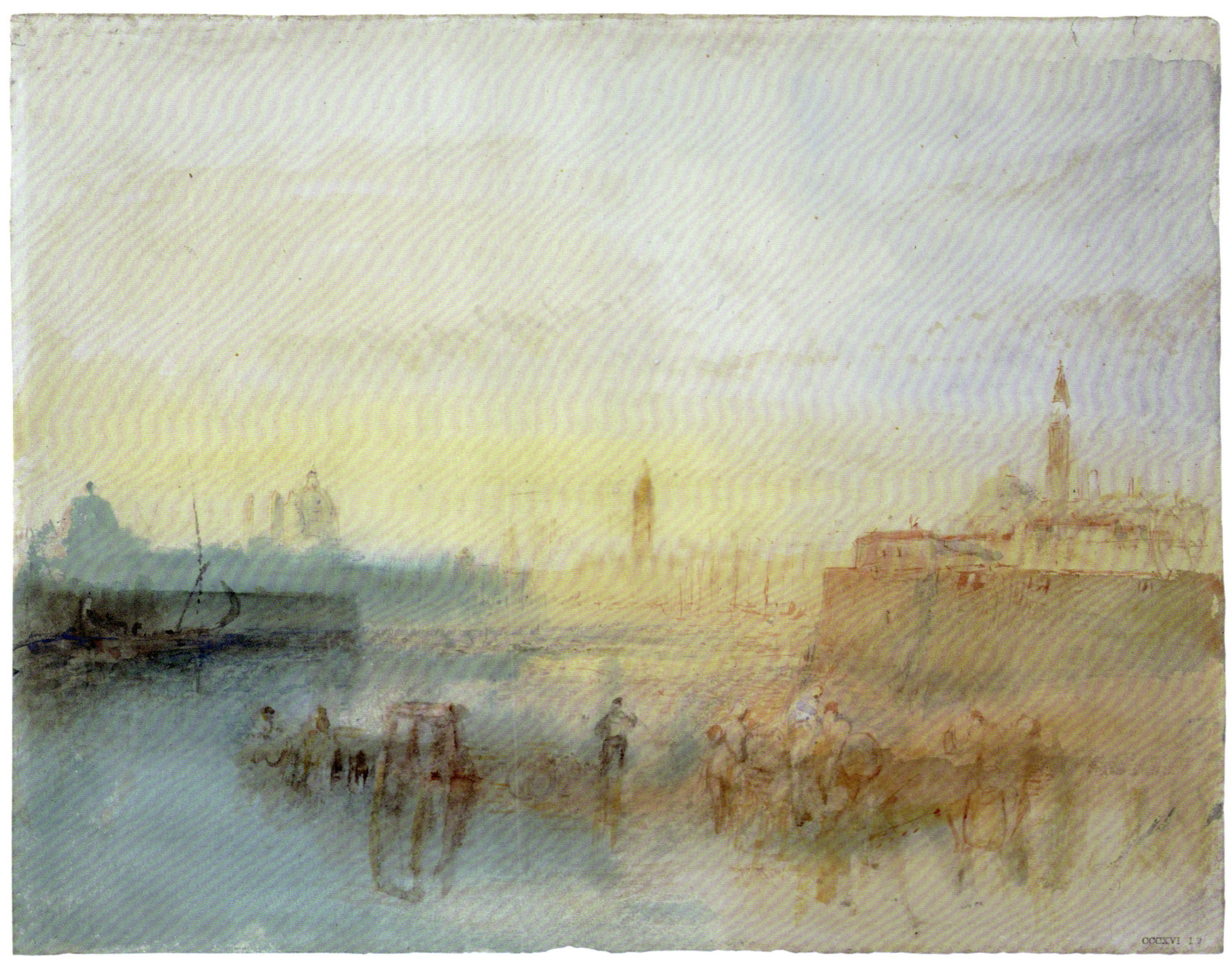

The Zitelle, Santa Maria della Salute, the Campanile and San Giorgio Maggiore from the Canale della Grazia 1840
Graphite, watercolour and pen on paper, 24.3 × 30.5

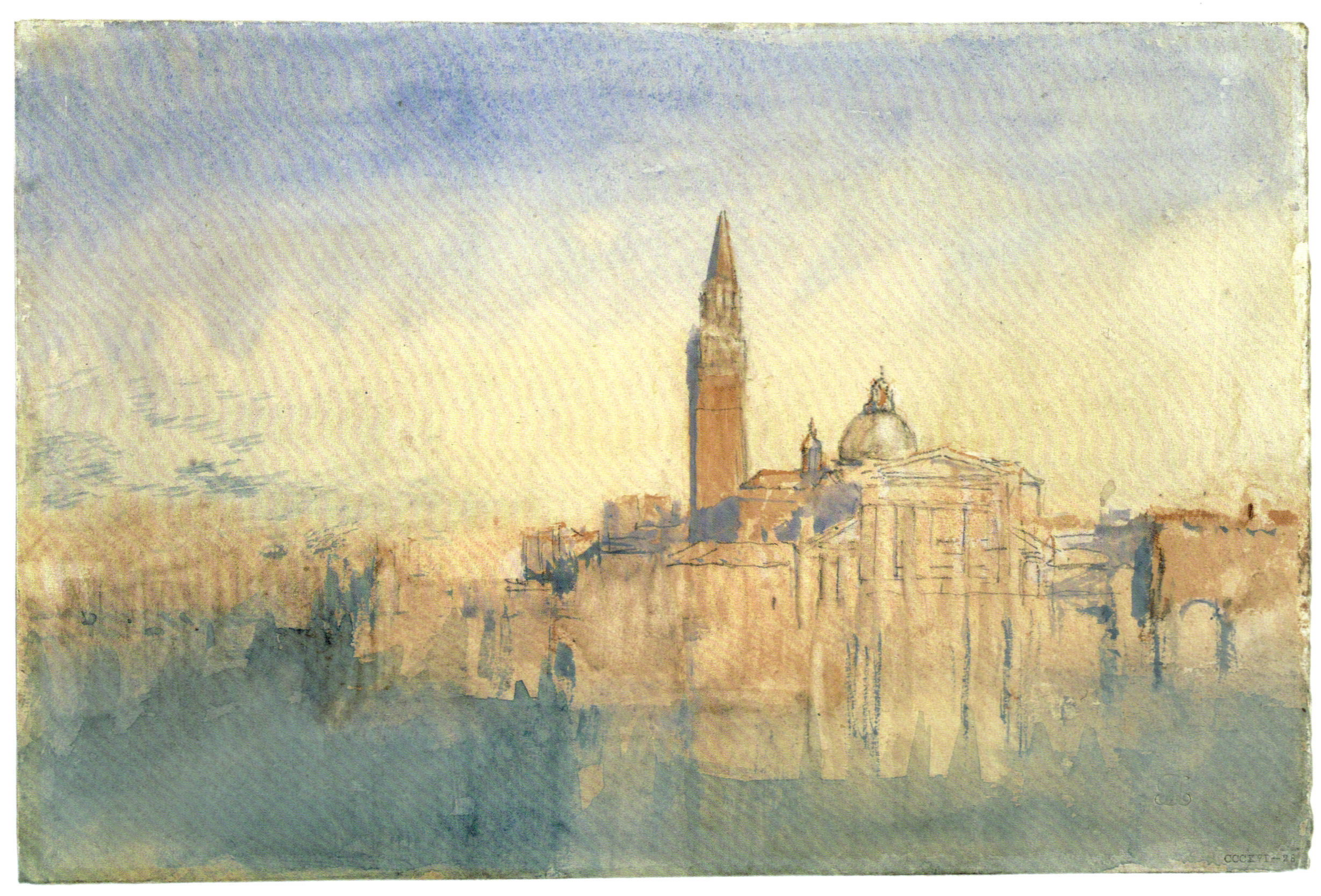

San Giorgio Maggiore at Sunset, from the Hotel Europa 1840
Graphite, watercolour and gouache on paper, 19.3 × 28.1

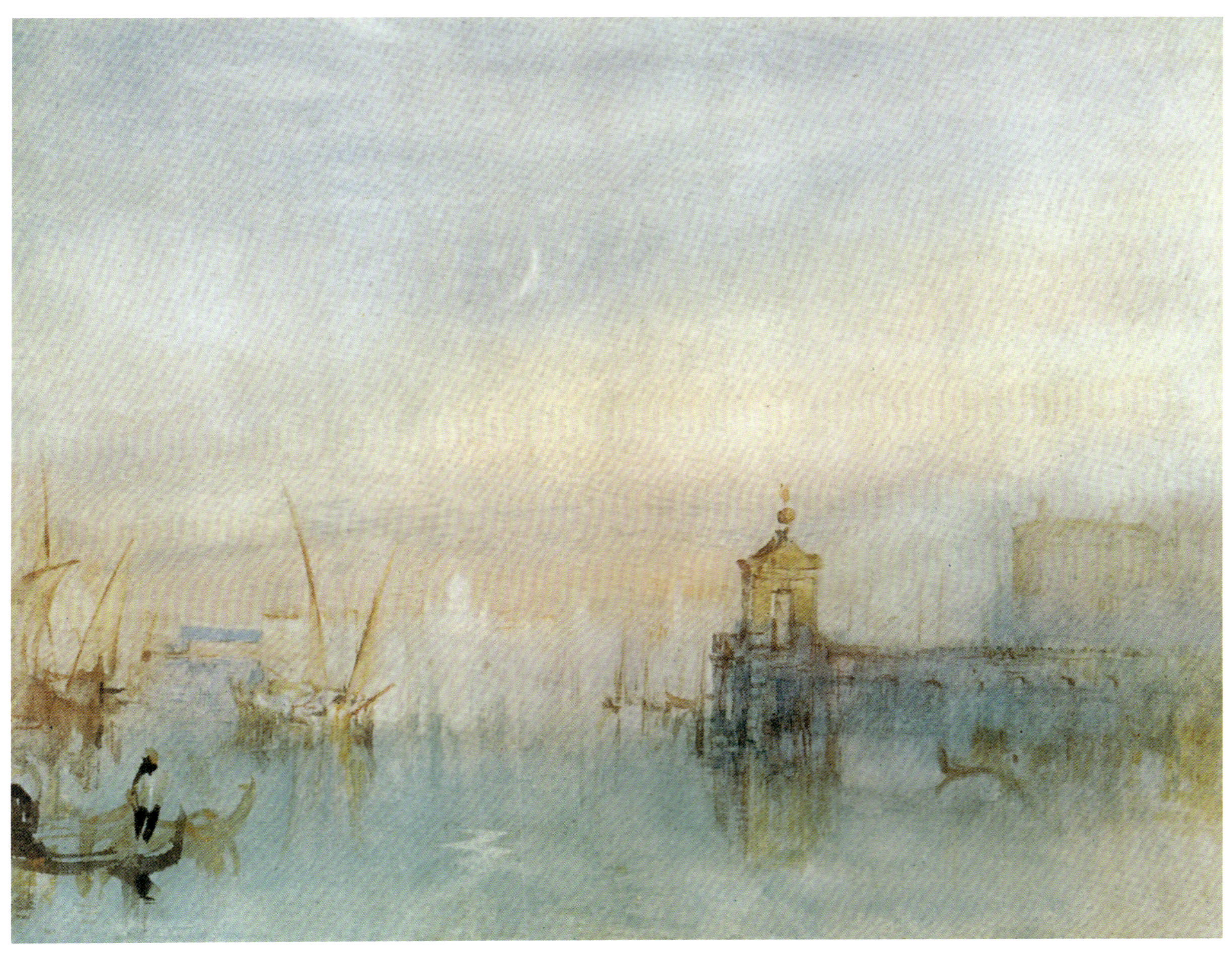

The New Moon (the Punta della Dogana, with the Zitelle beyond) 1840
Watercolour on paper, 23.8 × 30.3
Private collection

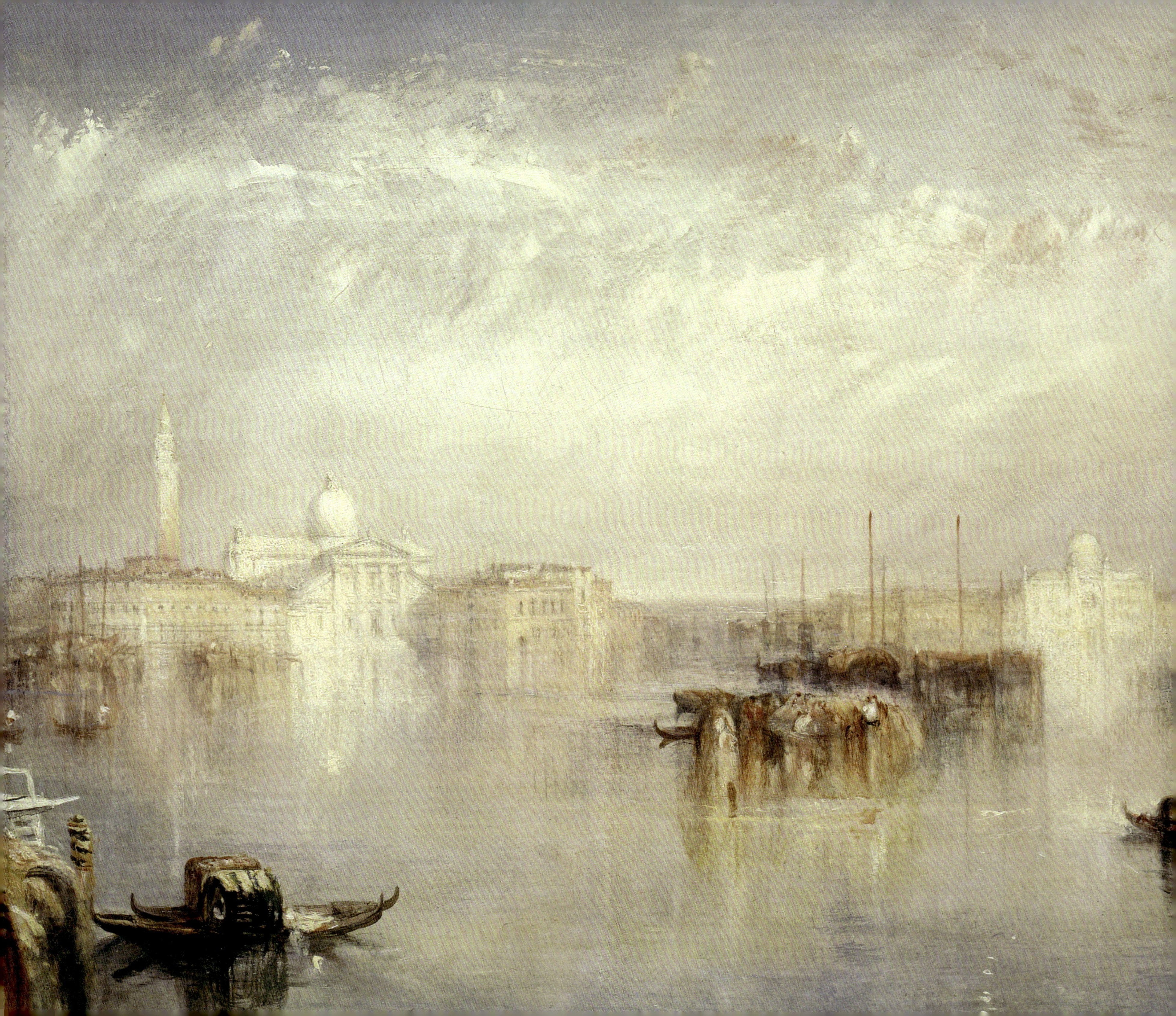

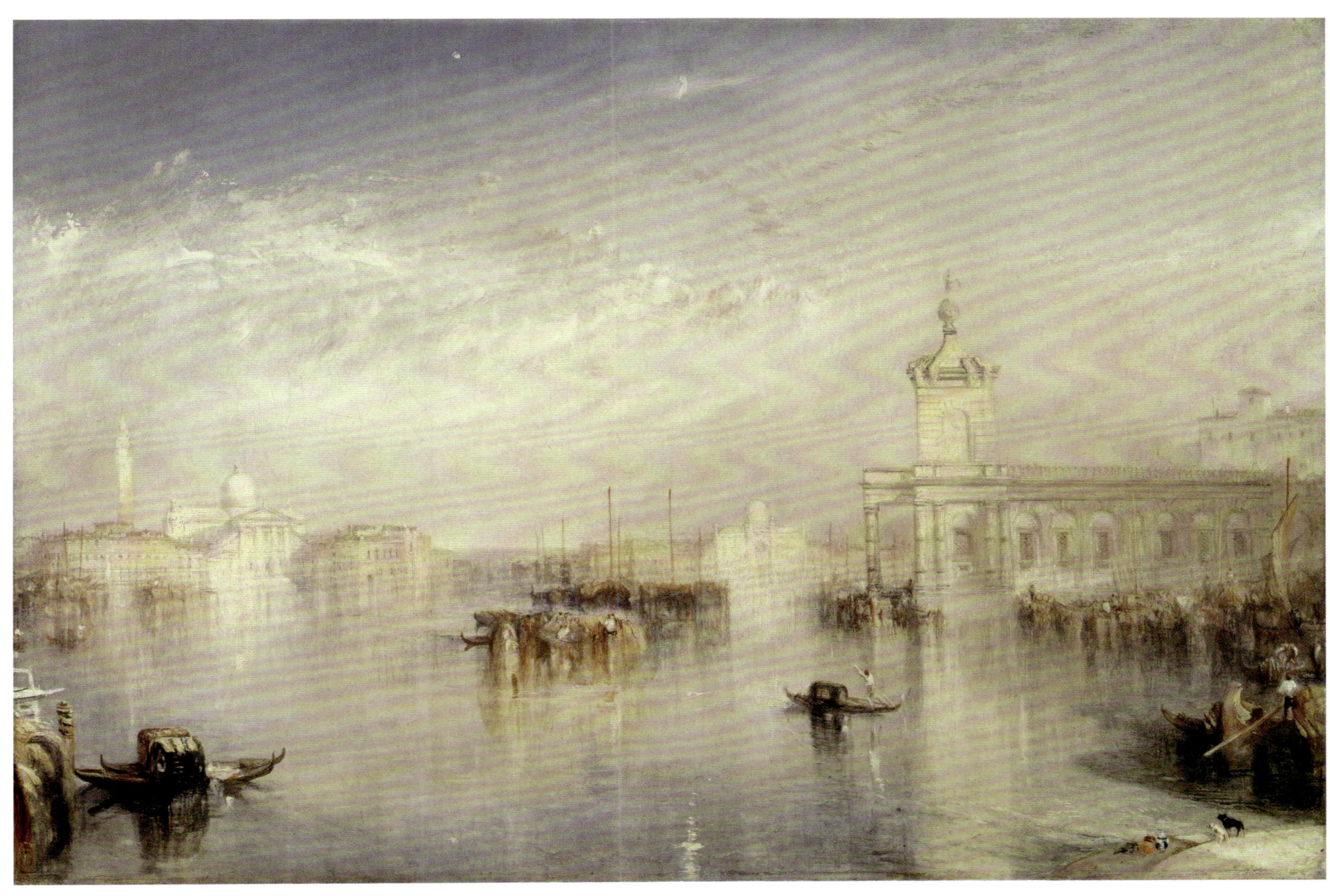

The Dogano, San Giorgio, Citella, from the Steps of the Europa
exhibited 1842 (*Citella* refers to the Zitelle church)
Oil paint on canvas, 61.6 × 92.7 (detail, opposite)

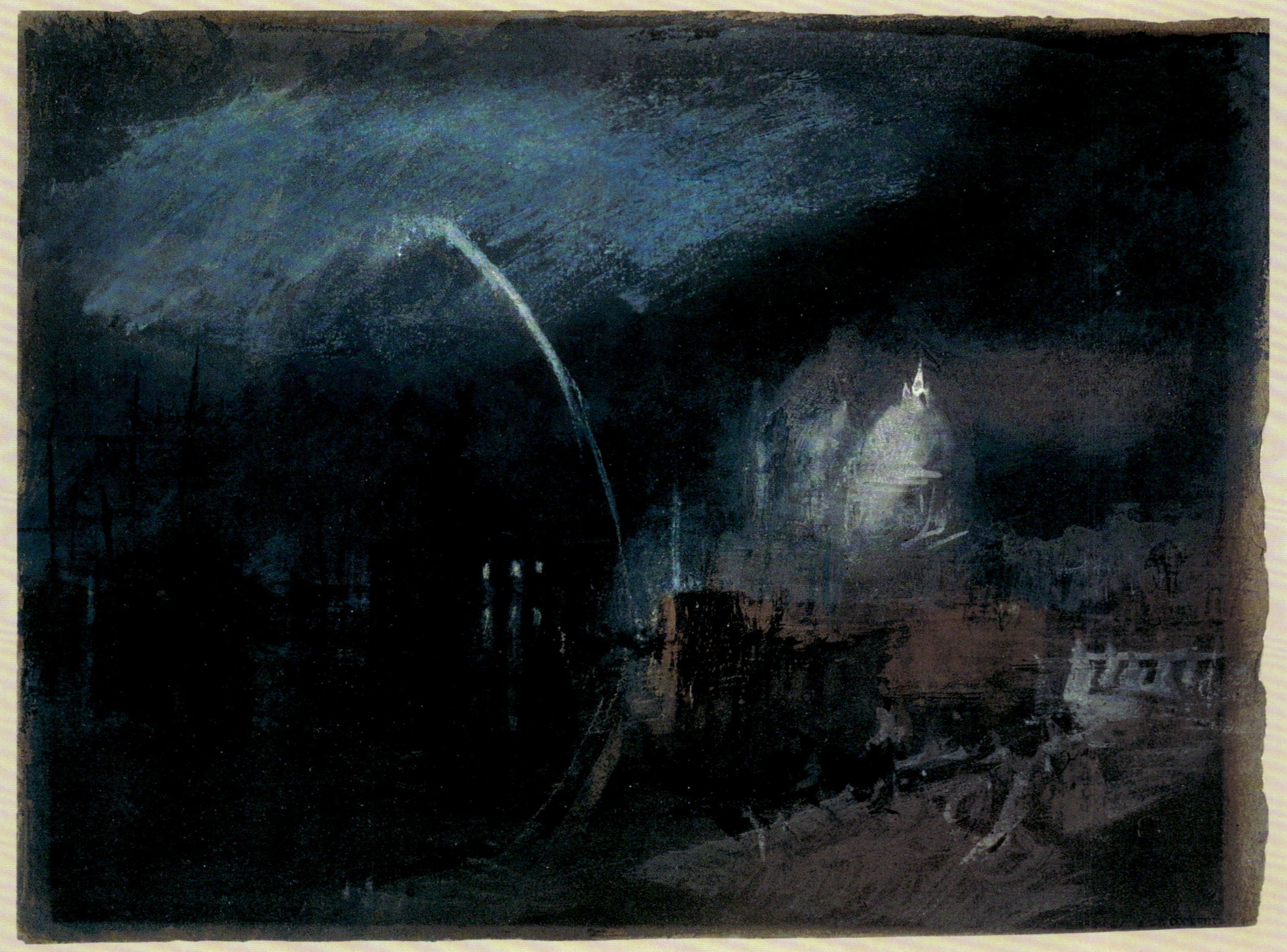

The Grand Canal

The Grand Canal, the longest and most richly adorned thoroughfare in Venice, snakes through and effectively bisects the city. Its unique character had been frequently depicted over the centuries, but no other artist has studied its architecture in such detail or its full length so comprehensively as Canaletto in his series of paintings, made from overlapping viewpoints that were widely reproduced as etchings by Antonio Visentini (1688–1782). Turner would have seen the prints, which perhaps explains why he repeated several of the same viewpoints along the canal in his sketches and watercolours. On a more prosaic note, however, it may be simply that both artists made use of the regular ferry points across the canal, which provided stable landing places from which to study and record each scene. Although Turner generally preferred to sketch quickly in pencil, his larger views of the Grand Canal were evidently occasionally developed on the spot in watercolour.

The influence of Canaletto can more certainly be detected in one of Turner's earliest Venetian oil paintings, looking down the Grand Canal from alongside the piazza beside the great domed church, Santa Maria della Salute (p.66). Conceived as a form of thanksgiving for the passing of the plague of 1629–30 (after it had killed about a third of the city's population) the church was designed by Baldassare Longhena (1598–1682), who lived to see it completed (but not consecrated) fifty years later. This luminous near-neighbour to Turner's lodgings at the Hotel Europa (visible among the palaces on the left) was built of brick and Istrian stone, and its principal dome dominates the lower part of the waterway in either direction. Turner generally cropped or blurred its full baroque extravagance, opting to represent it as a pale and ghostly presence, defined by shade as much as by either sun or moonlight.

Further up the canal, Turner was distracted by the contents of some of the buildings lying along its course, or nearby, down the labyrinthine alleys. Chief of these was the Gallerie dell'Accademia, a relatively new institution, set up to house paintings that had been dislodged from churches, palaces and public buildings across the city during the period of Napoleonic rule. Arguably the most celebrated work was Titian's *Assumption of the Virgin* 1515–18, temporarily moved to the Accademia from the Frari in the San Polo district. Turner also visited that great Franciscan church, as well as the neighbouring Scuola Grande di San Rocco, where he sketched and was profoundly impressed by the series of paintings by Tintoretto that it housed. Another detour took him to the Palazzo Pisani Moretta, where he had been asked to examine Paolo Veronese's celebrated evocation of *The Family of Darius before Alexander* c.1565–7 (now in the National Gallery, London), which had been the only painting in Venice that Goethe (1749–1832) praised two years earlier in his *Italienische Reise* (1817). One of Turner's partly coloured sketches was made from a mooring in front of the palace, focusing instead on the Mocenigo Palaces opposite, which (as his gondolier assuredly alerted him) had been the Venetian residence of Lord Byron.

Further up that side of the canal, Turner's sketches repeatedly emphasise the towering bulk of the Palazzo Grimani, which faces onto both the Grand Canal and the Rio San Luca. A sequence of studies on grey and blue paper explore this smaller canal, which Turner first encountered twenty years earlier when staying nearby at the neighbouring Albergo Leon Bianco.

Like most other British artists, Turner recognised the great potential of the Rialto bridge as a subject. Even before he arrived in Venice in 1819, he had produced a watercolour of it based on an outline by James Hakewill (Private collection; see the related study here, p.82). Once there he studied the reality from as many angles as possible on each of his visits. It was, of course, at that date the only pedestrian crossing on the entire length of the Grand Canal, straddling the pulsing centre of Venetian commerce.

Santa Maria della Salute, Night Scene with Rockets 1840
Watercolour and gouache on brown paper, 24 × 31.5

Just a short way up the canal lies the fish market, which was clearly
another subject with enduring appeal to Turner, who recorded the same
viewpoint again and again in his sketches, and perhaps in an oil study,
though no finished design materialised (Canaletto treated the scene in a
late canvas, now in the Gemäldegalerie, Berlin).

Although Turner conscientiously sketched the parade of palaces
between the fish market and the present train station on successive
visits, little of what he saw inspired him to get out his watercolours.
At that period, he would have found some of the buildings rather
dilapidated, including the picturesque Fondaco dei Turchi. On the other
hand, he would also have spotted the alterations and improvements that
had taken place between his first visit and his last, such as the addition
of a dome to the church of San Geremia, situated at the junction of the
Cannaregio Canal with the Grand Canal. But many of the buildings
Turner recorded at this end of the canal have since been lost. For
example, the church of Santa Lucia, formerly next to the church of the
Scalzi, has been replaced by the eponymous station, now the teeming
threshold into Venice for many visitors.

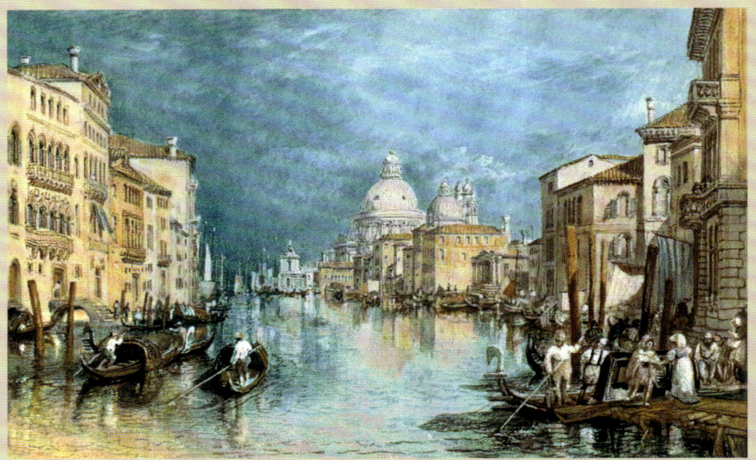

The Grand Canal, with the Salute, Venice c.1818–20
Watercolour on paper, 14 × 21.5
Private collection

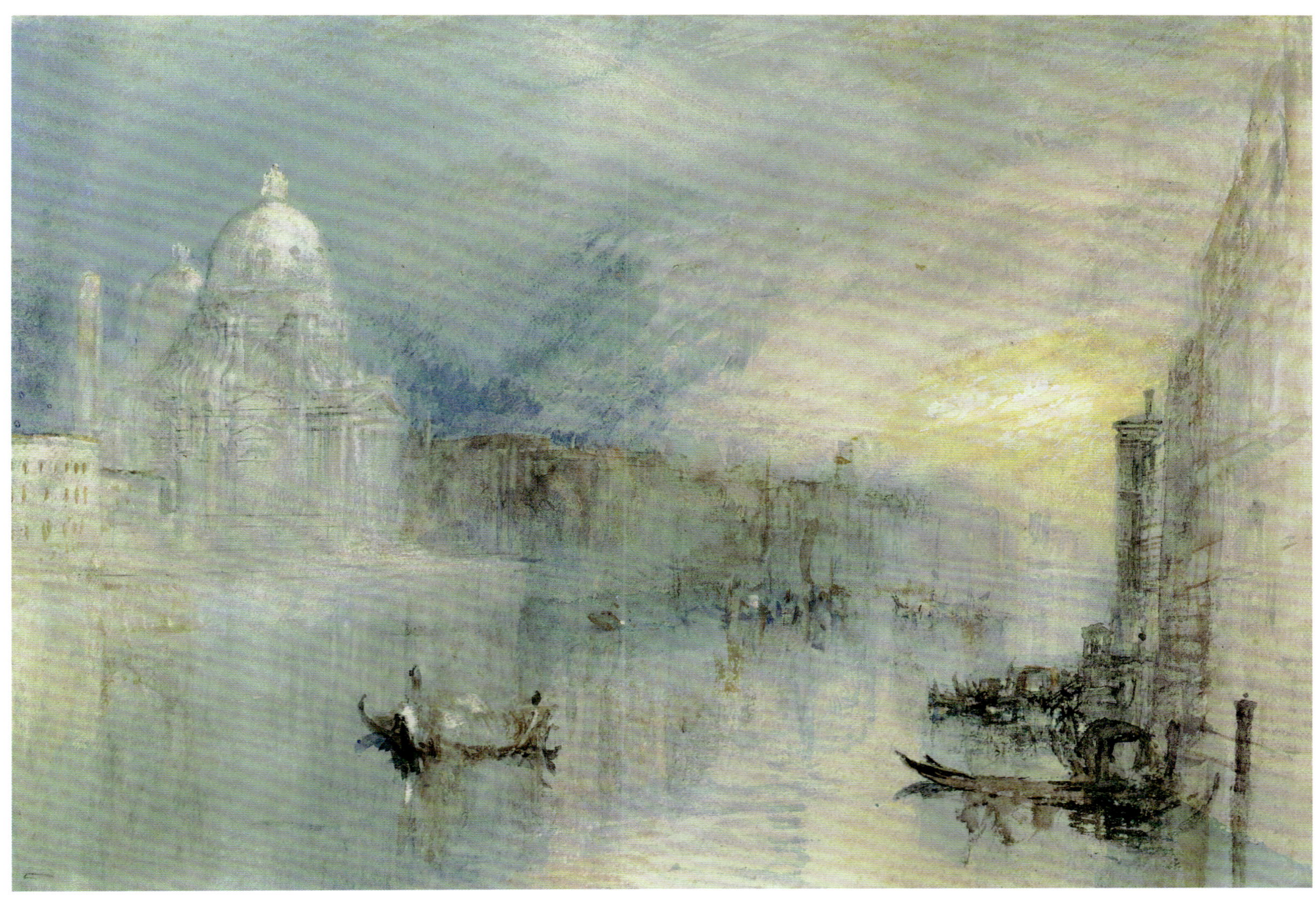

The Grand Canal with Santa Maria della Salute,
from near the Hotel Europa 1840
Graphite, watercolour and gouache, with some scraping-out on paper, 22 × 31.8
Private collection

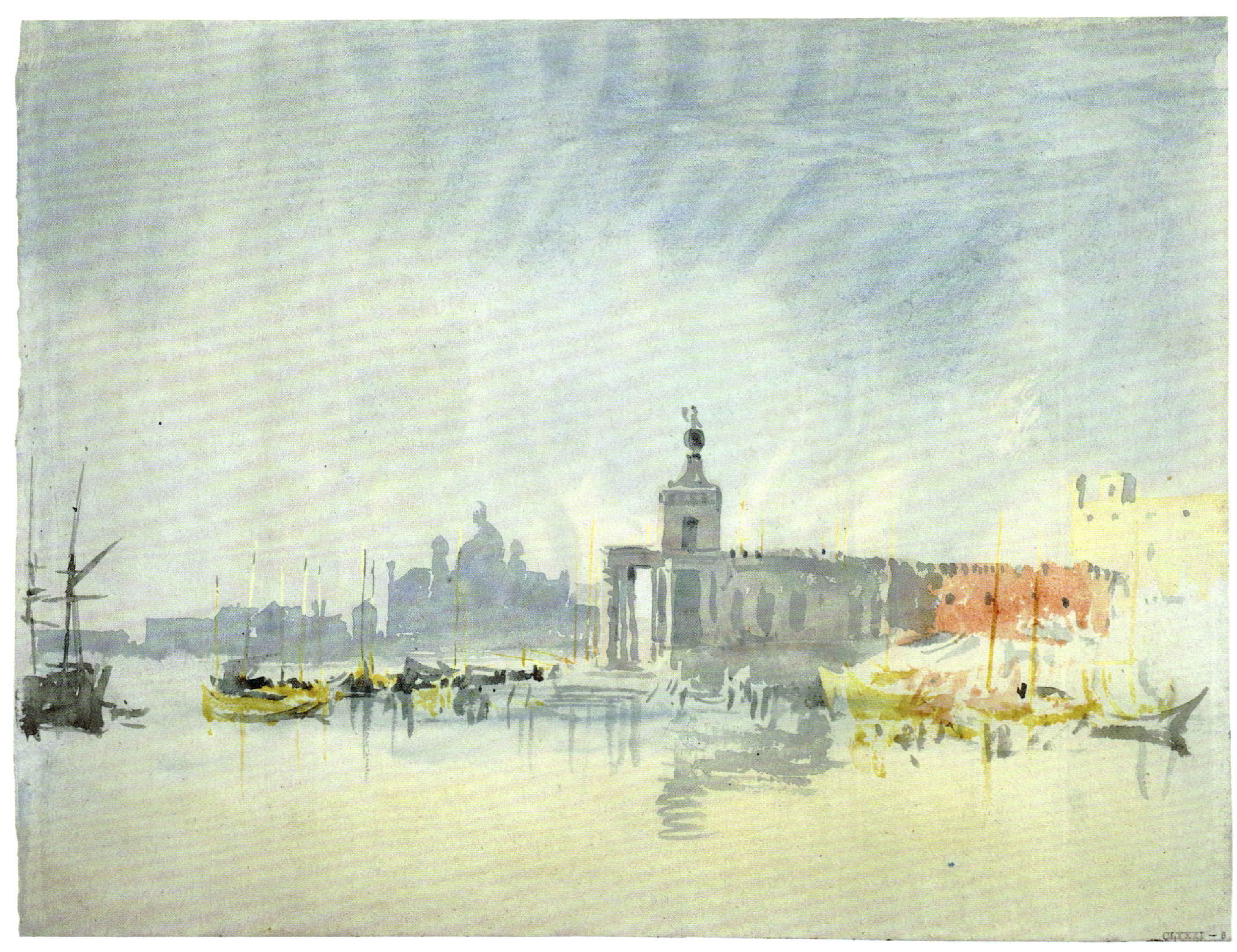

The Punta della Dogana, with the Zitelle in the Distance – Early Morning
from the Como and Venice Sketchbook 1819
Watercolour on paper, 22.3 × 28.5

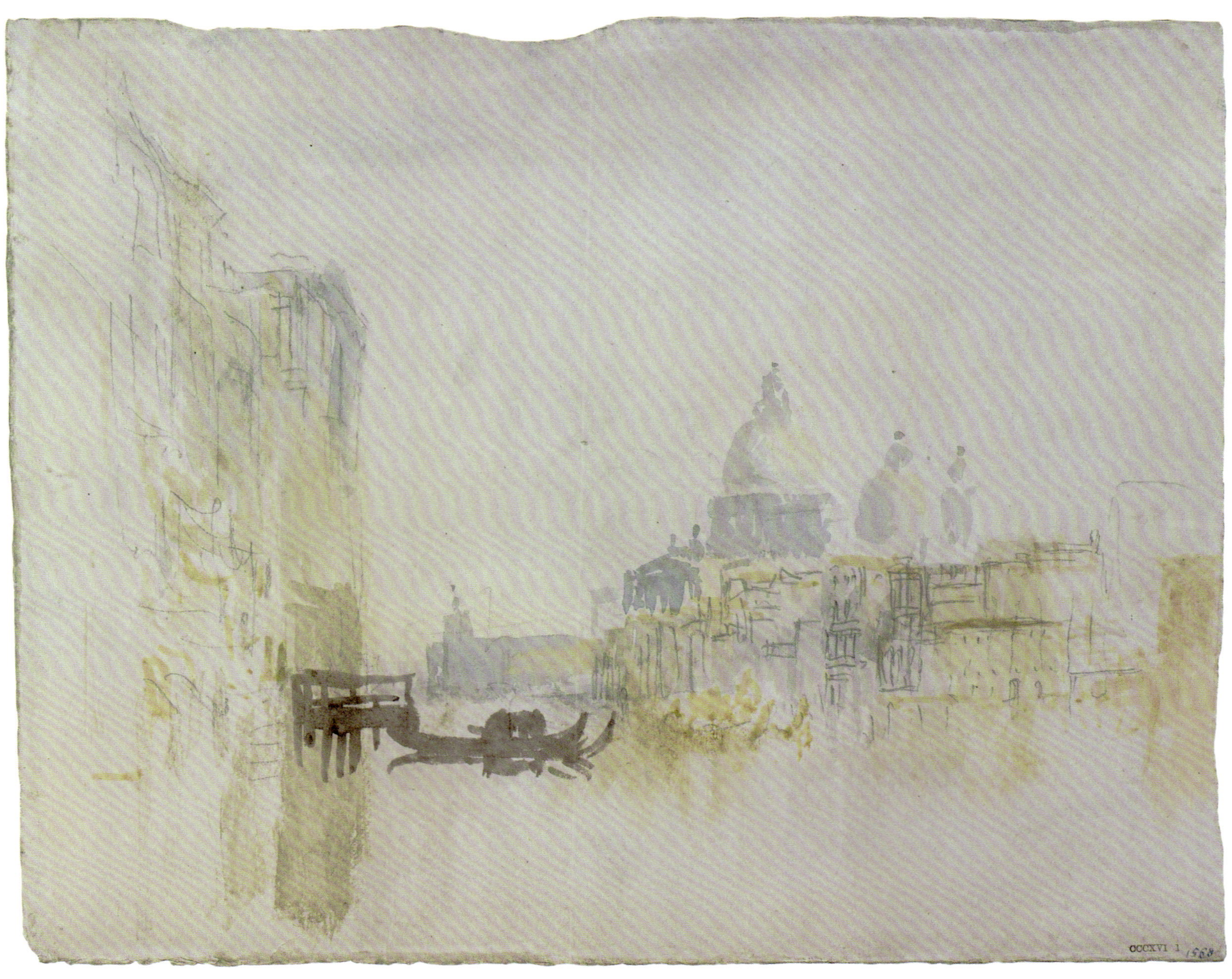

Santa Maria della Salute with the Traghetto San Maurizio 1840
Graphite and watercolour on paper, 24.5 × 30.4

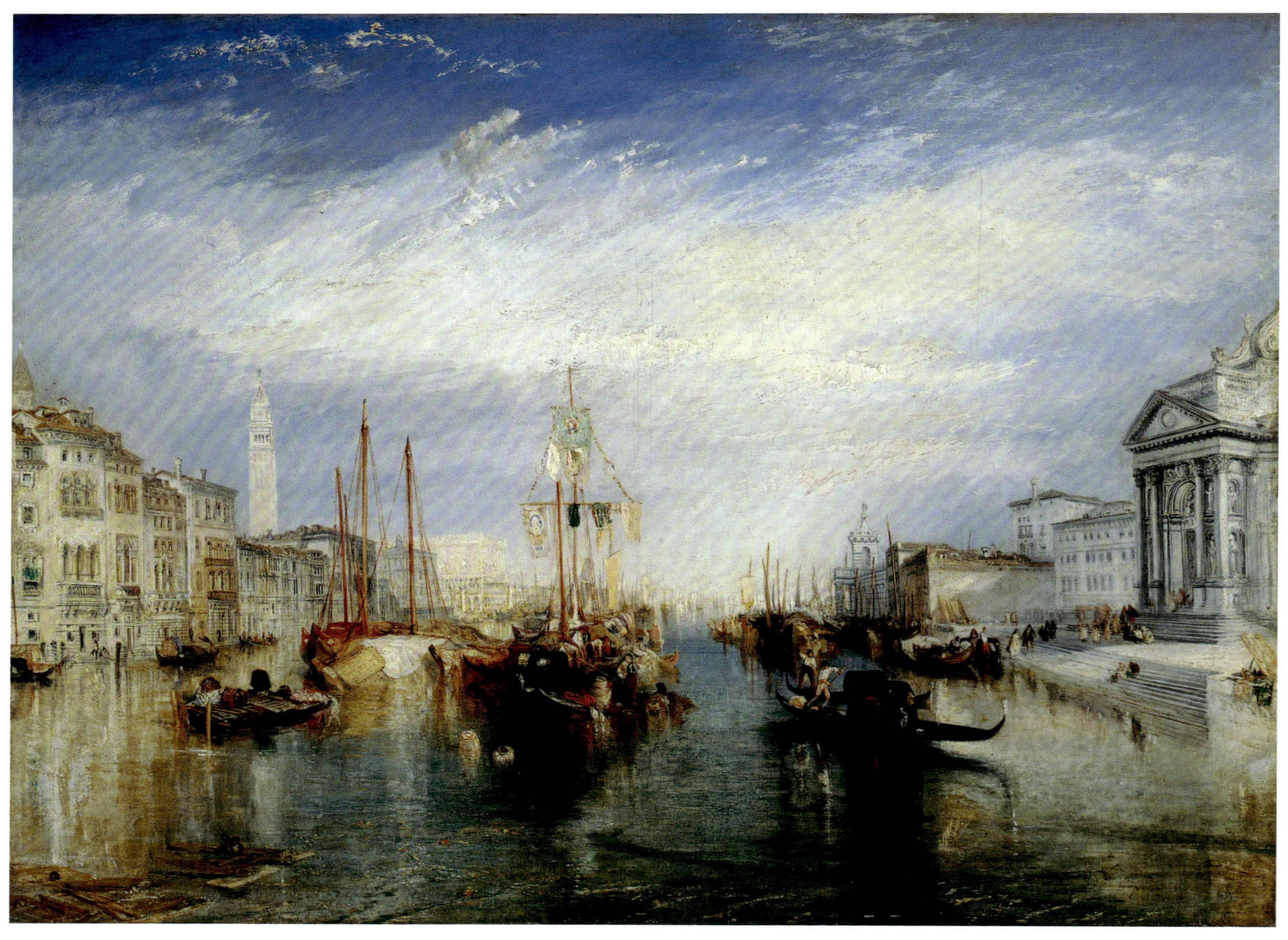

Venice, from the Porch of Madonna della Salute exhibited c.1835
Oil paint on canvas, 91.4 × 122.2
The Metropolitan Museum of Art, New York

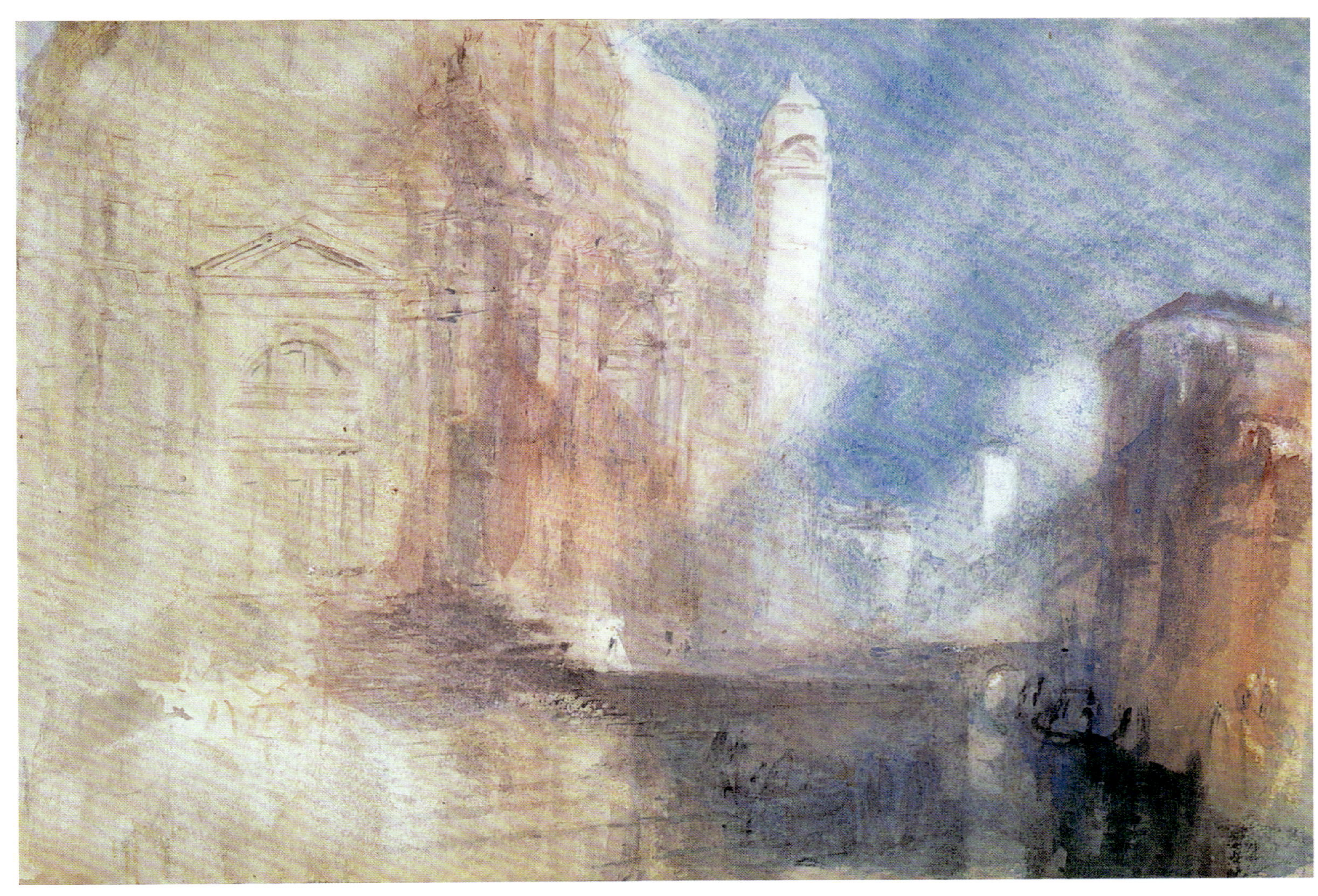

The North-Western Façade of Santa Maria della Salute 1840
Watercolour, gouache and pen and ink on paper, 22.2 × 32
National Galleries Scotland, Edinburgh

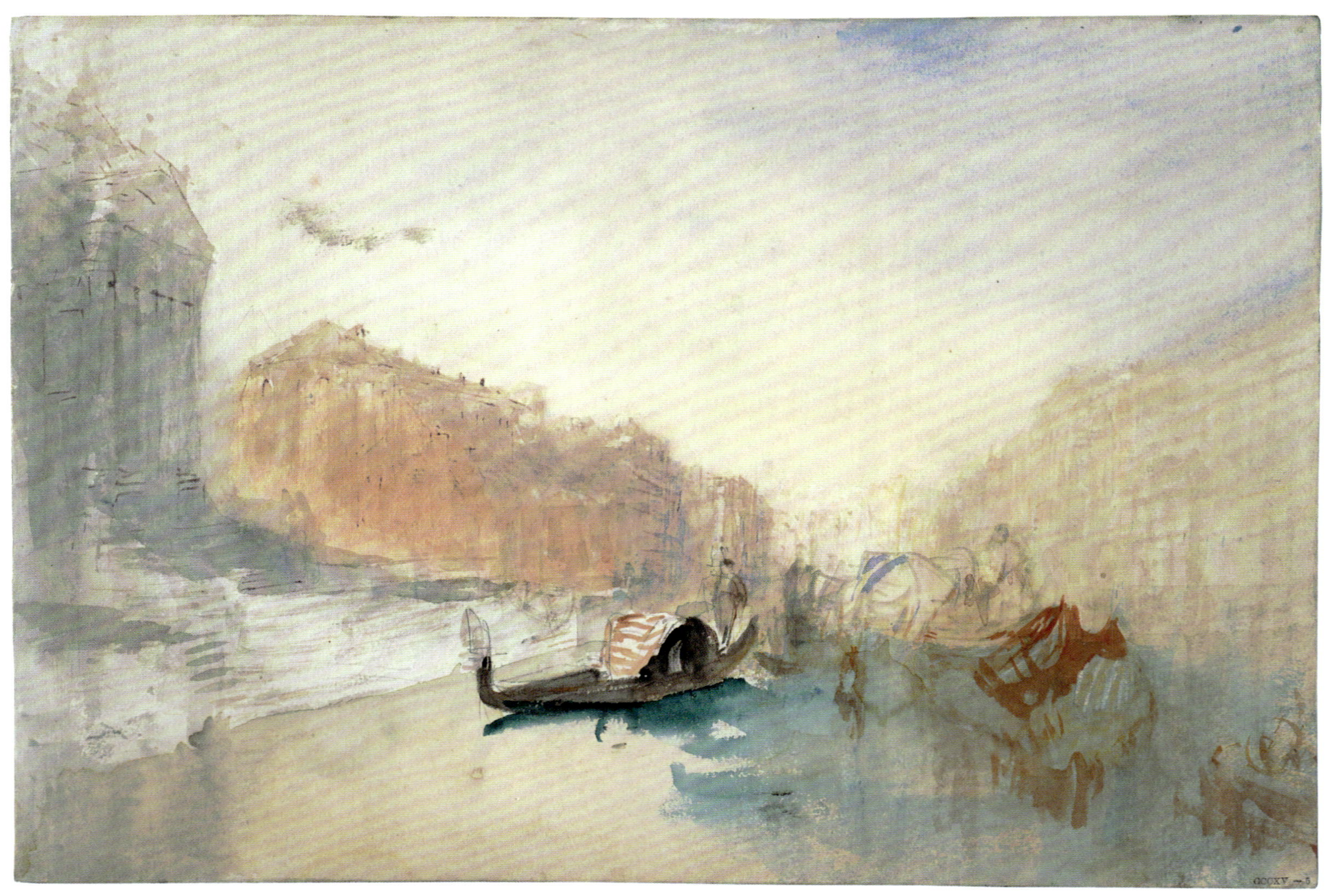

The Steps of Santa Maria della Salute, looking up the Grand Canal
from the Grand Canal and Giudecca Sketchbook 1840
Watercolour on paper, 22.1 × 32.2

The incongruous line of grey smoke hovering above the suppressed
Abbey of San Gregorio emanated from a chimney added to the
building once it was converted to industrial purposes for the state mint
(the nearby Zecca).

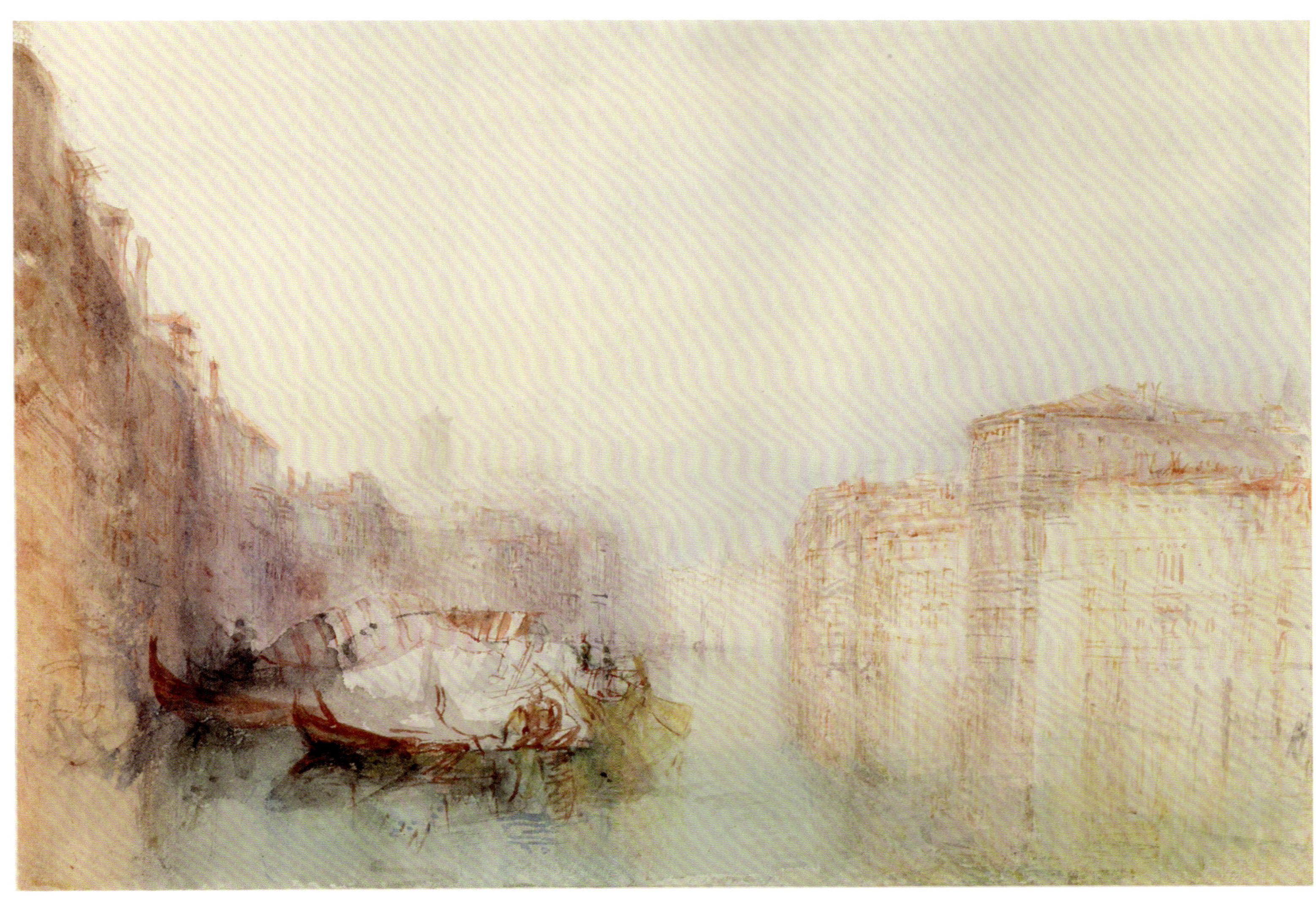

*Looking up the Grand Canal towards the Palazzo Corner della
Ca' Grande, from alongside the Abbazia di San Gregorio, near Santa Maria
della Salute* 1840
Watercolour, 22 × 31.6
Private collection

The Grand Canal looking towards the Palazzo Contarini degli Scrigni, with the Barbaro and Cavalli Palaces on the right, from near the Traghetto di San Vio from the Venice sketchbook 1833
Graphite on paper, 10.9 × 20.3

The Accademia from the Grand Canal 1840
Watercolour with pen and reddish-brown ink on paper, 21.7 × 31.8
Ashmolean Museum, Oxford

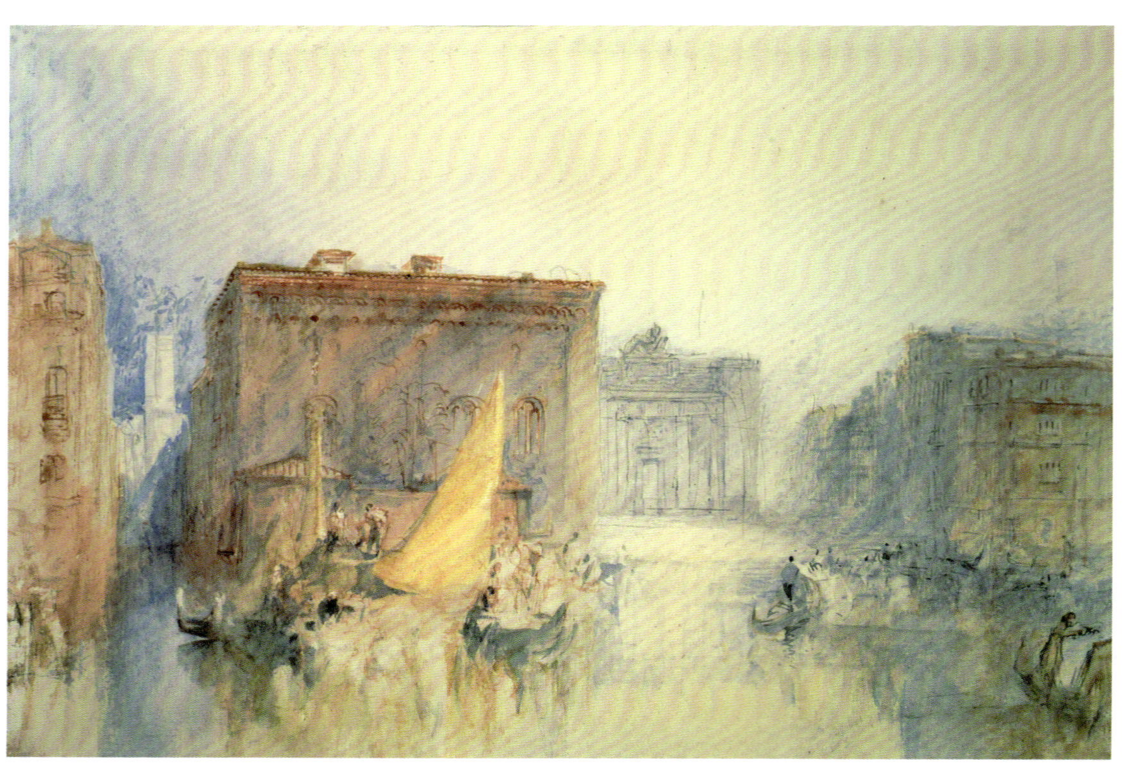

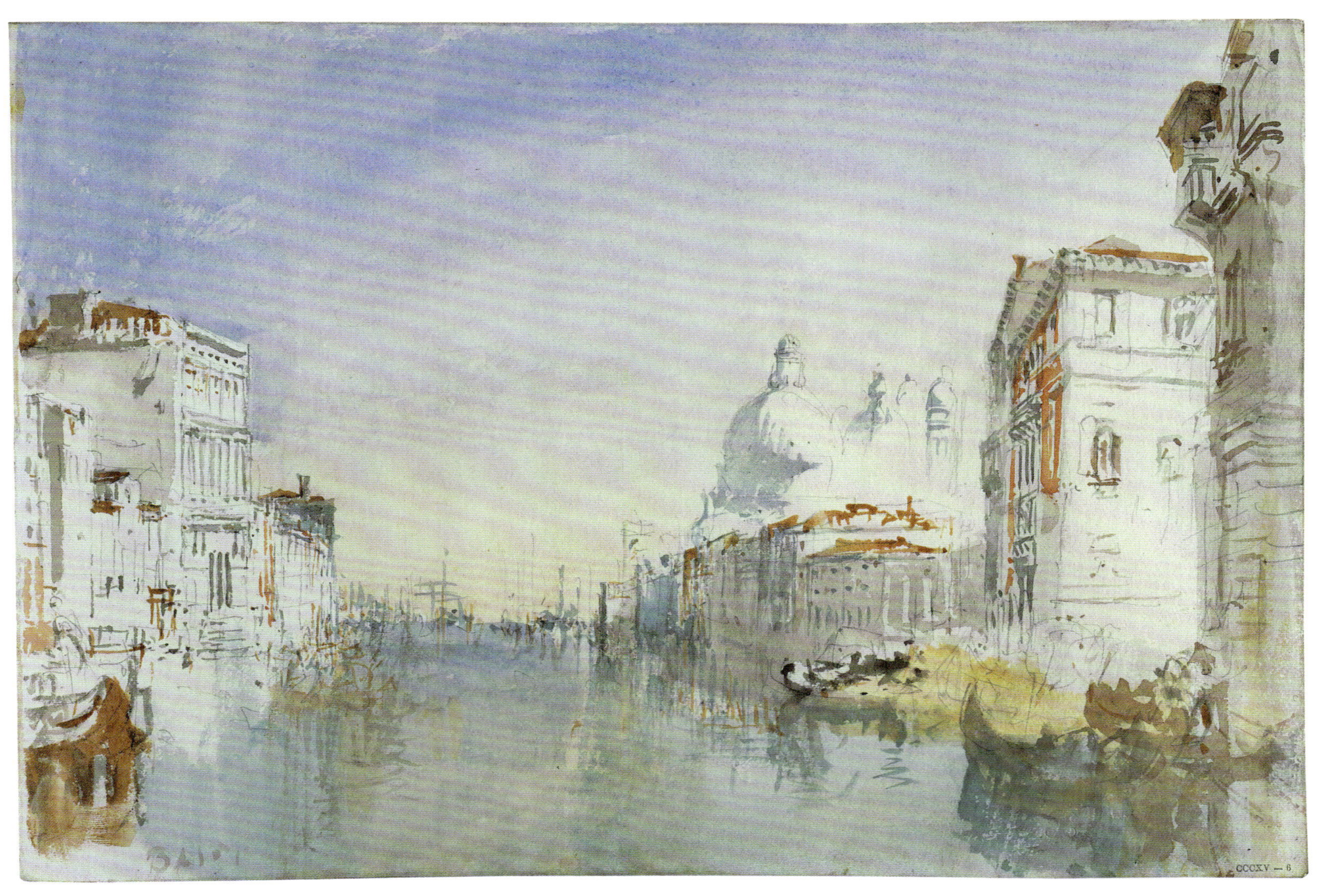

Looking down the Grand Canal to Palazzo Corner della Ca' Grande
and Santa Maria della Salute from the Grand Canal and Giudecca
Sketchbook 1840
Graphite and watercolour on paper, 22.1 × 32.2

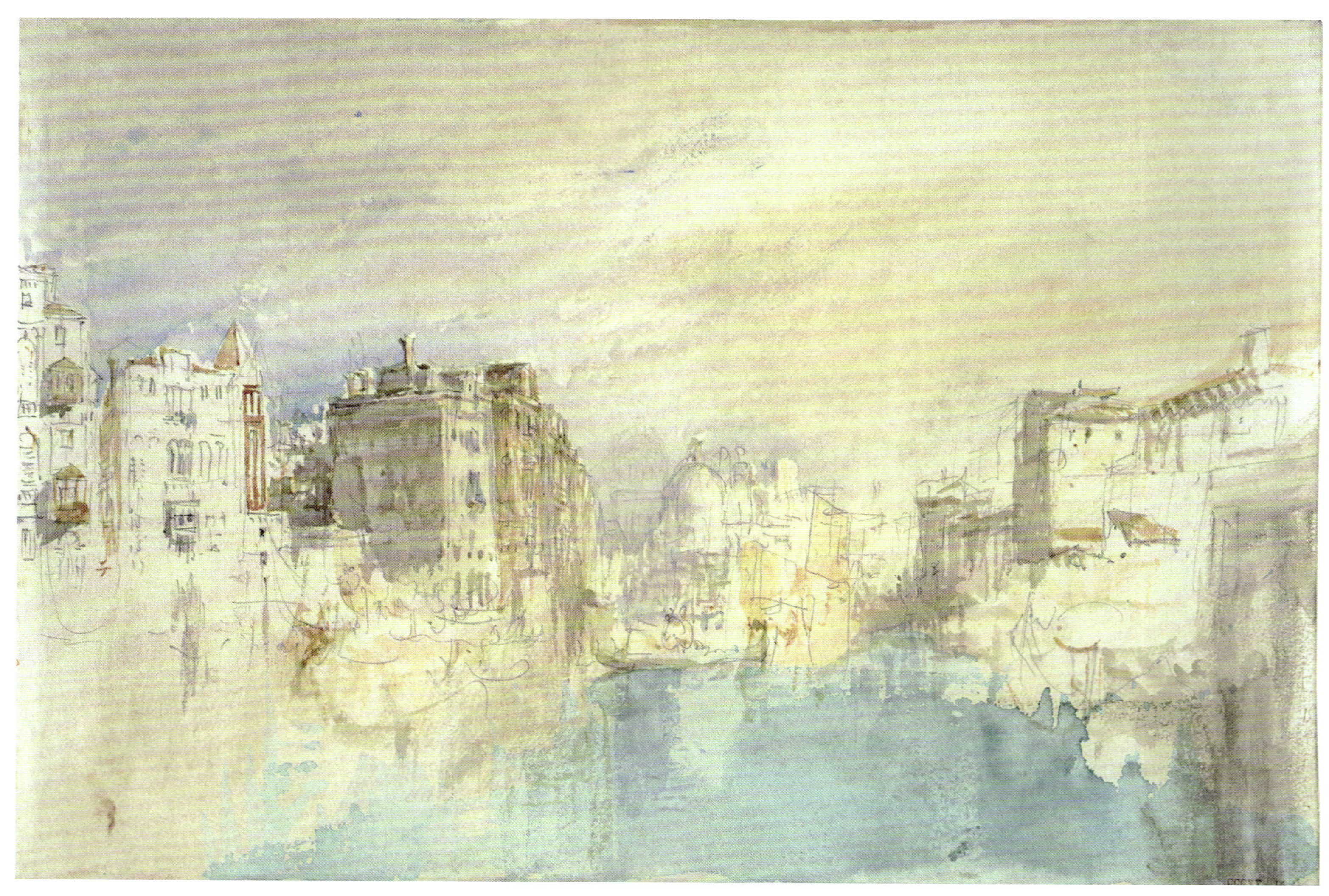

The Grand Canal from near the Accademia, with the Campanile of San Vidal, and Santa Maria della Salute in the Distance from the Grand Canal and Giudecca Sketchbook 1840
Graphite and watercolour on paper, 22.1 × 32.2

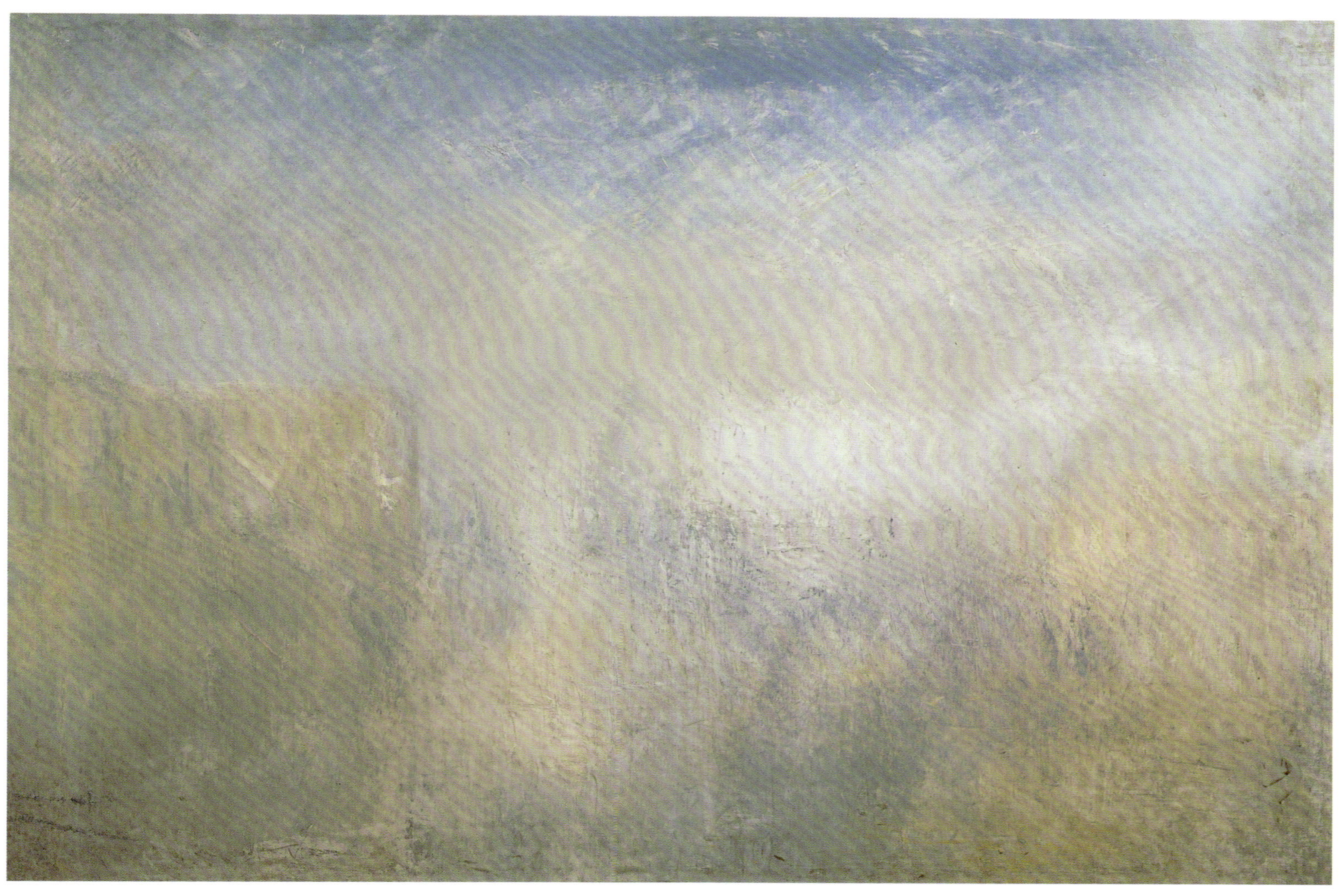

Venice with the Salute c.1844
Oil paint on canvas, 62.2 × 92.7

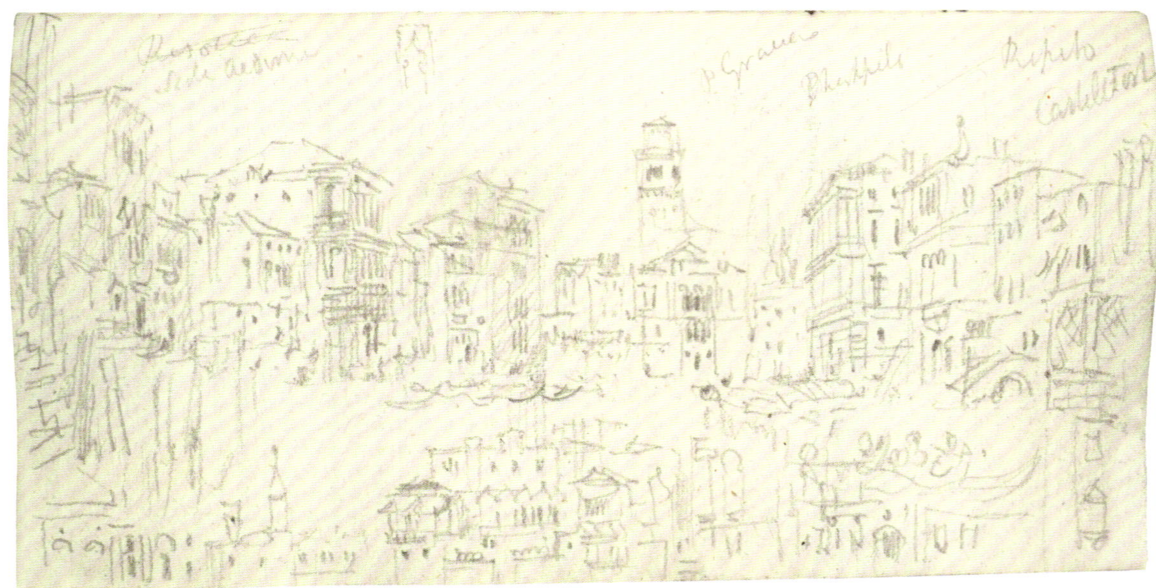

On the Grand Canal looking towards the Palazzo Balbi and the Campanile of the Frari, at the bend of the canal, with the Rezzonico and Foscari palaces on the left, and the Ca' del Duca and the Palazzo Grassi on the right; a supplementary sketch below continues the palaces on the right side of the main view from the Venice sketchbook 1833

Graphite on paper, 10.9 × 20.3

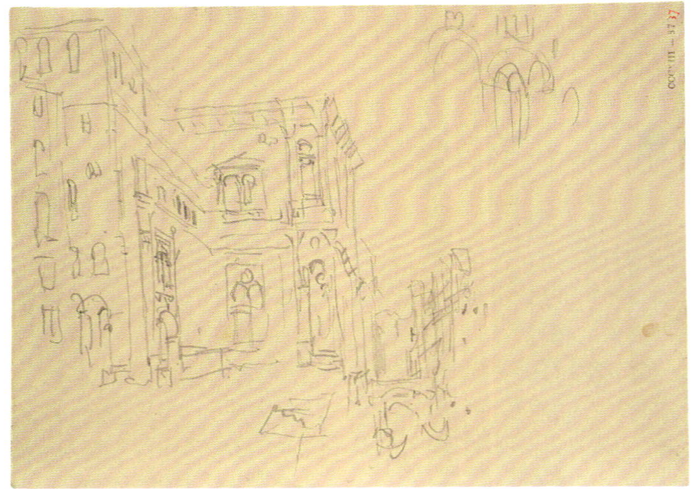

The Scuola Grande di San Rocco, on the Rio della Frescada from the Venice and Botzen sketchbook 1840

Graphite on paper, 17.3 × 12.3

The Apse and Campanile of Santa Maria dei Frari from the Campo San Rocco from the Venice and Botzen sketchbook 1840

Graphite on paper, 12.3 × 17.3

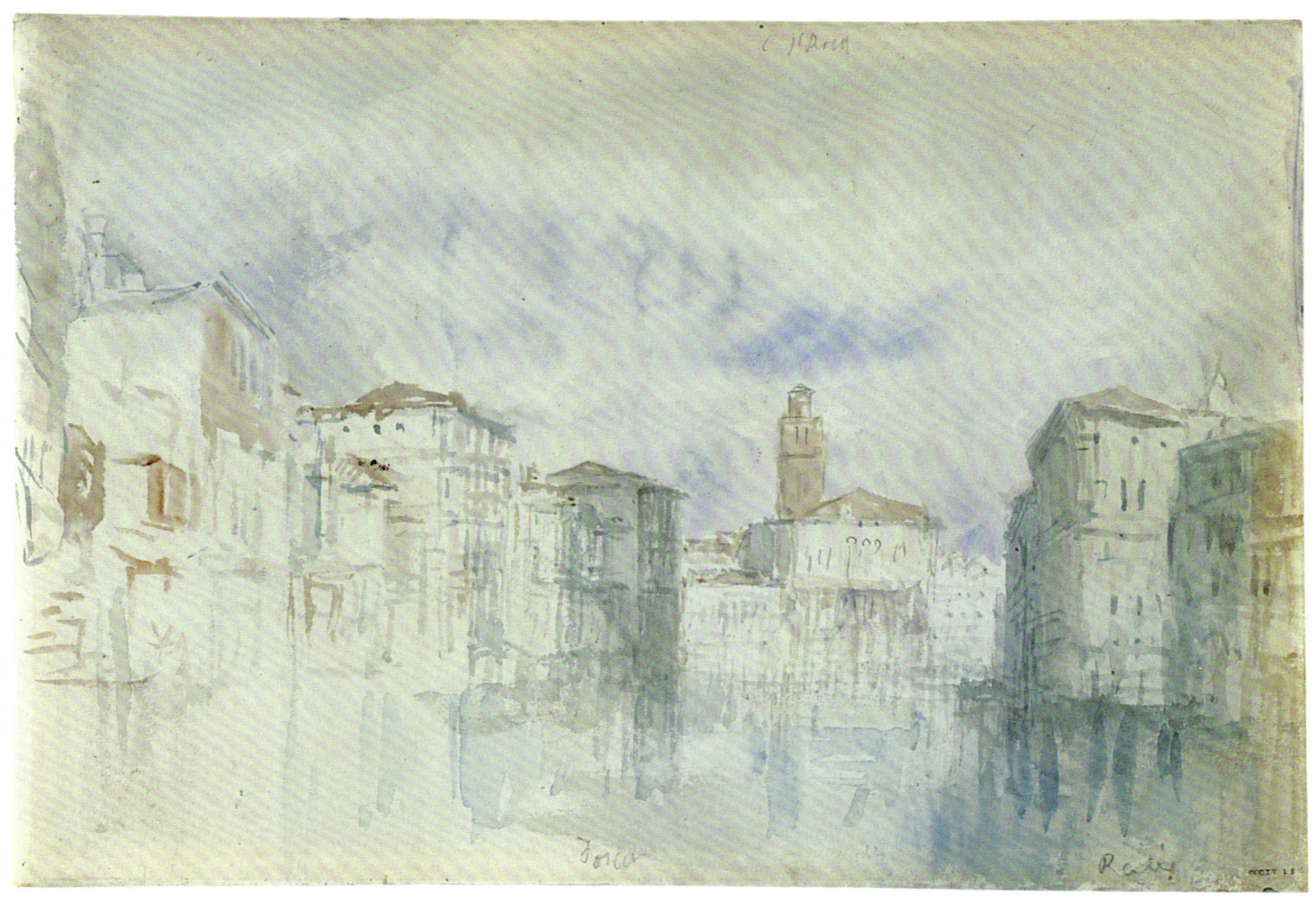

*The Grand Canal Looking towards the Palazzo Balbi and Campanile of
the Frari* from the Grand Canal and Giudecca Sketchbook 1840
Graphite and watercolour on paper, 22.2 × 32

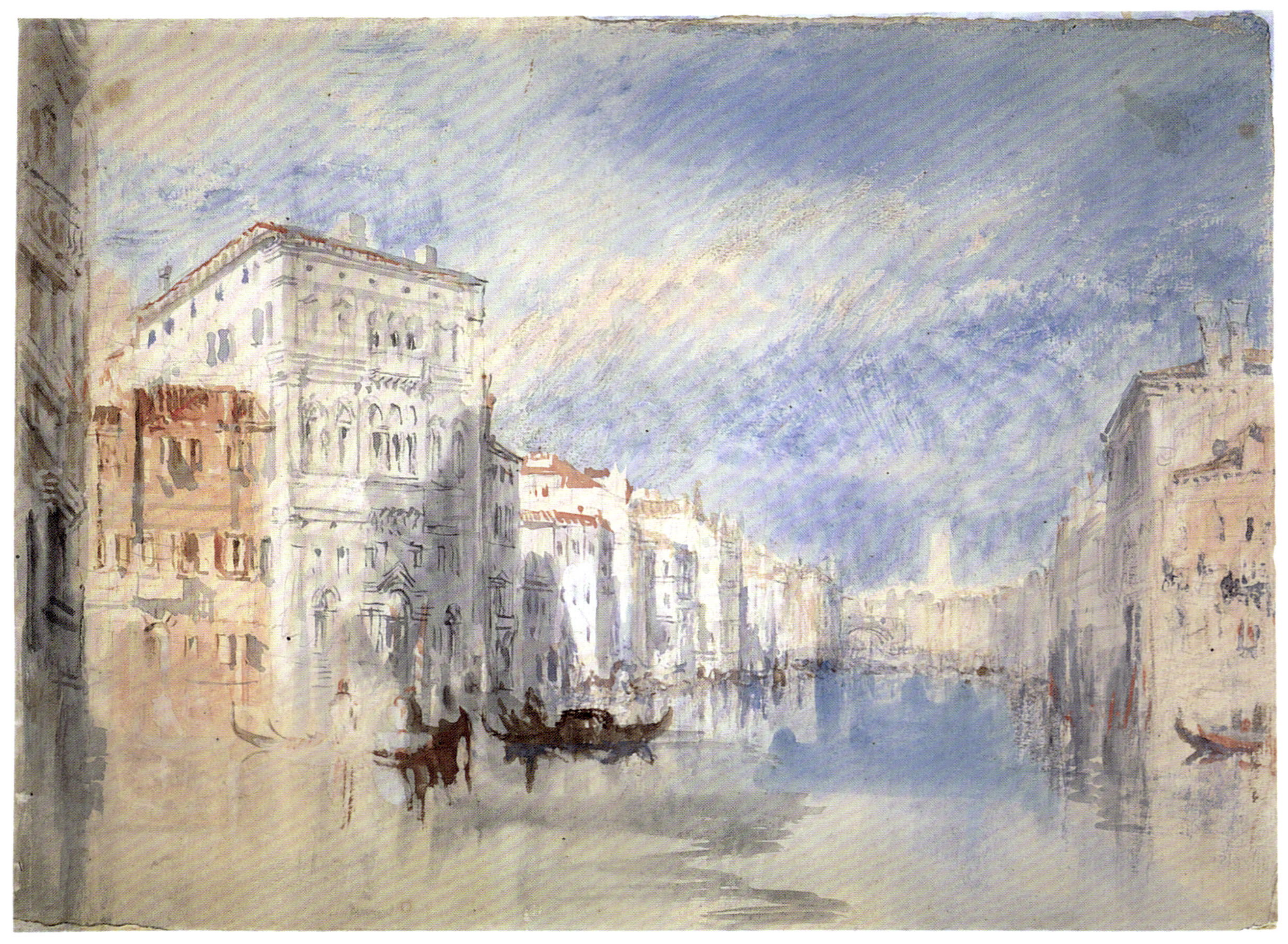

The Palazzo Balbi on the Grand Canal ?1833/1840
Graphite, watercolour and gouache on buff paper, 23.1 × 30.7
National Galleries Scotland, Edinburgh

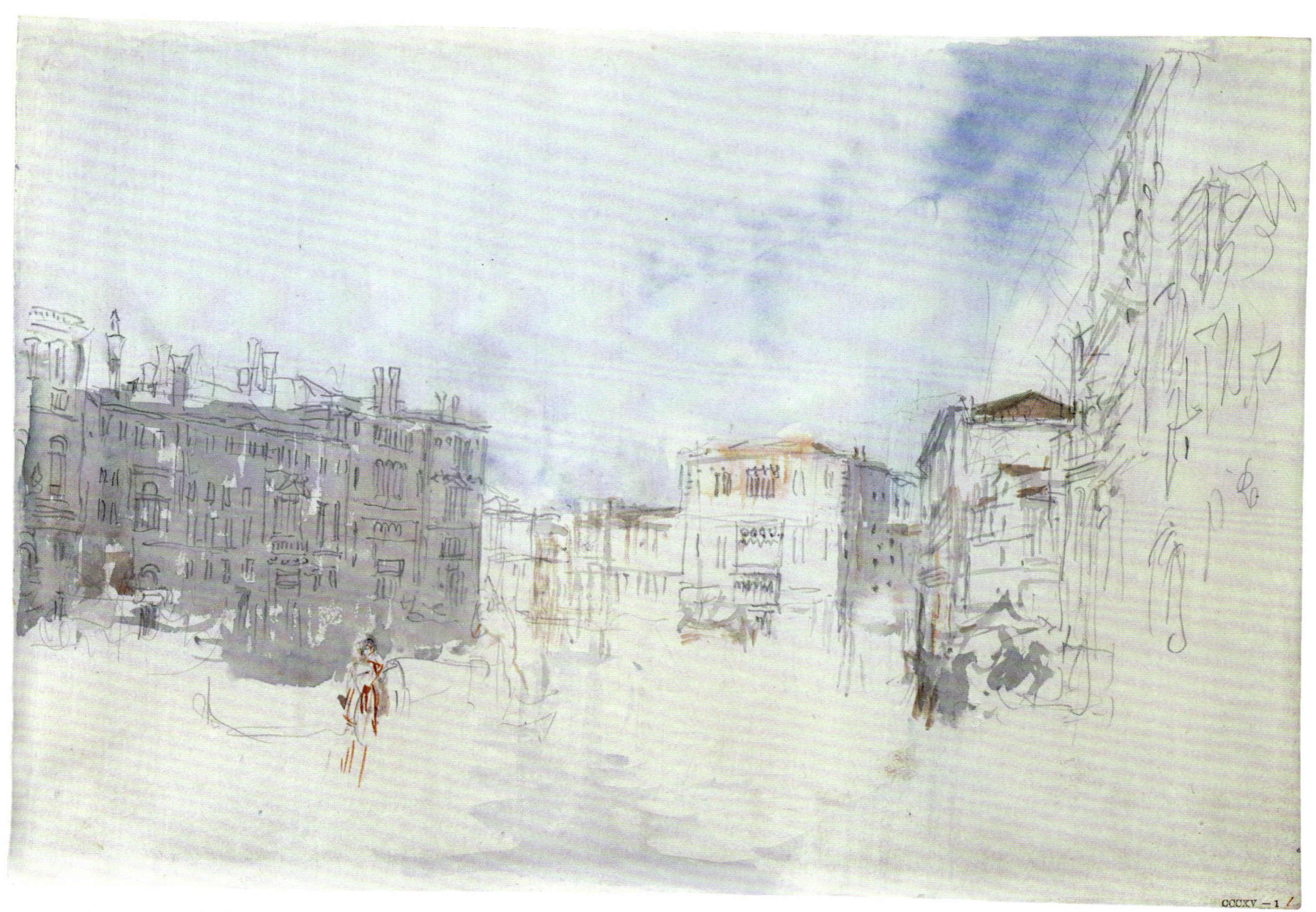

On the Grand Canal, looking towards the Mocenigo Palaces, with the Palazzo Foscari beyond from the Grand Canal and Giudecca Sketchbook 1840
Graphite and watercolour on paper, 22.1 × 32.2

The Pisani Moretta and the Barbarigo della Terrazza palaces on the Grand Canal from the Milan to Venice Sketchbook 1819
Graphite on paper, 11.2 × 18.5

Looking down the Grand Canal towards the Palazzo Pisani-Moretta and the Palazzo Barbarigo della Terrazza, from near the Palazzo Grimani 1840
Graphite, watercolour and gouache, with pen and ink, on grey paper, 19.1 × 28.1

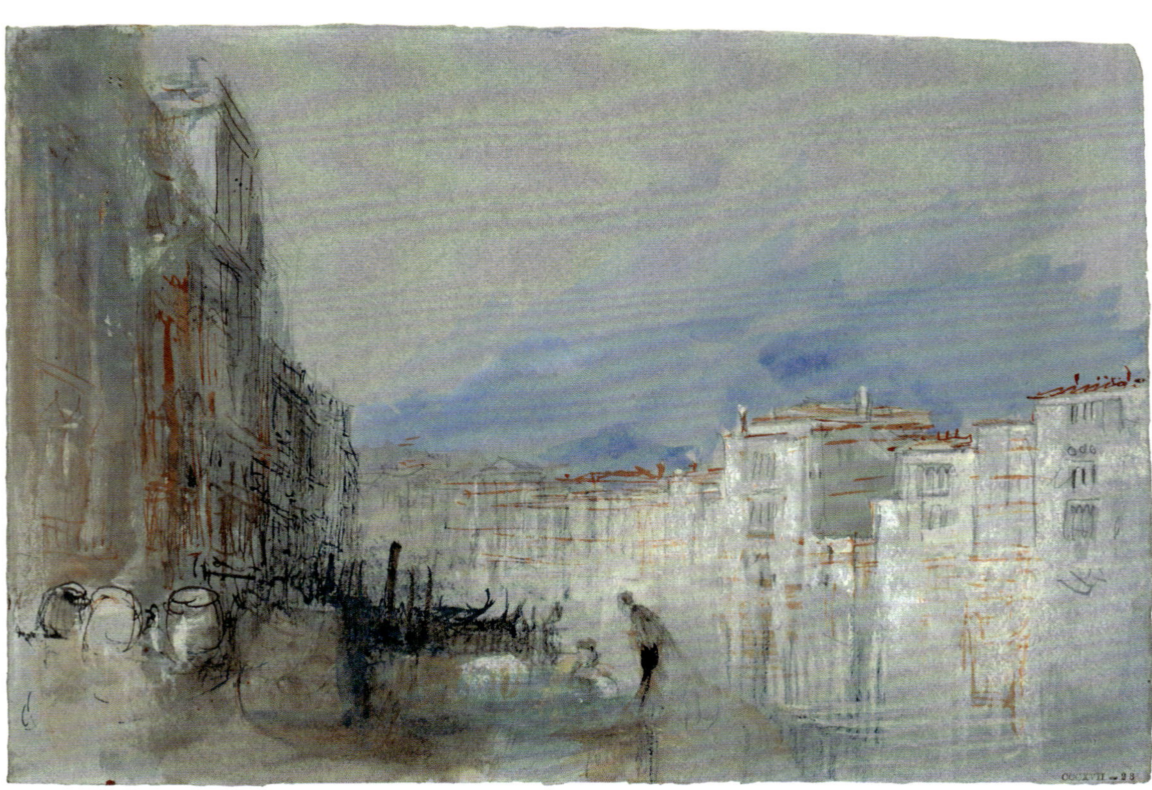

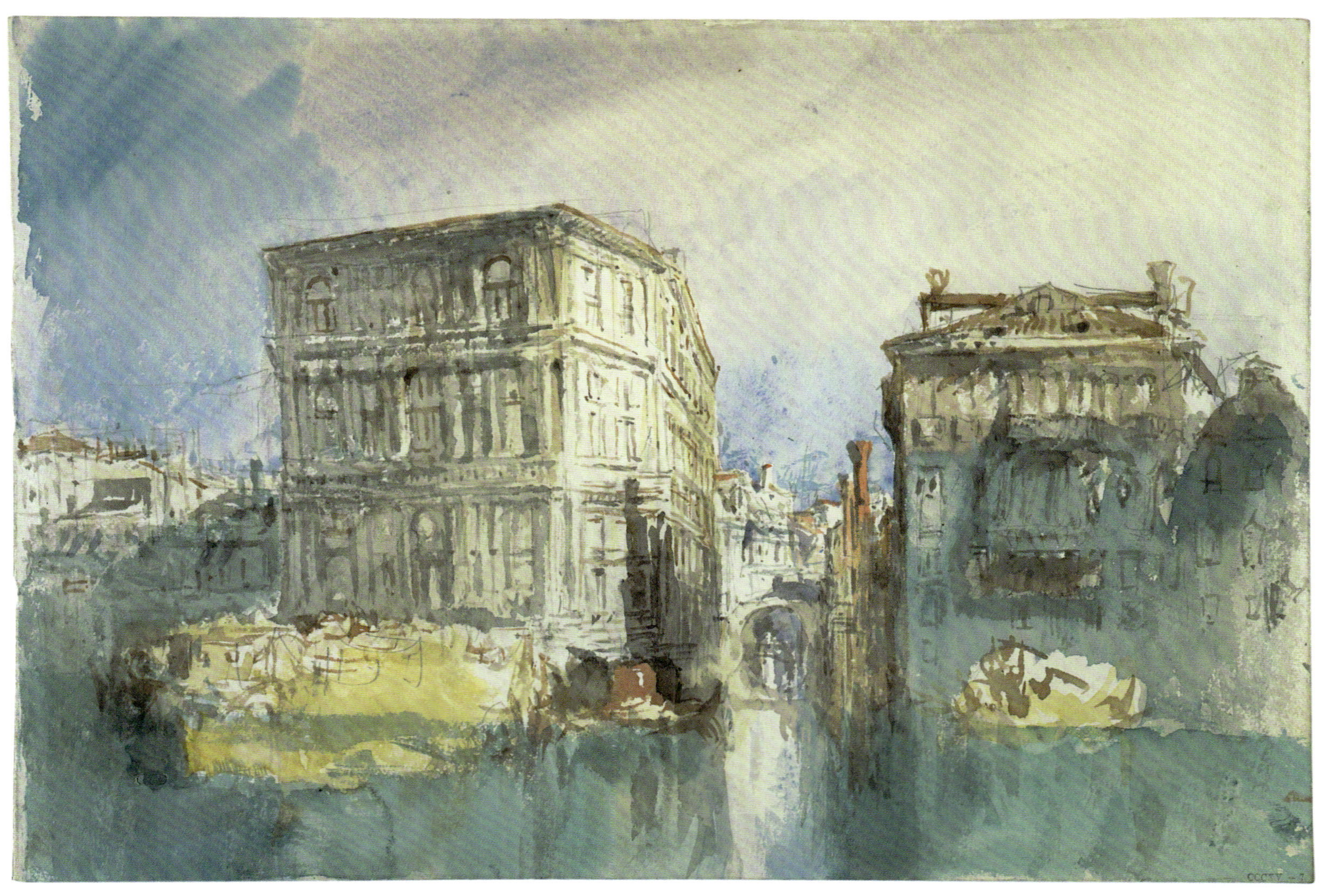

The Palazzo Grimani and the Palazzo Corner Contarini dei Cavalli,
with the Rio di San Luca from the Grand Canal and Giudecca
Sketchbook 1840
Graphite and watercolour on paper, 22.1 × 32.2

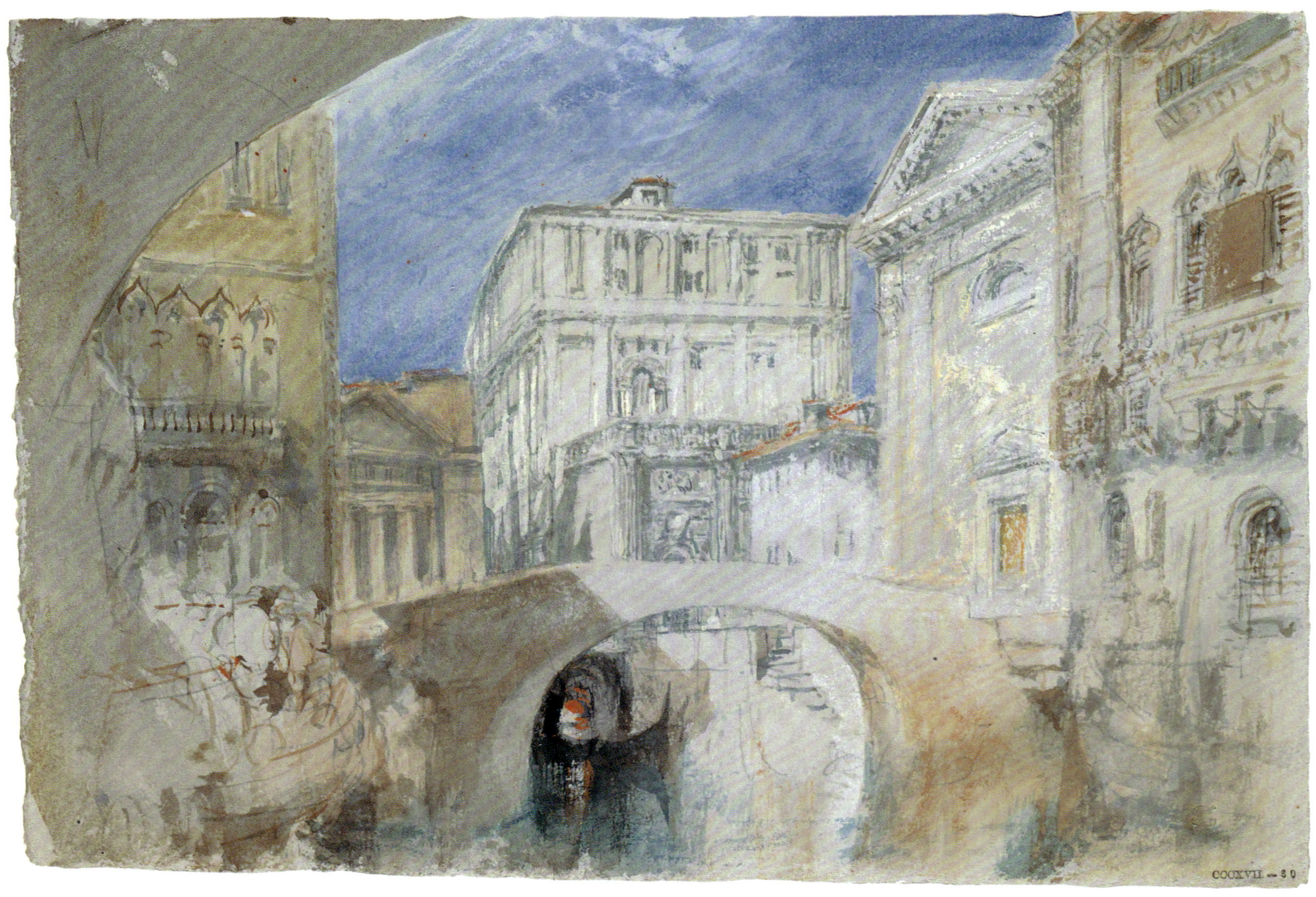

The Church of San Luca and the Back of the Palazzo Grimani
from the Rio di San Luca 1840
Graphite, watercolour and gouache on grey paper, 19.4 × 27.9

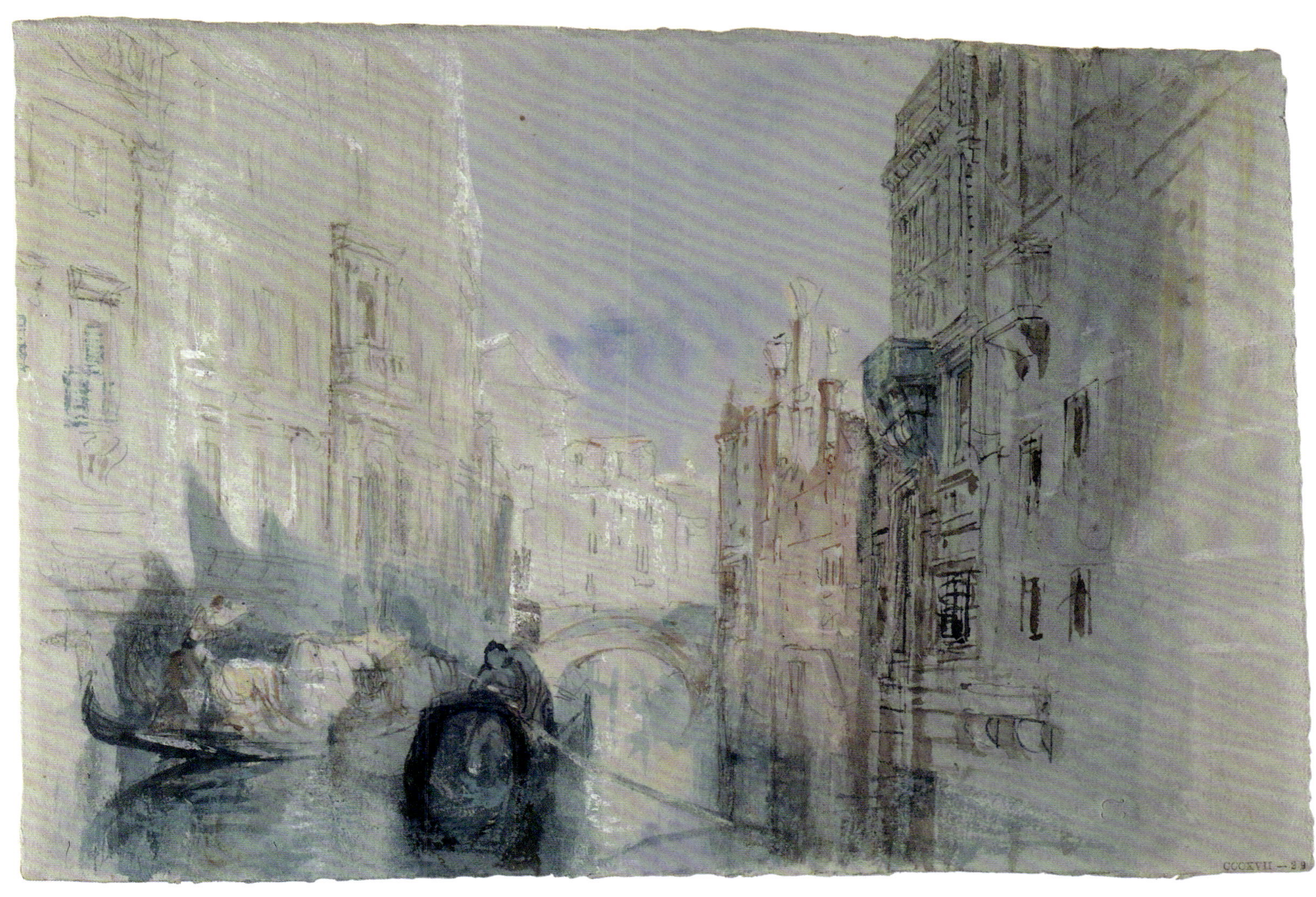

The Rio di San Luca alongside the Palazzo Grimani,
with the Church of San Luca 1840
Gouache, graphite and watercolour on grey paper, 19.1 × 28.1

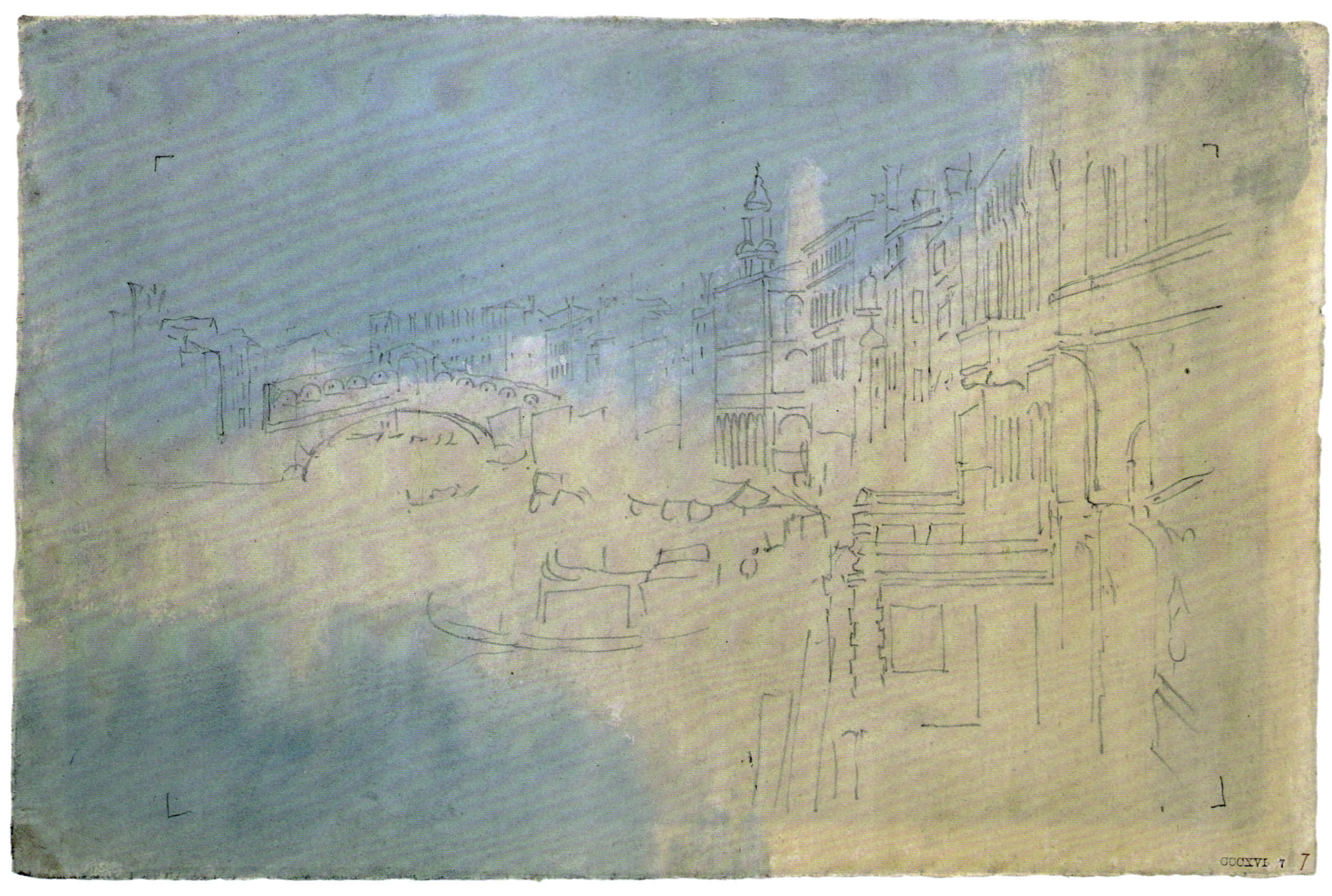

The Rialto from the Albergo Leon Bianco, traced from a Drawing by James Hakewill c.1818
Graphite and watercolour on paper, 18.2 × 26.6

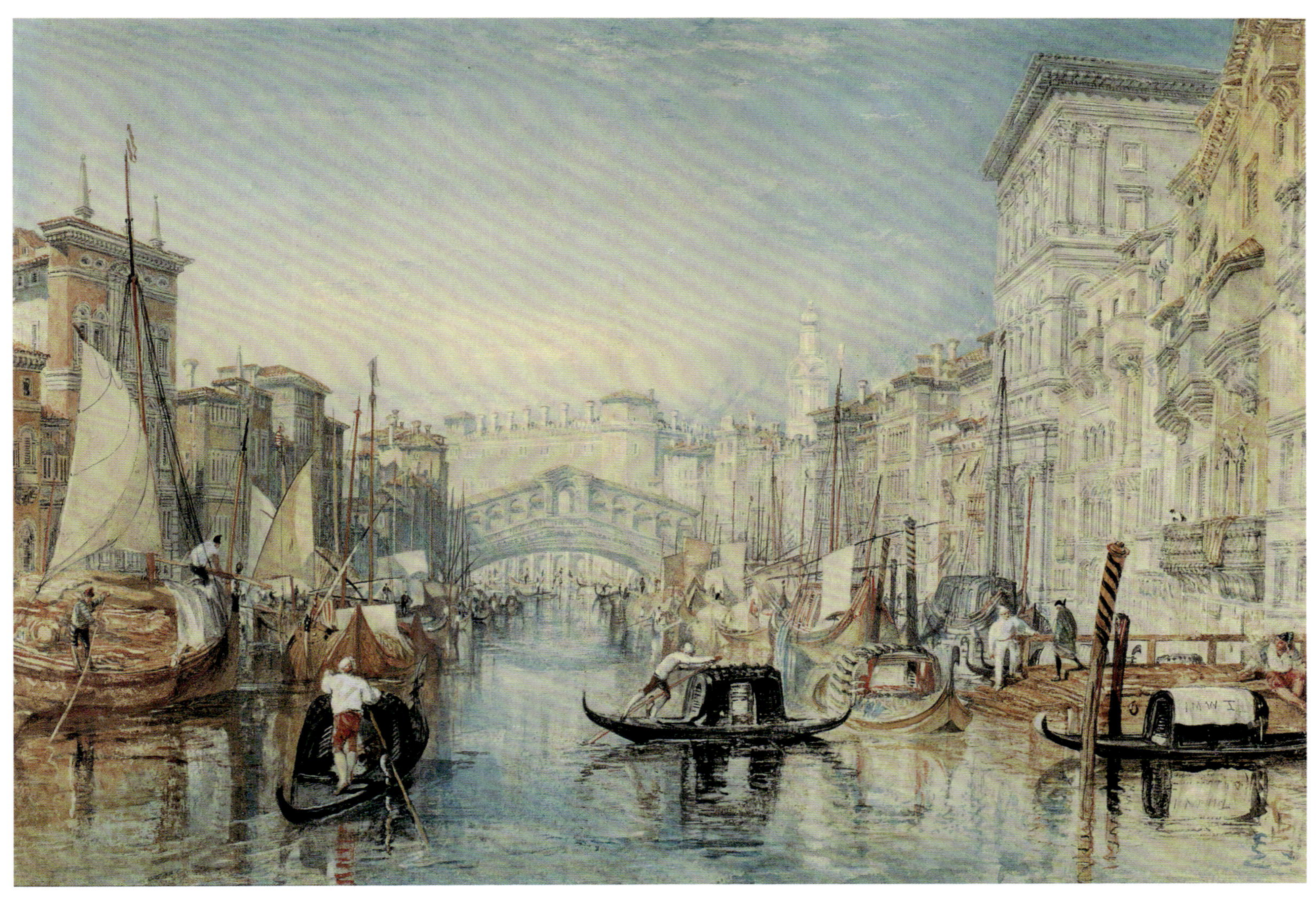

The Rialto, Venice 1820–1
Graphite and watercolour on white wove paper, 28.6 × 41.3
Indianapolis Museum of Art, Indiana

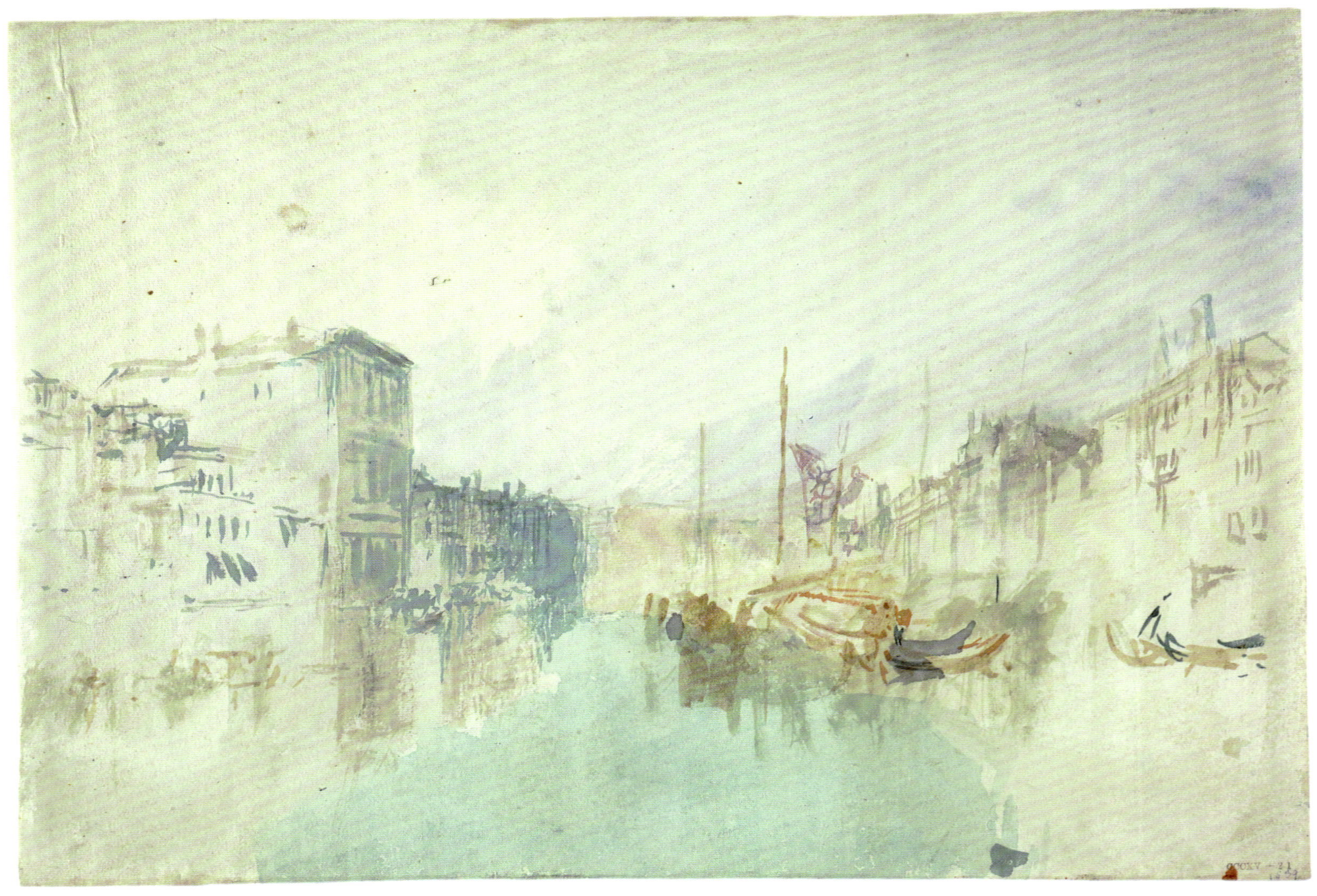

The Grand Canal, Looking towards the Palazzo Grimani from the Grand
Canal and Giudecca Sketchbook 1840
Graphite and watercolour on paper, 22.1 × 32.2

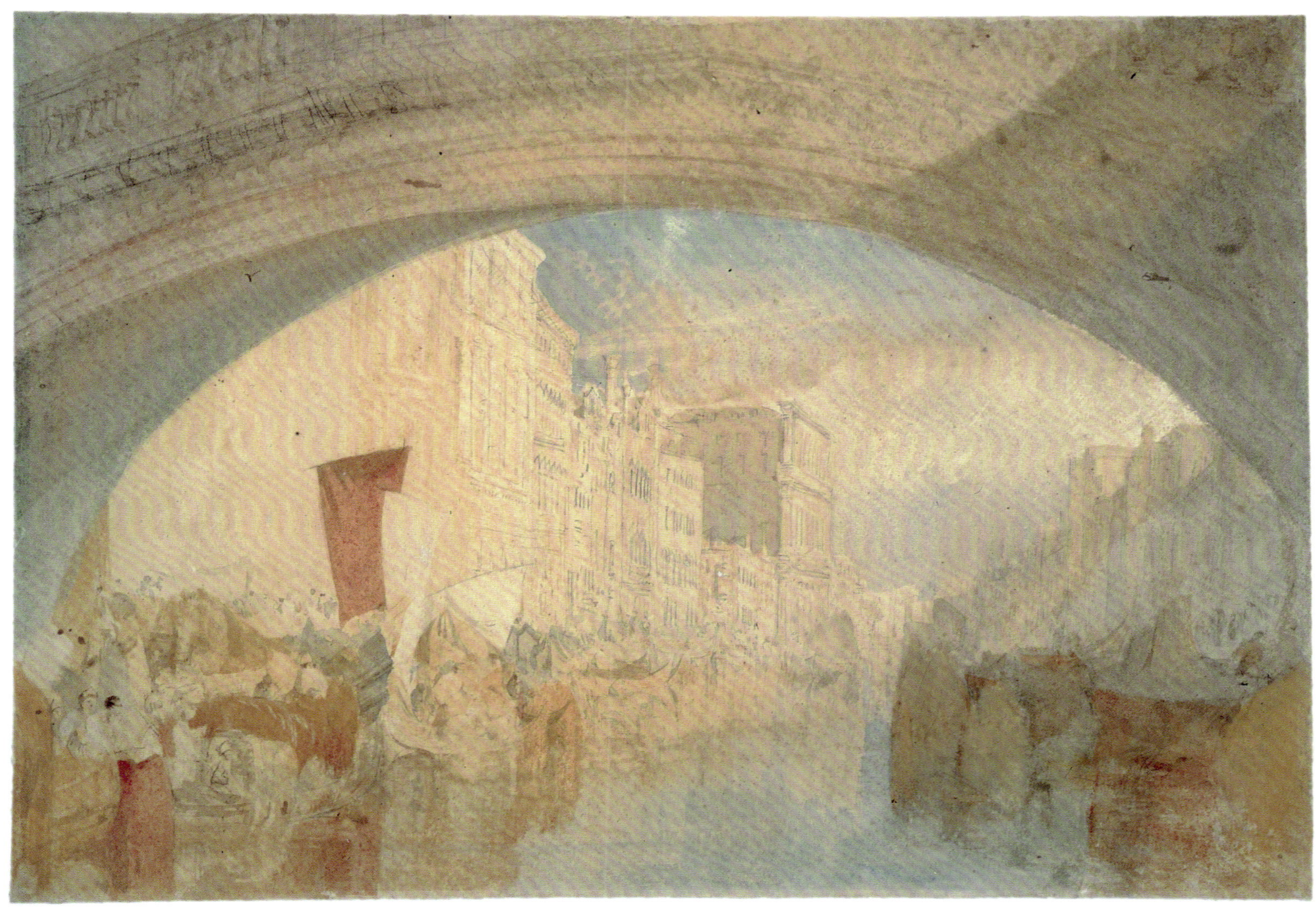

The Grand Canal, with the Palazzo Grimani, from below the Rialto Bridge
?1819/1833
Watercolour, graphite and gouache with white highlights on paper, 28.4 × 40.6
National Gallery of Ireland, Dublin

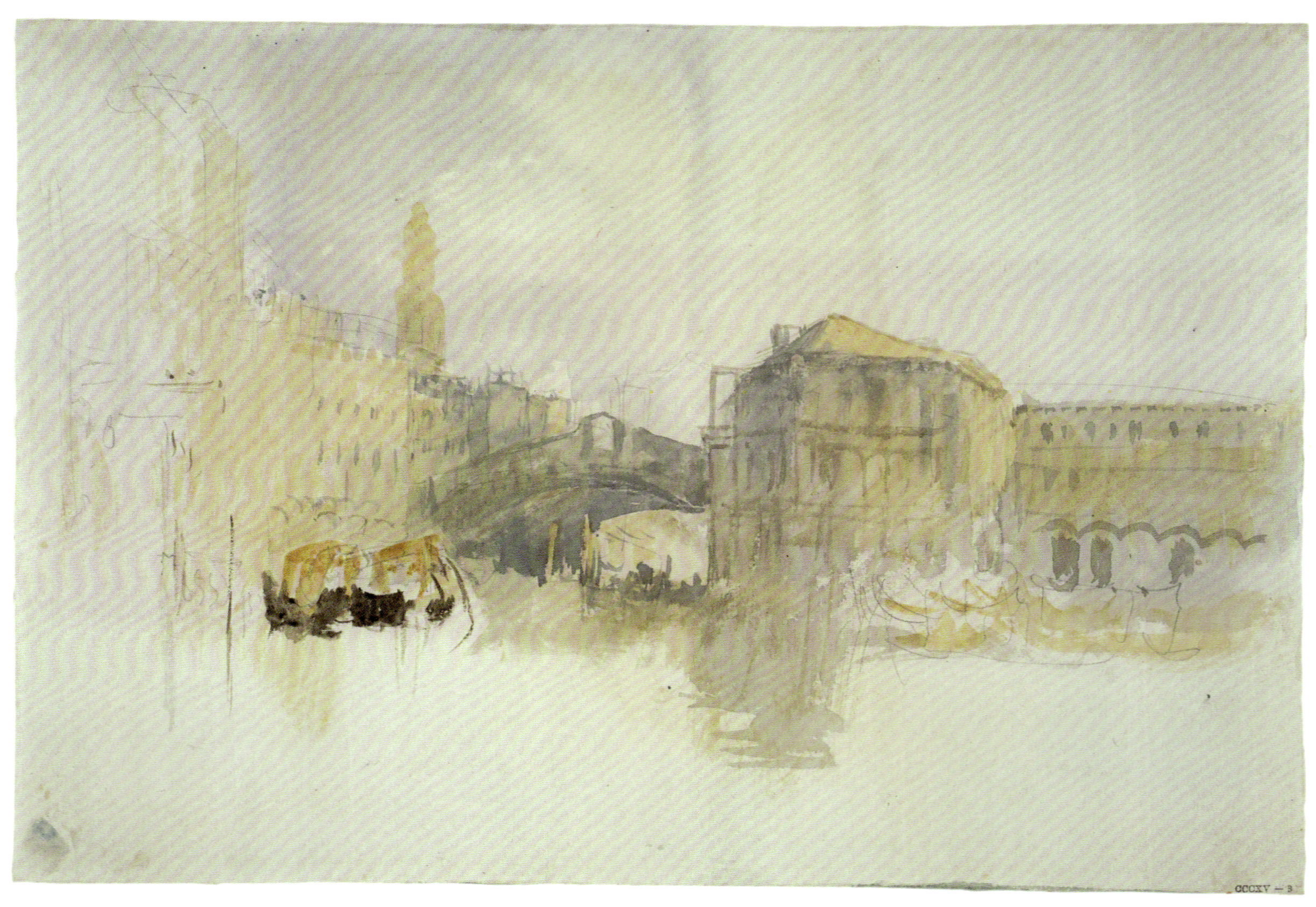

The Rialto Bridge from the North, with the Palazzo dei Camerlenghi from
the Grand Canal and Giudecca Sketchbook 1840
Watercolour on paper, 22.1 × 32.2

86

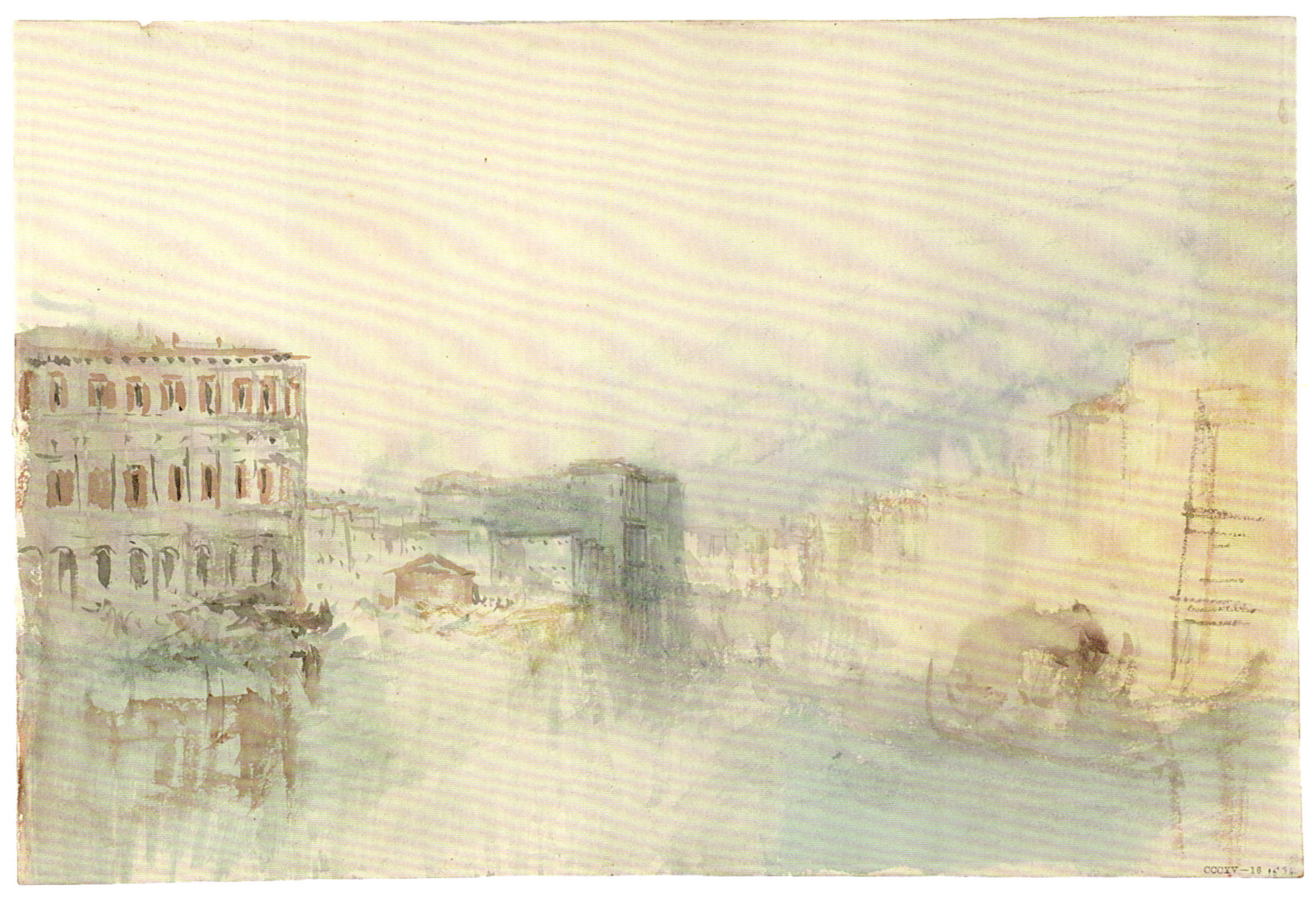

The Fabbriche Nuove and the Pesacaria (the Fish Market) on the Grand Canal from the Grand Canal and Giudecca Sketchbook 1840
Watercolour on paper, 22.1 × 32.2

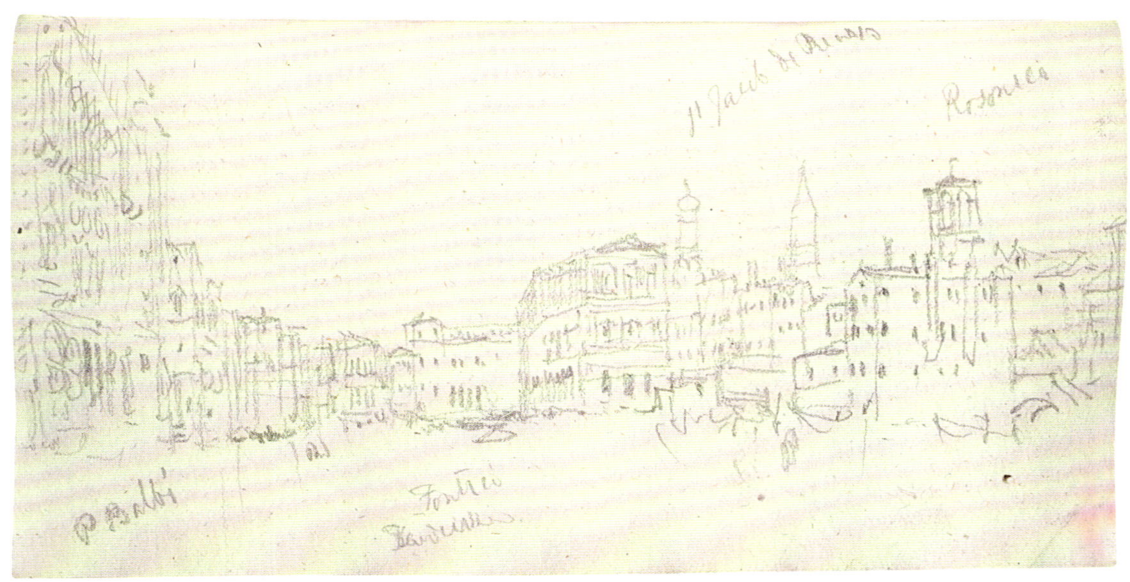

*The Grand Canal from near
Ca' Doro, looking towards the
Pescaria and the Fabbriche Nuove,
with the Fondaco dei Tedeschi in the
distance. The bell-towers are those
of San Giovanni Elemosinario,
San Marco and San Bartolomeo
(from right to left)* from the
Venice sketchbook 1833
Graphite on paper, 10.9 × 20.3

*The Grand Canal looking towards
the Pescaria and the Fabbriche
Nuove* from the Grand Canal and
Giudecca Sketchbook 1840
Graphite and watercolour on paper,
22.1 × 32.2

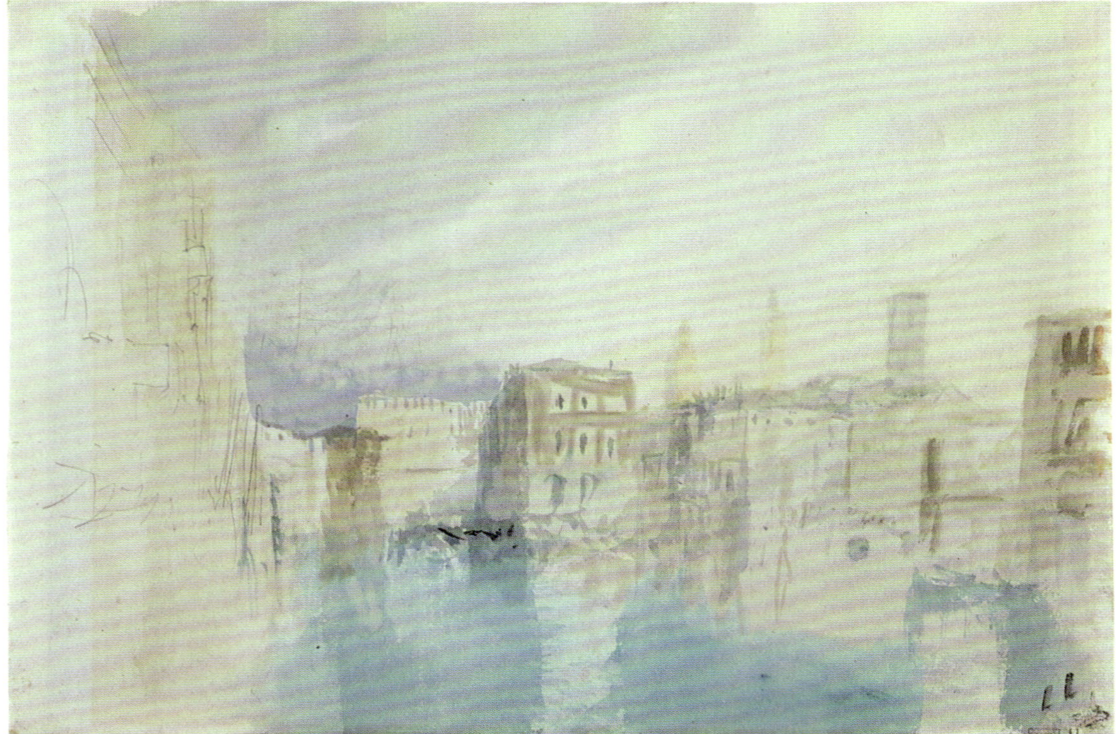

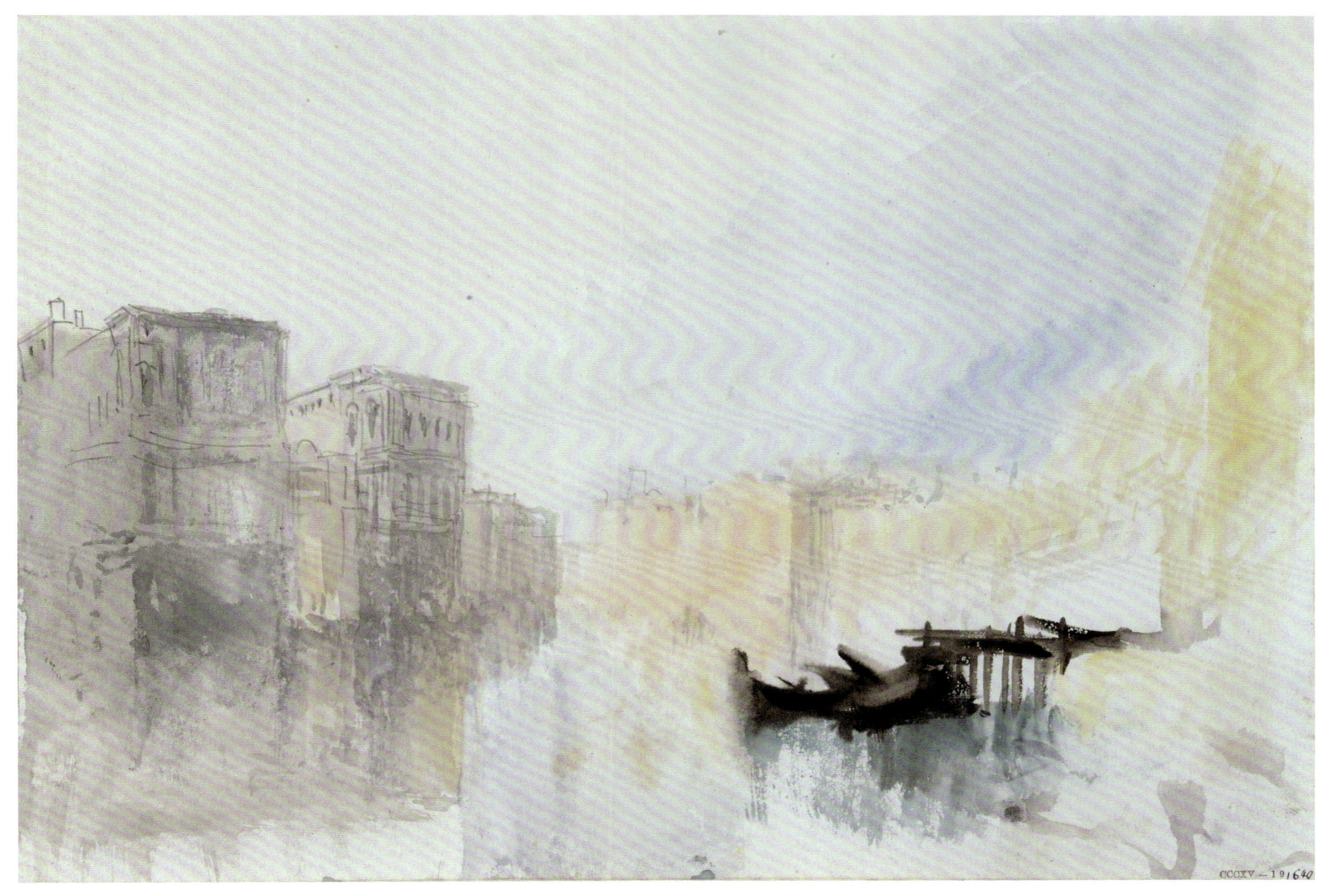

The Grand Canal from the Traghetto di San Felise, with Ca' Corner della Regina and Ca' Pesaro on the Left from the Grand Canal and Giudecca Sketchbook 1840
Graphite and watercolour on paper, 22.1 × 32.2

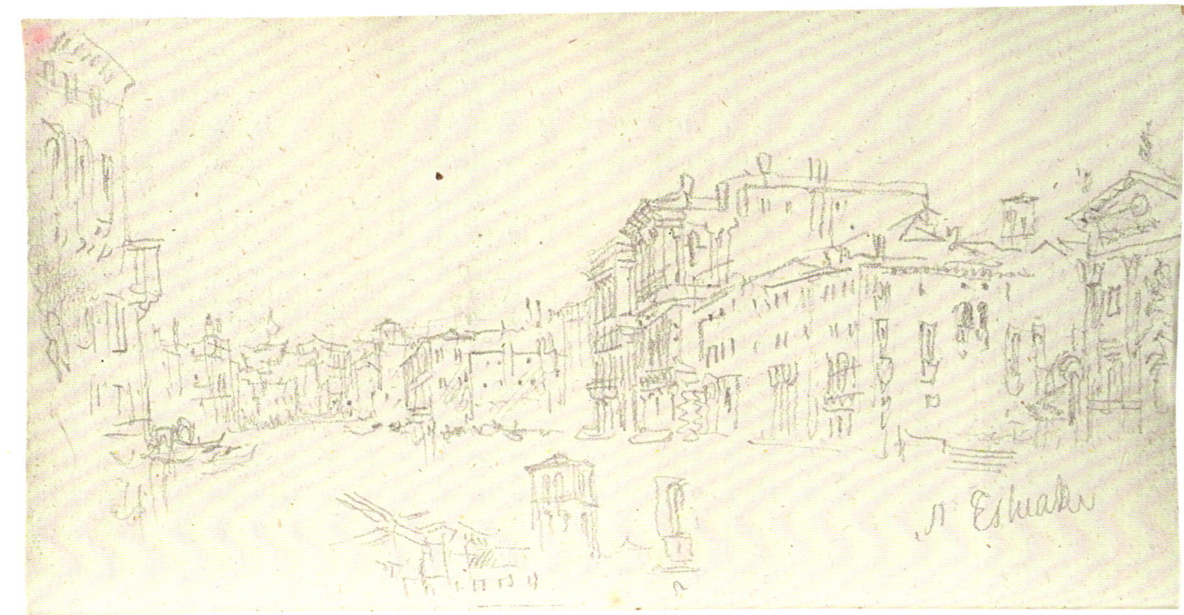

Views up and down the Grand Canal from opposite San Stae (also known as Sant'Eustachio), with the Ca' Pesaro and Ca' Corner della Regina in one direction, and the Fondaco dei Turchi, the Church of San Geremia and the Palazzo Vendramin Calergi in the other from the Venice sketchbook 1833
Graphite on paper, 10.9 × 20.3

90

The Fondaco dei Tuchi, the Deposito del Megio and the Palazzo Belloni-Battagia, with the Campanile of Santi Apostoli in the distance from the Venice Sketchbook 1833
Graphite on paper, 10.9 × 20.3

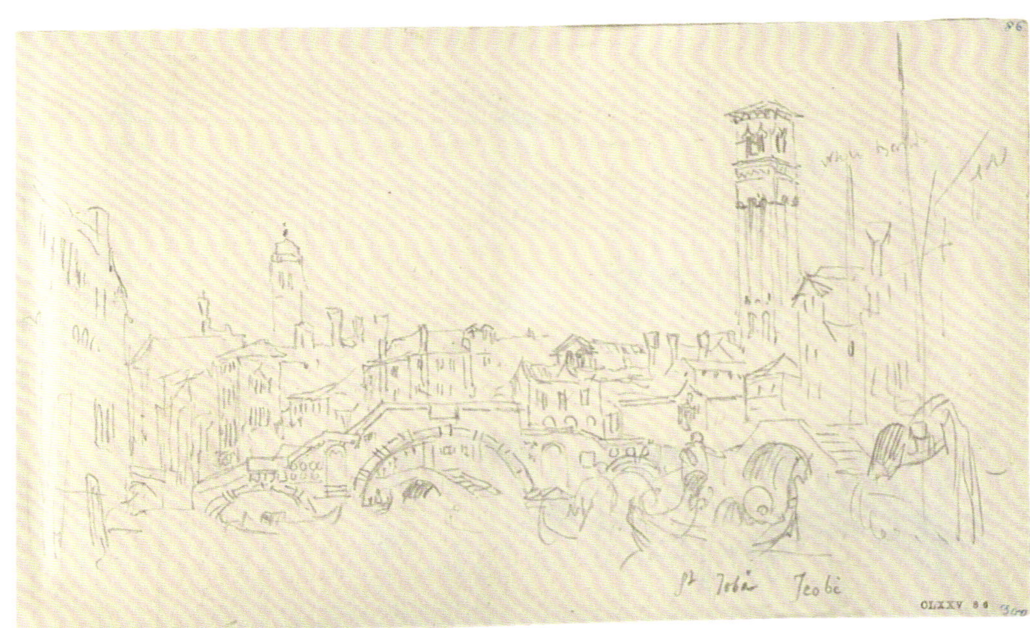

The Ponte dei Tre Archi on the Cannaregio Canal, with the Campanile of San Giobbe from the Milan to Venice Sketchbook 1819
Graphite on paper, 11.2 × 18.5

Looking down the Grand Canal from San Simeone Piccolo (on the right), with the Chiesa di Santa Lucia (now destroyed and replaced by the railway station) and beyond to the churches of the Scalzi and San Geremia from the Venice Sketchbook 1833
Graphite on paper, 10.9 × 20.3

San Nicolò da Tolentino from the Junction of the Grand Canal with the Rio dei Tolentini from the Venice to Ancona Sketchbook 1819
Graphite on paper, 11.1 × 18.4

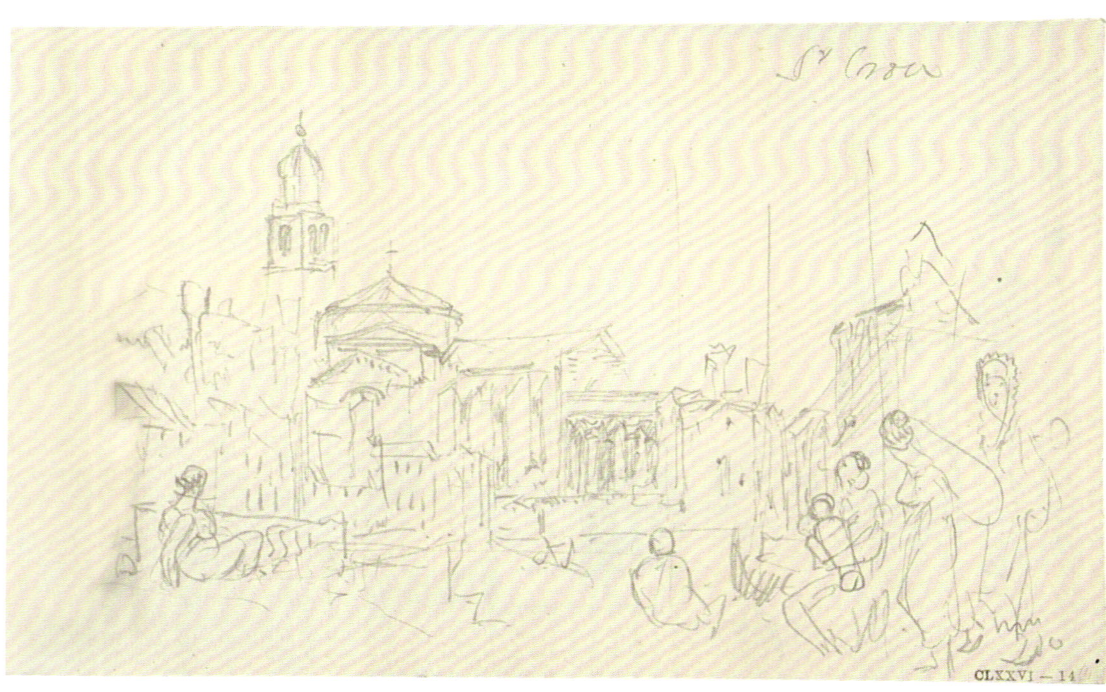

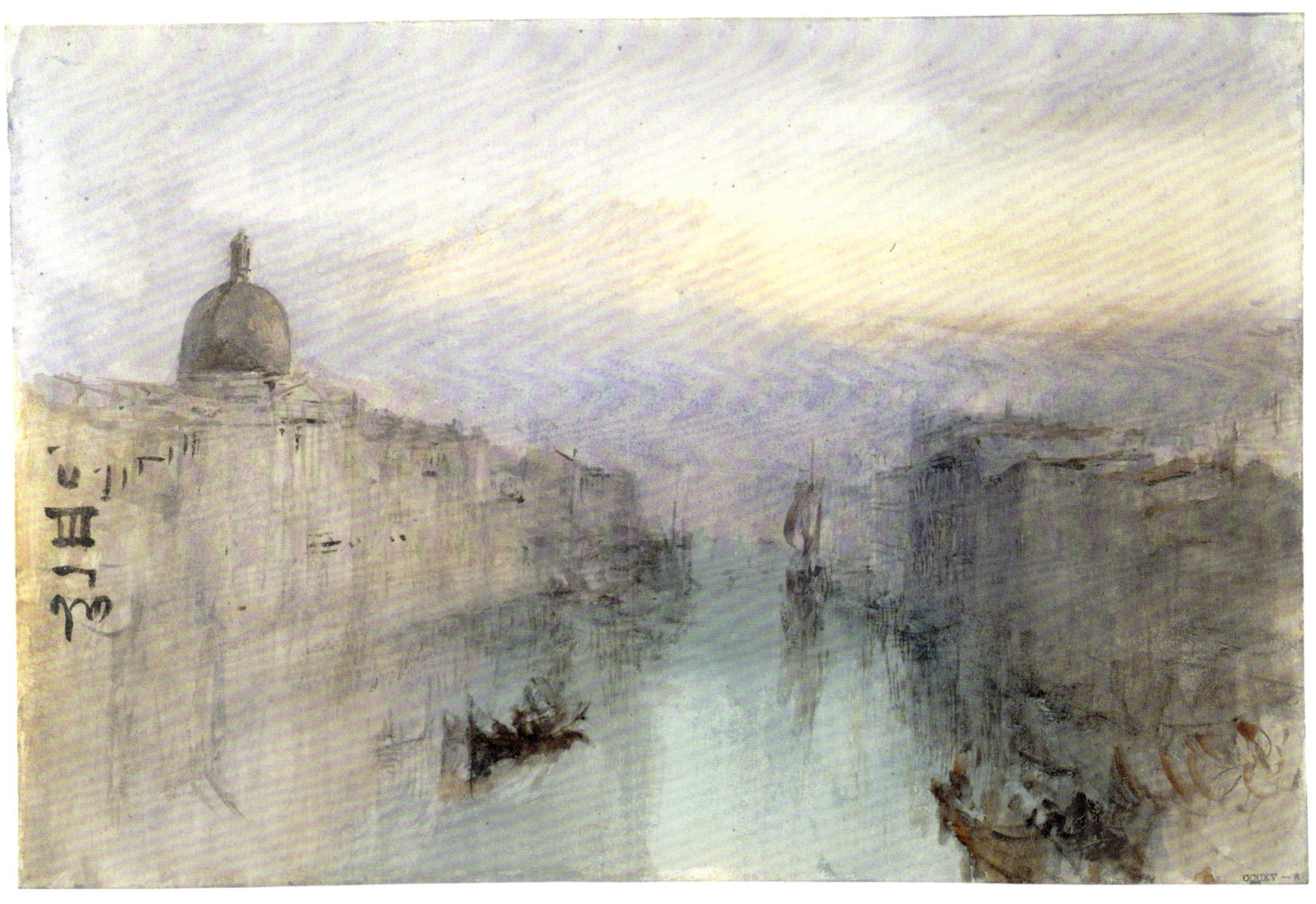

The Upper End of the Grand Canal, with San Simeone Piccolo, Dusk
from the Grand Canal and Giudecca Sketchbook 1840
Watercolour, gouache and pen and ink on paper, 22.1 × 32.2

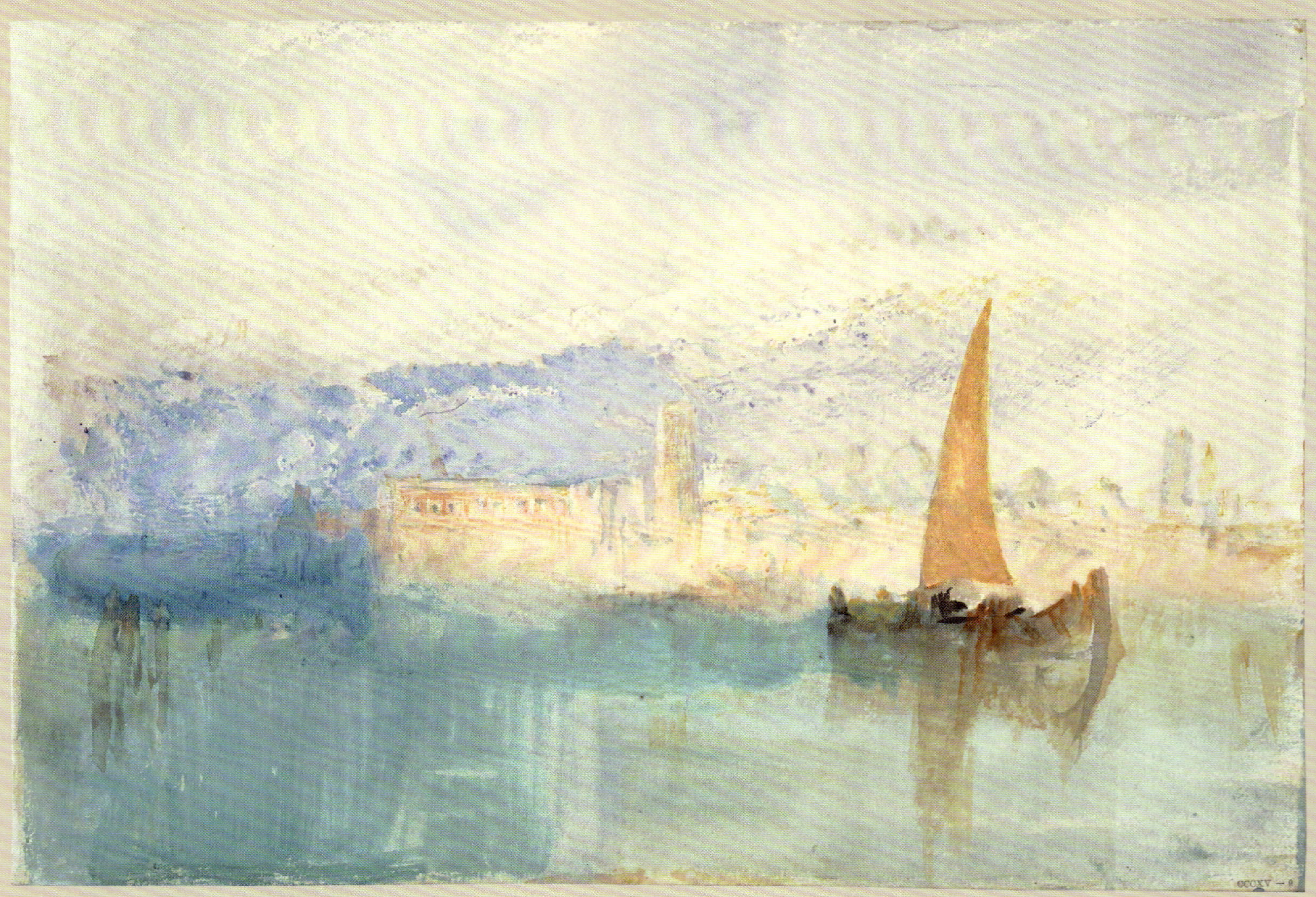

94

Dorsoduro and the Giudecca Canal

The south-western quarter of Venice is the area that has changed the most since Turner's time, as a result of industrialisation and tourism. It is consequently the least recognisable in the images he made here. Now dominated by the regenerated docks, this peripheral neighbourhood was formerly a modest peninsula, peopled by fishermen, with their own traditions. The settings Turner depicted are now difficult to pinpoint and remain elusive. They are perhaps best glimpsed in the imagination, a factor that enhances their intrinsic poetic mystery.

When painting his watercolours, Turner selected his favourite hour of twilight, which justified his lack of detail in his realisation of the buildings, as well as the way he clothed the whole setting in the kind of indistinctness for which his later works became infamous with critics. One image probably shows the former convent island of Santa Chiara, at the landward end of the Grand Canal, with a range of the city's towers and domes above the rooftops, contributing to the impression of a place found only in fairytales (opposite). For the next scene Turner had moved beyond the deconsecrated church of Santa Marta to look back towards the rising moon, with the island of San Secondo off to the left. Despite the late hour, Turner shows boatmen transporting produce, perhaps to the church which had been commissioned by the army as a store (p.97).

Turner had only skirted the area during his first stay in Venice, as part of a quick circumnavigation of the Giudecca Canal. In fact he never made the kind of fastidious architectural sketches that he undertook elsewhere in the city, and instead tended to record the key features in isolation, prioritising the churches (though often without any notes to clarify their names). Such a fragmented approach made it difficult to recreate accurately the true spatial relationships of any vista subsequently, and it was why he struggled when naming some of the pictures; for example, there is no church dedicated to San Benedetto in the area he depicts in one of his most famous views of the city (Frontispiece; perhaps the most popular with Turner's later nineteenth-century admirers).

Despite these shortcomings in his field notes, the western Giudecca was a place that resonated in his later work. Much of this has to do with the width and openness of the canal, which enabled him to produce expansive prospects of Venice, where the waterfronts on either side frame the natural drama of light – whether sunrise or sunset – infusing and transforming the space in between. Turner also evidently delighted in the steady crescendo of expectation dictated by the natural curve of the Giudecca Canal, which sweeps round finally to present the full glory of the Molo and the Riva degli Schiavoni stretched out in front of the viewer in a way that is even more satisfying than the view when arriving from the sea (p.103).

In his earliest depictions of the Giudecca, dating from 1840–1, it is possible to detect his desire to emulate the greatest of Canaletto's pictures (p.102 and p.105). This group of canvases are drenched in the sparkling sunlight of midday, with wispy cirrus and banks of stratocumulus cloud encroaching on the infinite blue sky. The effect serves to intensify the brilliance of the marble stonework throughout each image, at the same time interspersing the artfully placed vessels with shimmering reflections.

A Boat near Santa Chiara from the Grand Canal and Giudecca Sketchbook 1840
Watercolour on paper, 22.1 × 32.2

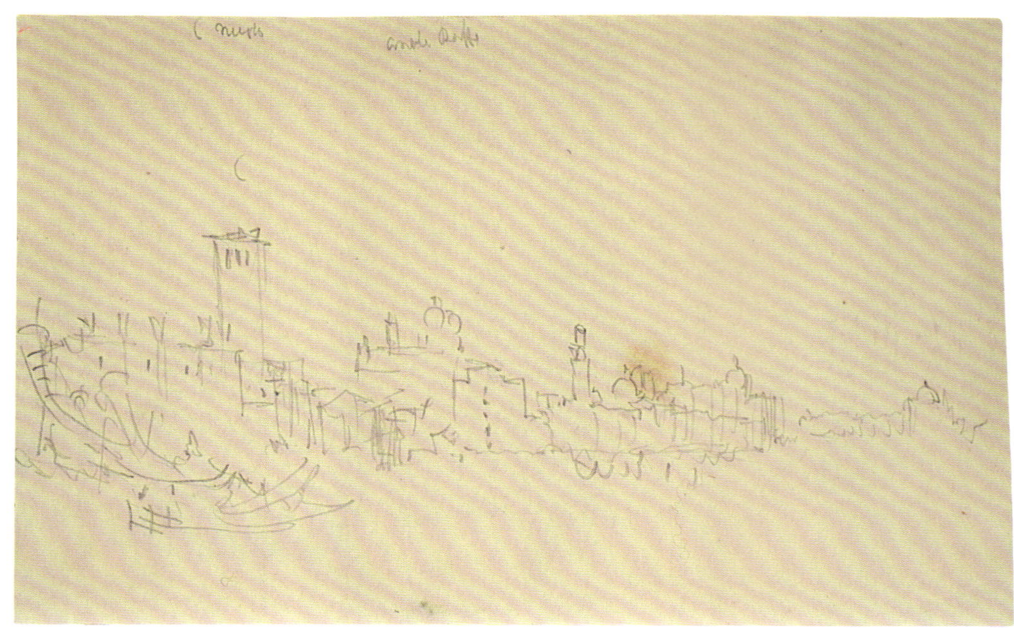

*From Santa Marta looking down the Giudecca
Canal, with the bell-towers of San Nicolò dei
Mendicoli, Angelo Raffaele, the Carmini, San
Sebastiano, and the domes of the Salute, the
Gesuati and the Zitelle beyond* from the Venice;
Passau to Wurzburg Sketchbook 1840
Graphite on paper, 19.8 × 12.6

Venice – Sunset, a Fisher exhibited 1845
Oil paint on canvas, 61.3 × 92.1

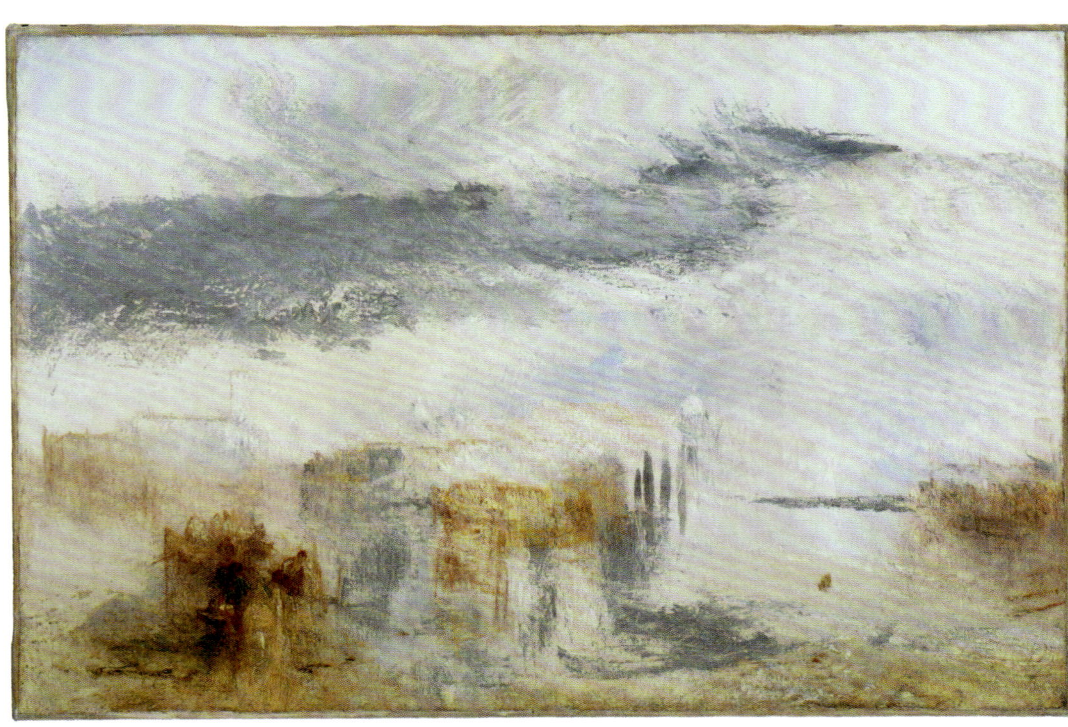

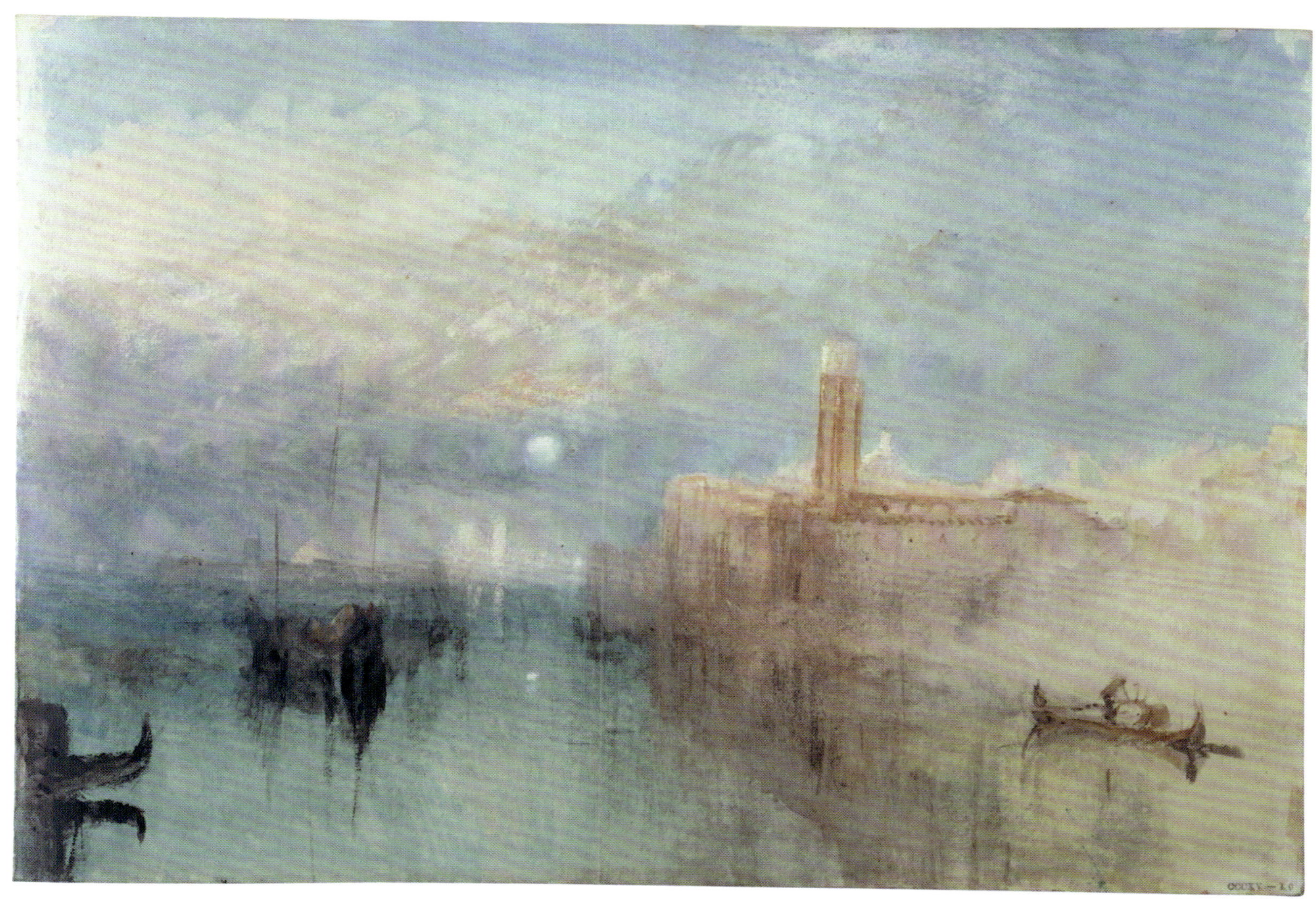

Venice, Moonrise; Santa Marta with San Secondo beyond
from the Grand Canal and Giudecca Sketchbook 1840
Watercolour on paper, 22.1 × 32.2

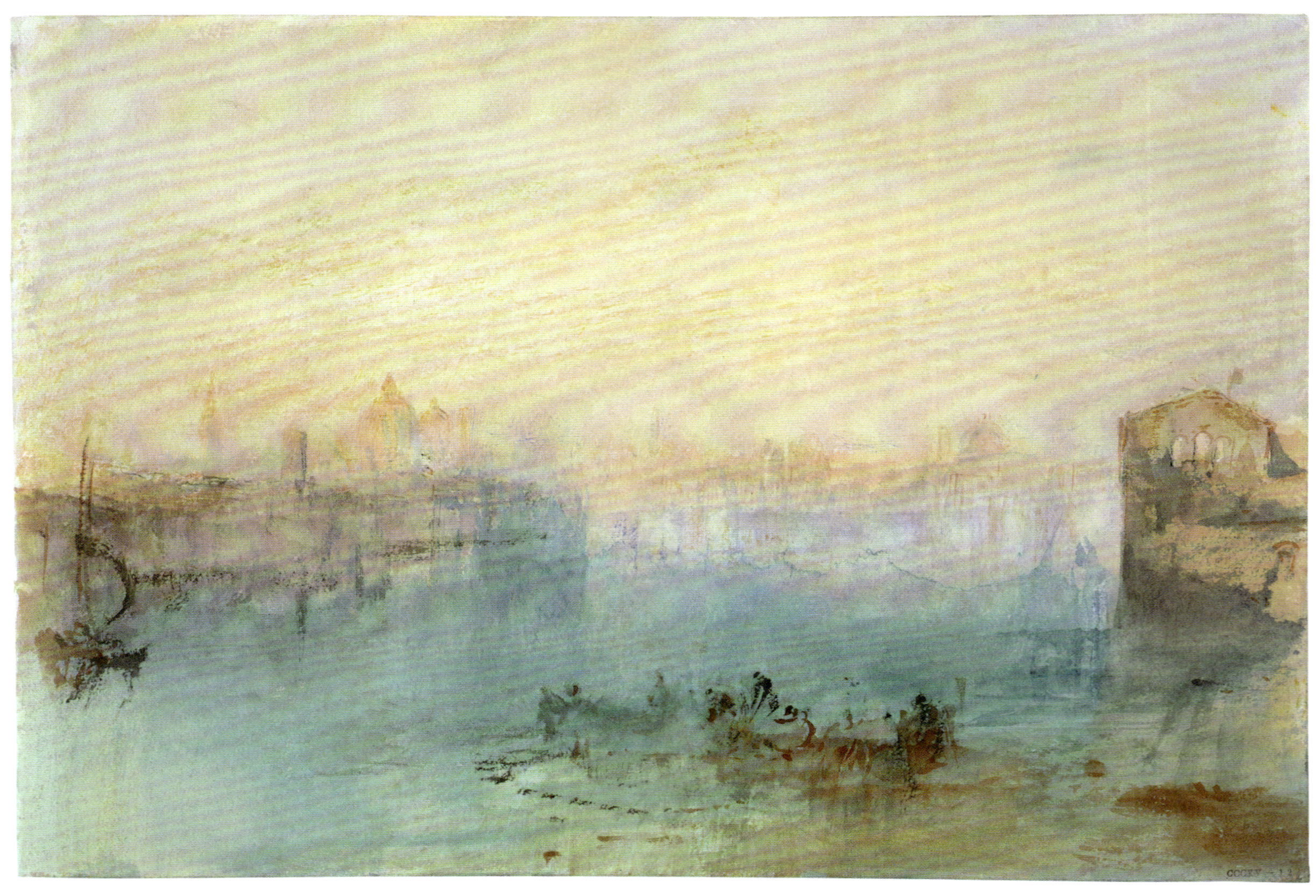

The Western End of the Giudecca Canal from near the Convent of Santi Biagio e Cataldo from the Grand Canal and Giudecca Sketchbook 1840
Watercolour on paper, 22.1 × 32.2

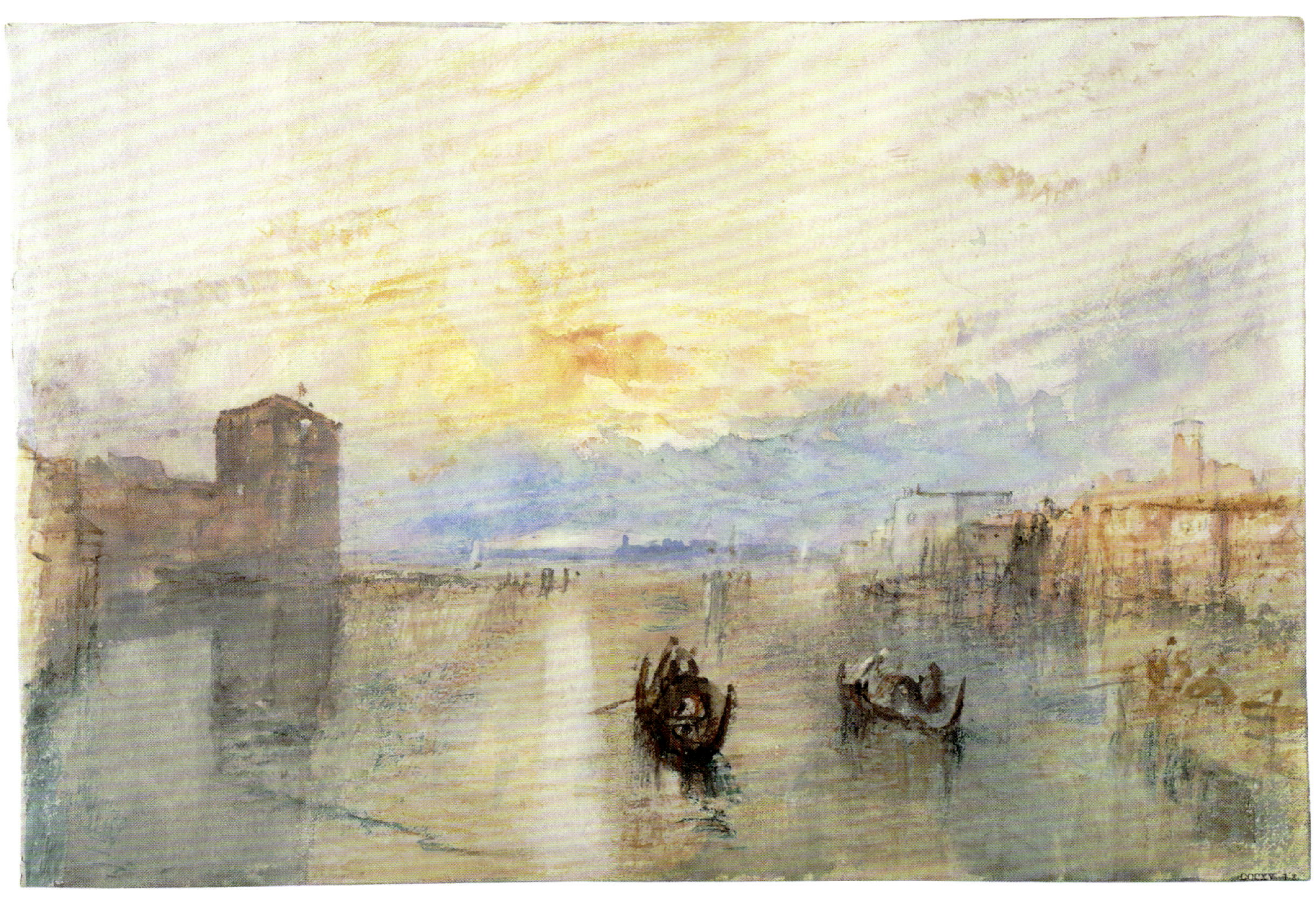

The Giudecca Canal, Looking towards Fusina at Sunset from the Grand
Canal and Giudecca Sketchbook 1840
Graphite, watercolour and crayon on paper, 22.1 × 32.2

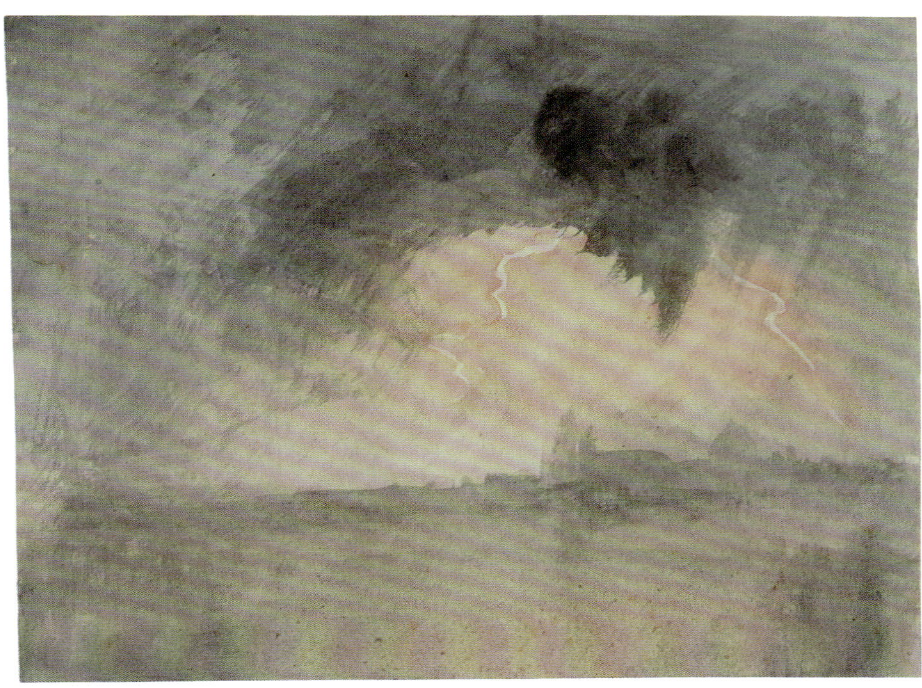

*A Recollection of Venice: the Giudecca Canal in a Storm
(formerly known as 'Catania')* c.1819–20
Watercolour on paper, 23.1 × 28.1
Museum of Fine Arts, Boston, Massachusetts

Churches along the Giudecca Canal from the Venice and
Botzen Sketchbook 1840
Graphite on paper, 12.3 × 17.3

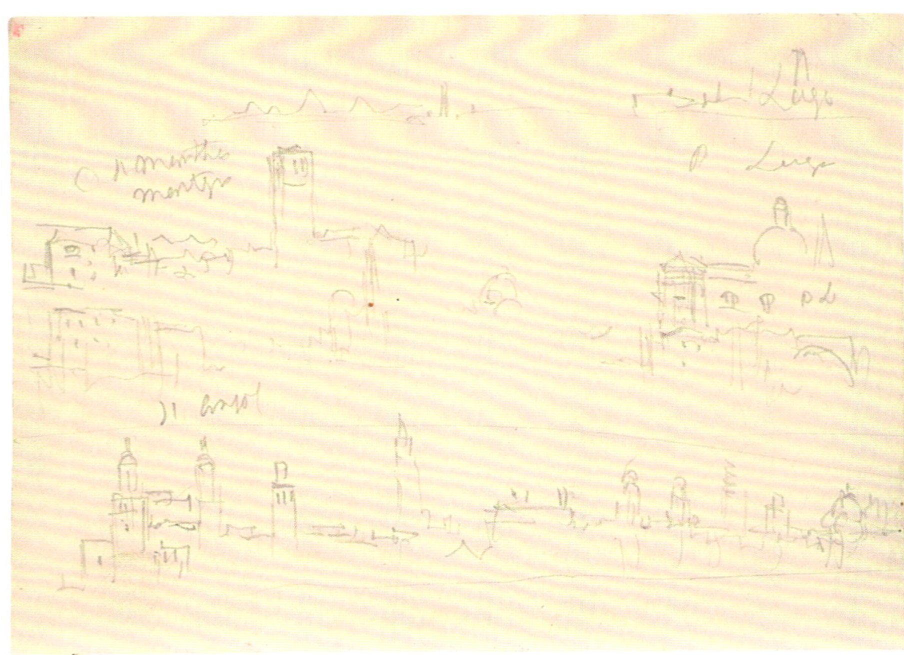

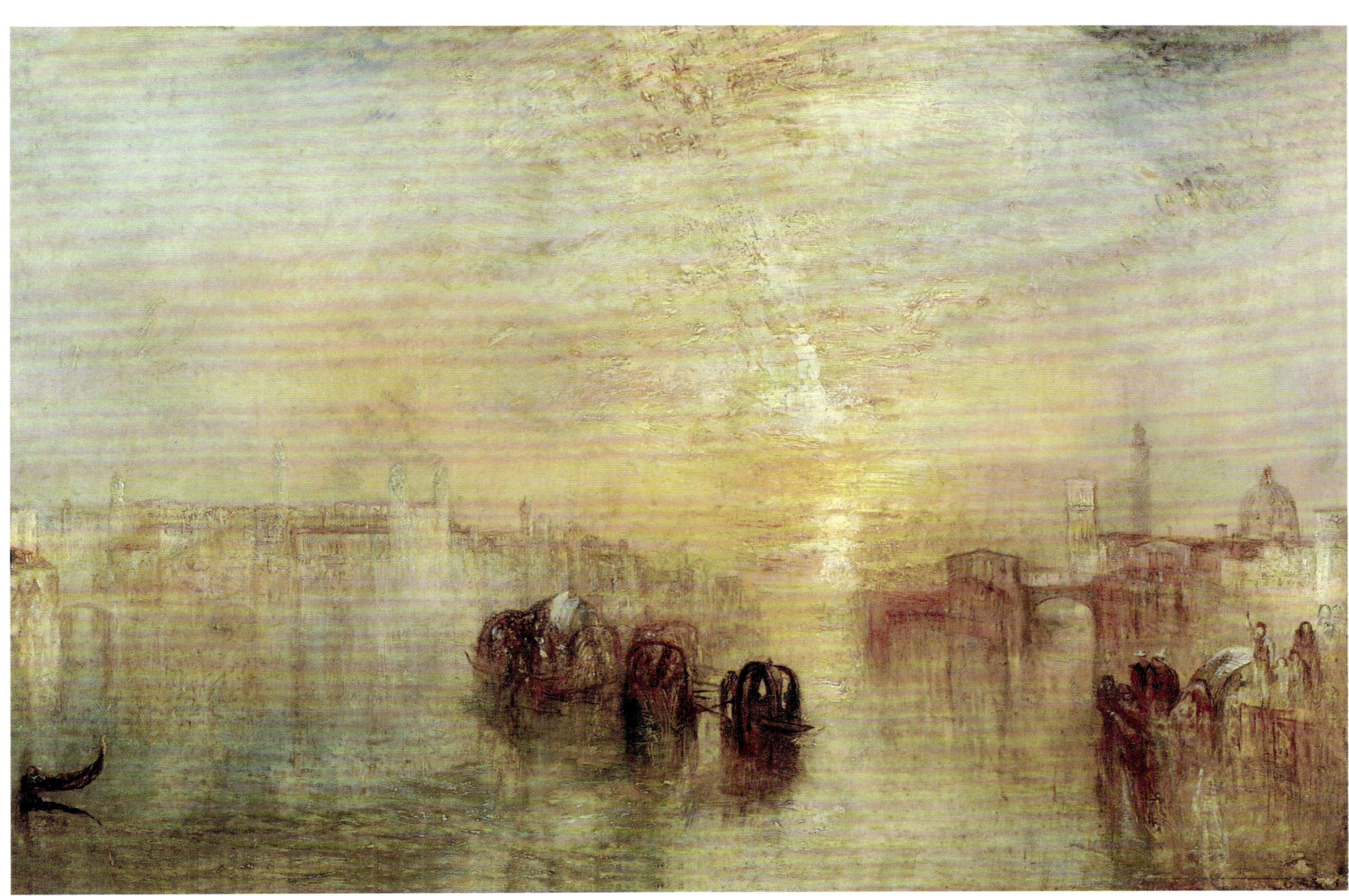

Going to the Ball (San Martino) exhibited 1846
Oil paint on canvas, 61.6 × 92.4

There has been confusion over the titles of Turner's last views of Venice, emanating from the artist himself, who was confused about the names of the churches along the Giudecca. This scene shows a sunrise, and so might actually be the picture he exhibited in 1846 as *Returning from the Ball (St Martha)*.

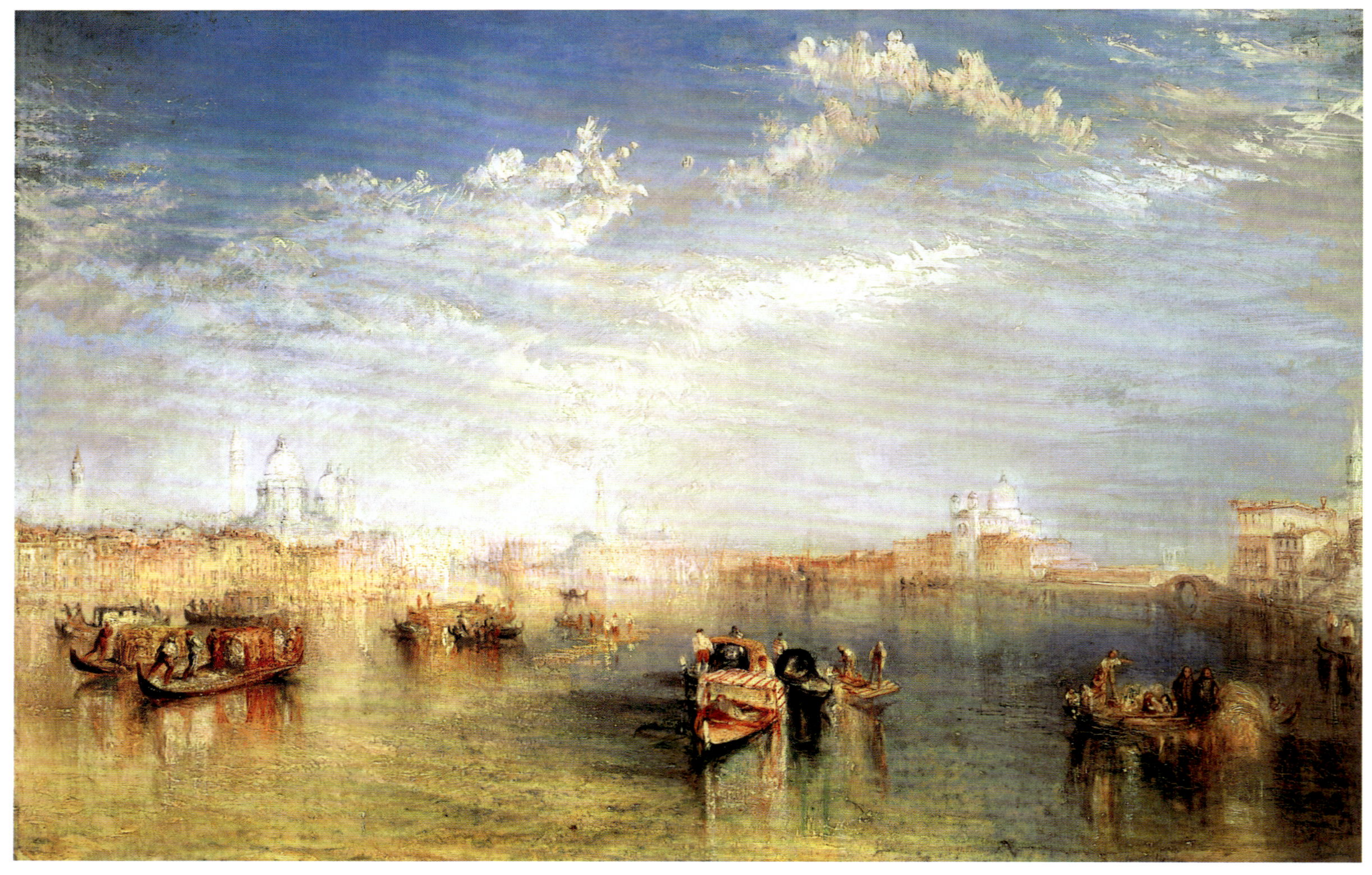

Giudecca, la Donna della Salute and San Georgio exhibited 1841
Oil paint on canvas, 61 × 91.5
Private collection

In 1841 two of Turner's three paintings of the Giudecca Canal adopted the spelling 'San Georgio', rather than 'San Giorgio'. This may have been a typesetting error, or an alternative contemporary usage, as was the case with his allusion to Canaletto in the title of his 1833 picture (p.11).

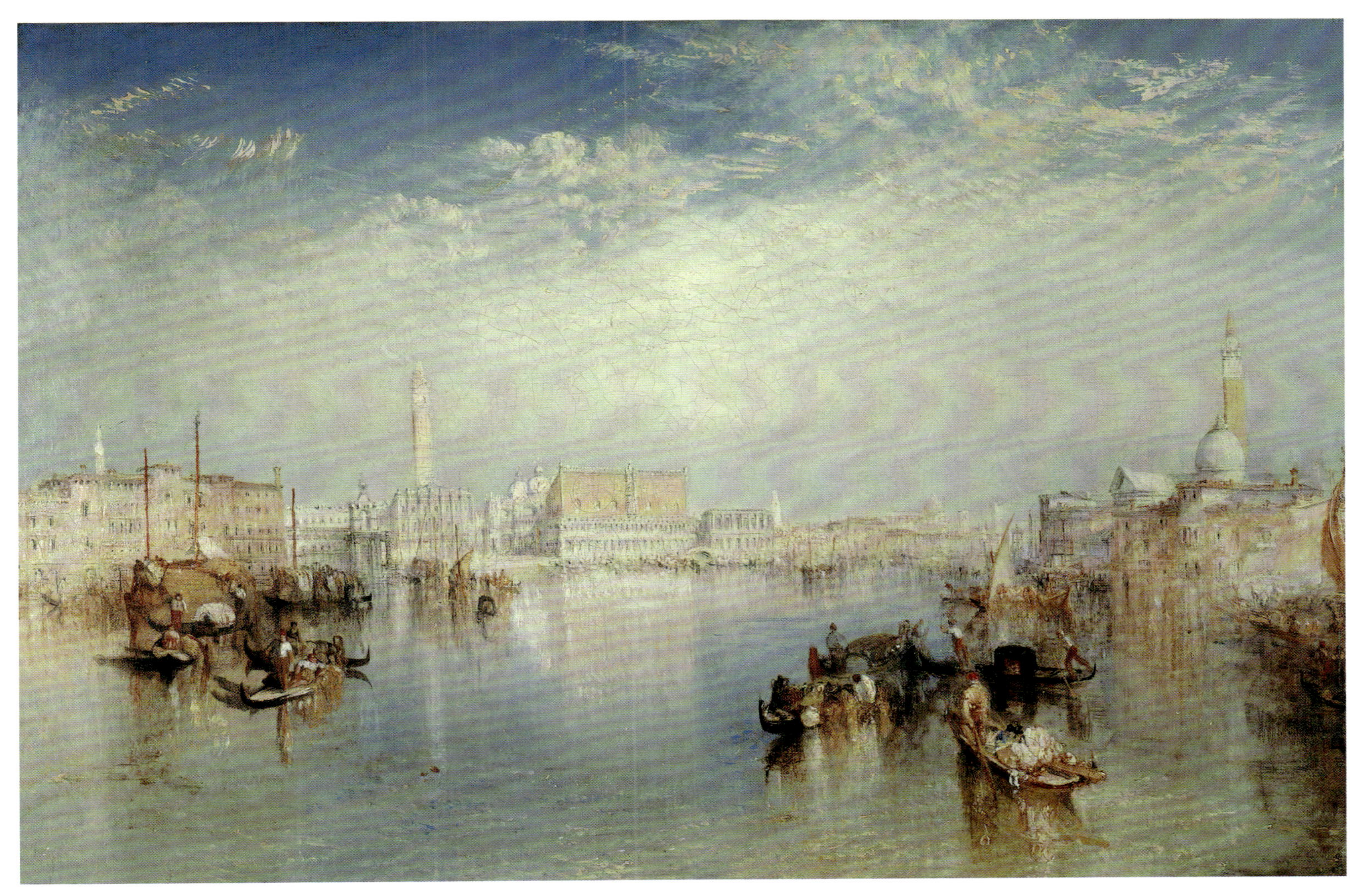

Ducal Palace, Dogano, with Part of San Georgio, Venice exhibited 1841
Oil paint on canvas, 63.5 × 93
Allen Memorial Art Museum, Oberlin College, Ohio

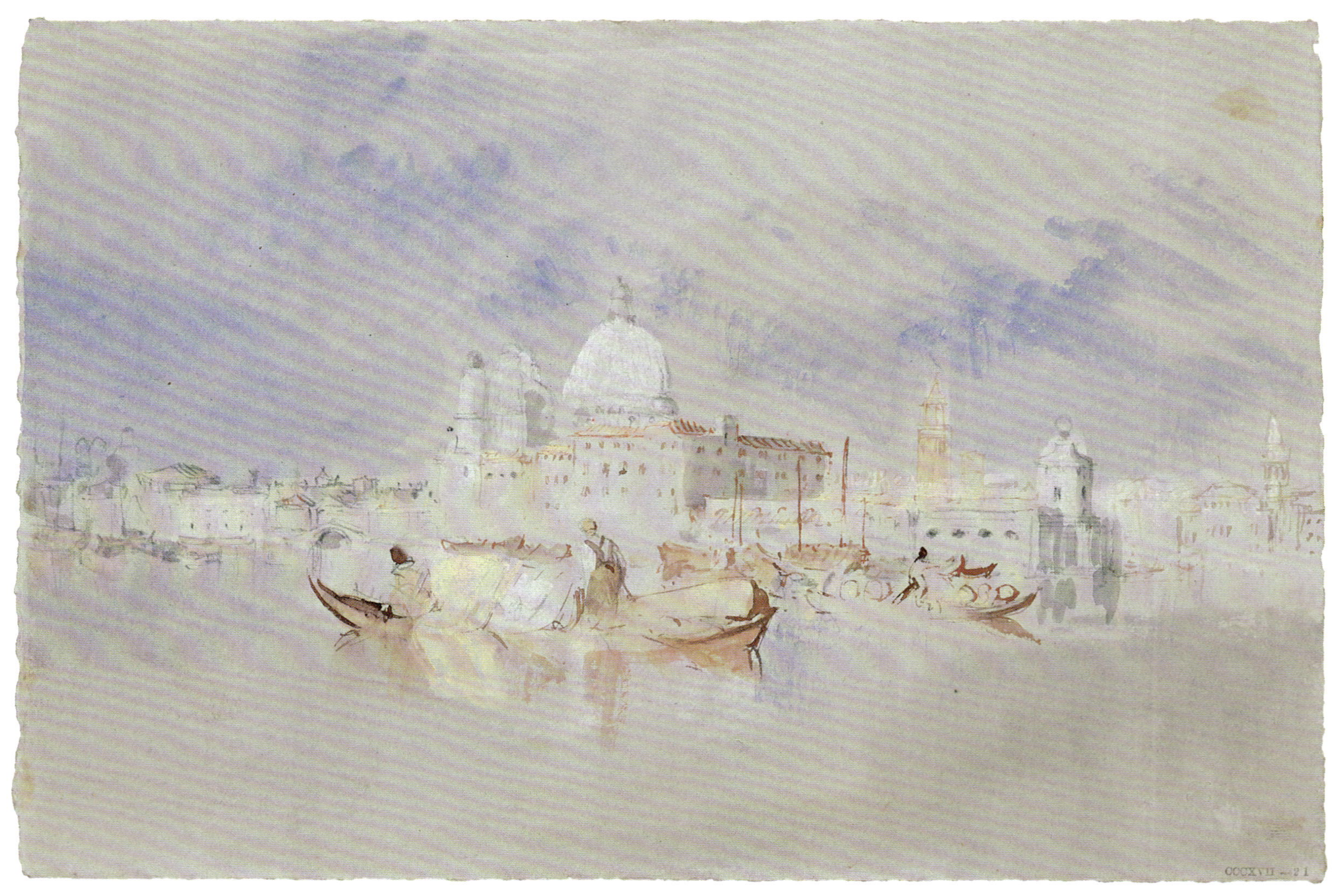

Boats in front of the Dogana and Santa Maria della Salute c.1833 or 1840
Graphite, watercolour and gouache on grey paper, 19 × 28.1

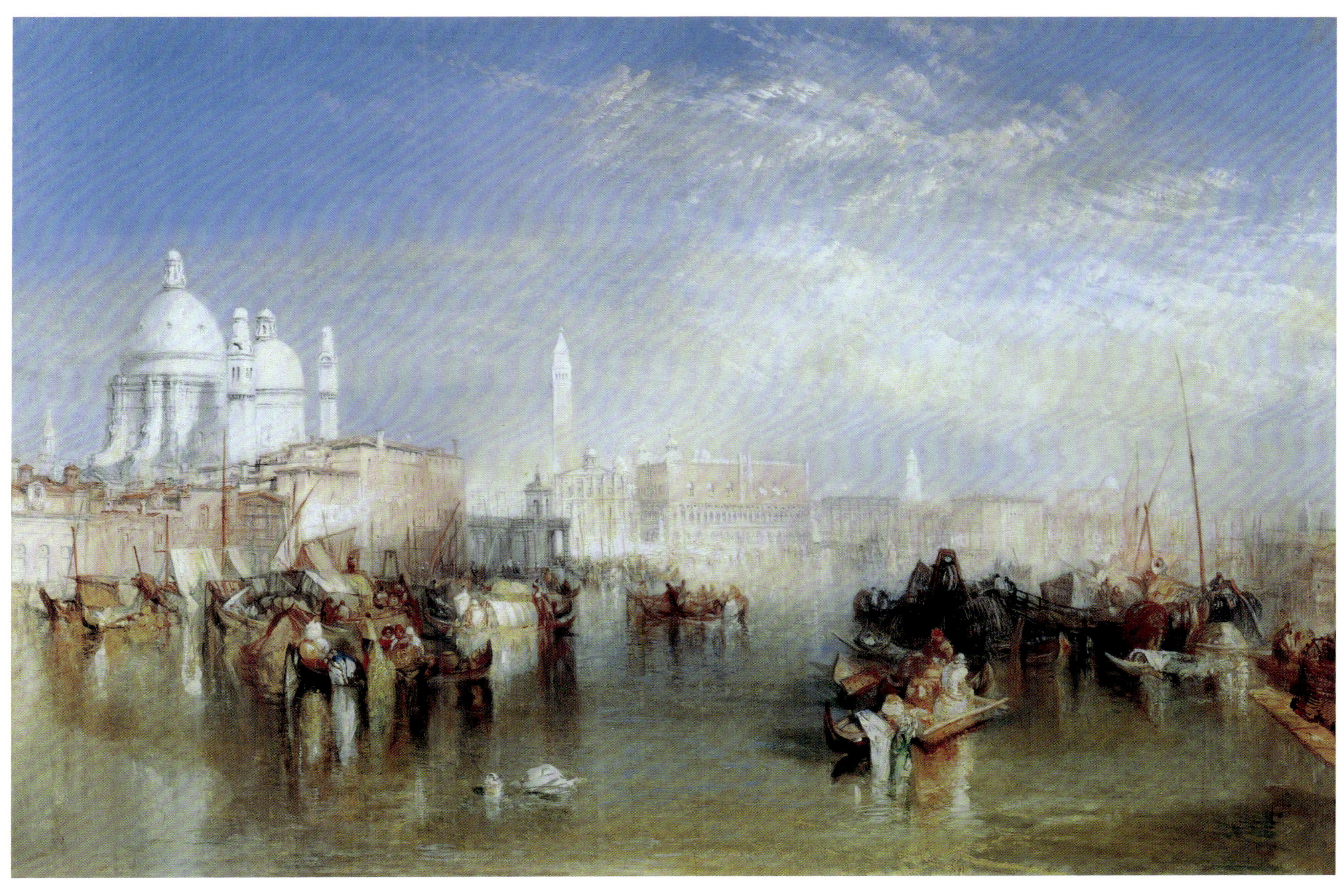

Venice from the Canale della Giudecca, Chiesa di S.Maria della Salute
exhibited 1840
Oil paint on canvas, 61 × 91.4
Victoria & Albert Museum, London

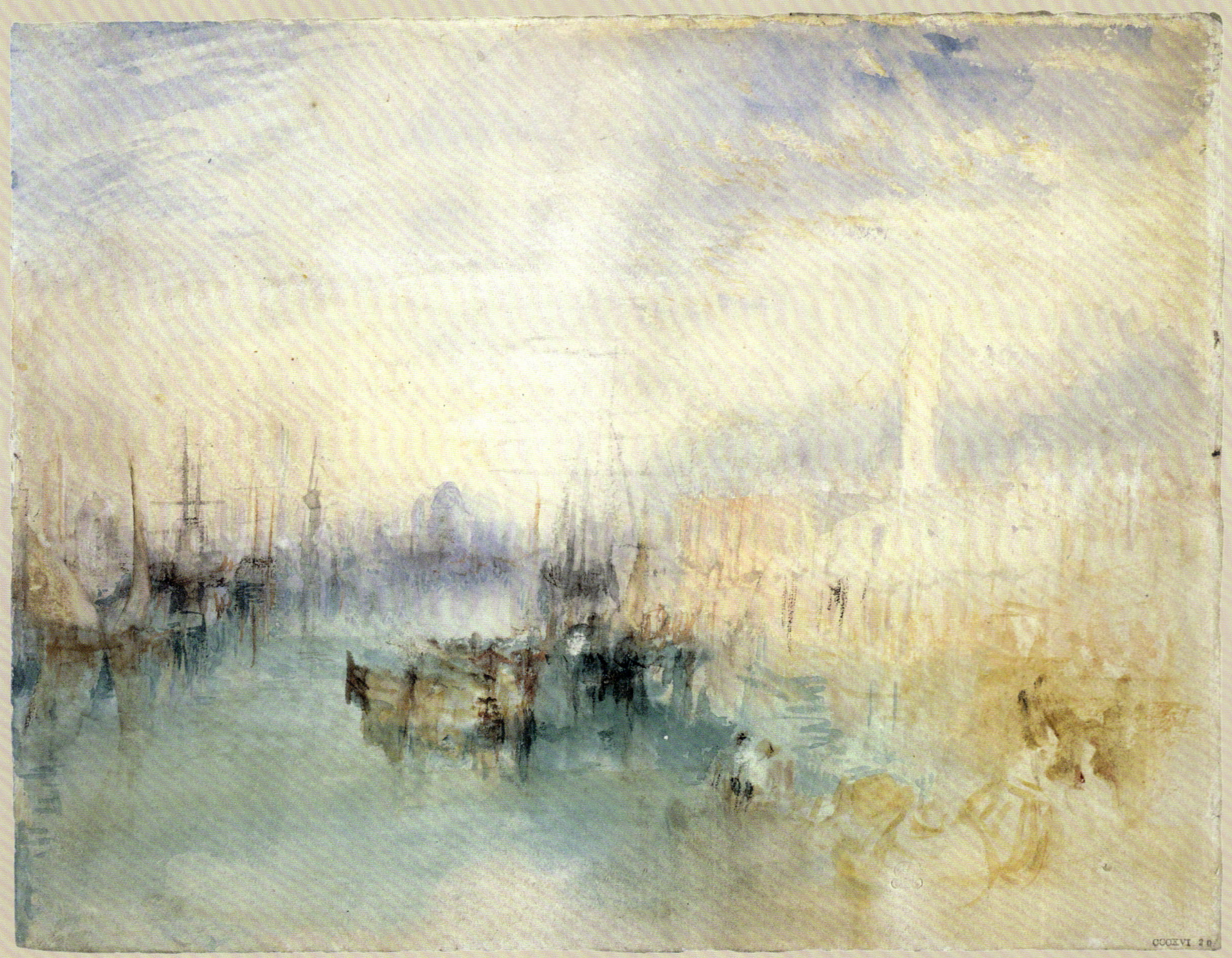

Eastwards towards the Arsenale

Back at the Bacino in the heart of Venice, several of the watercolours connected to Turner's final visit evoke the sudden incursion of summer storm clouds, which bear down on the famous waterfront to obscure or transform its monuments, while soaking the city and its inhabitants alike. Turner's washes of watercolour were the perfect medium in which to recreate so vividly an impression of being in the midst of the heavy downpour. These images preserve a sense of how he layered overlapping washes of wet colour, allowing them to blur into each other to give a compelling approximation of the storm in suspended motion. Each is completed by the addition of deft calligraphic marks to introduce the silhouette of a gondolier making haste to escape the choppy waters.

Turner deployed a similarly reductive, almost impressionistic form of notation for many of his other colour studies when painting his progress along the Riva degli Schiavoni. Moving from sheet to sheet, he defined the great landmarks along the Venetian quayside using seemingly child-like blocks, towers and domes. Nevertheless, these simplified forms belie the underlying close scrutiny Turner had paid to all of the details he depicted as part of the process of sketching. There may have been an exception to this principle, because as he moved towards and around the intimidating walls of the legendary shipyards of the huge Arsenale (then occupied by the Austrians), he may have felt the need to exercise caution, and to sketch surreptitiously, in case he was mistaken for a spy (p.113).

As in the western district of Dorsoduro, Turner was captivated in the Castello area by the activities of the fishermen. In his pencil and watercolour sketches he repeatedly recorded the distinctive profiles of different types of Venetian boats, and especially the fishing vessels known as bragozzi, which frequently had their canvas sails painted with patterns or symbols (pp.110–11). Spotting one featuring a glowing sun, conjoined with a new moon, Turner's imagination was fired, resulting in the ominous painting *The Sun of Venice going to Sea* (p.111). In that work, the sail acts as a painted canvas, carrying an image of sunset, which Turner (in a poem composed to supplement the picture) pessimistically predicted would be a time of reckoning for the fishing boat. Here, once again, he was defining the contemporary city through representatives of the most quotidian aspect of Venetian life, rather than its fabulous past.

In exploring eastern Venice, like most tourists, Turner fastened on the churches that punctuate the bewildering maze of canals and winding streets as his reference points, seeking to differentiate them as useful landmarks. His pencil sketches of San Pietro di Castello, the original cathedral of Venice, are among his most rudimentary, and were very probably made after dark. This would explain the imprecision of his recollection of the church and its bell-tower at dawn (p.115); though the golden effect he created testifies to the revelatory sensations he presumably experienced when seeing it at some point. Elsewhere on his wanderings through the more central neighbourhoods of the Castello district, it is clear from the low perspective he adopted in his sketches that he was being conducted from place to place in a gondola, rather than relying on his own homing instincts to get back to the Hotel Europa.

Shipping off the Riva degli Schiavoni, from near the Ponte dell'Arsenale 1840
Watercolour on paper, 24.3 × 30.6

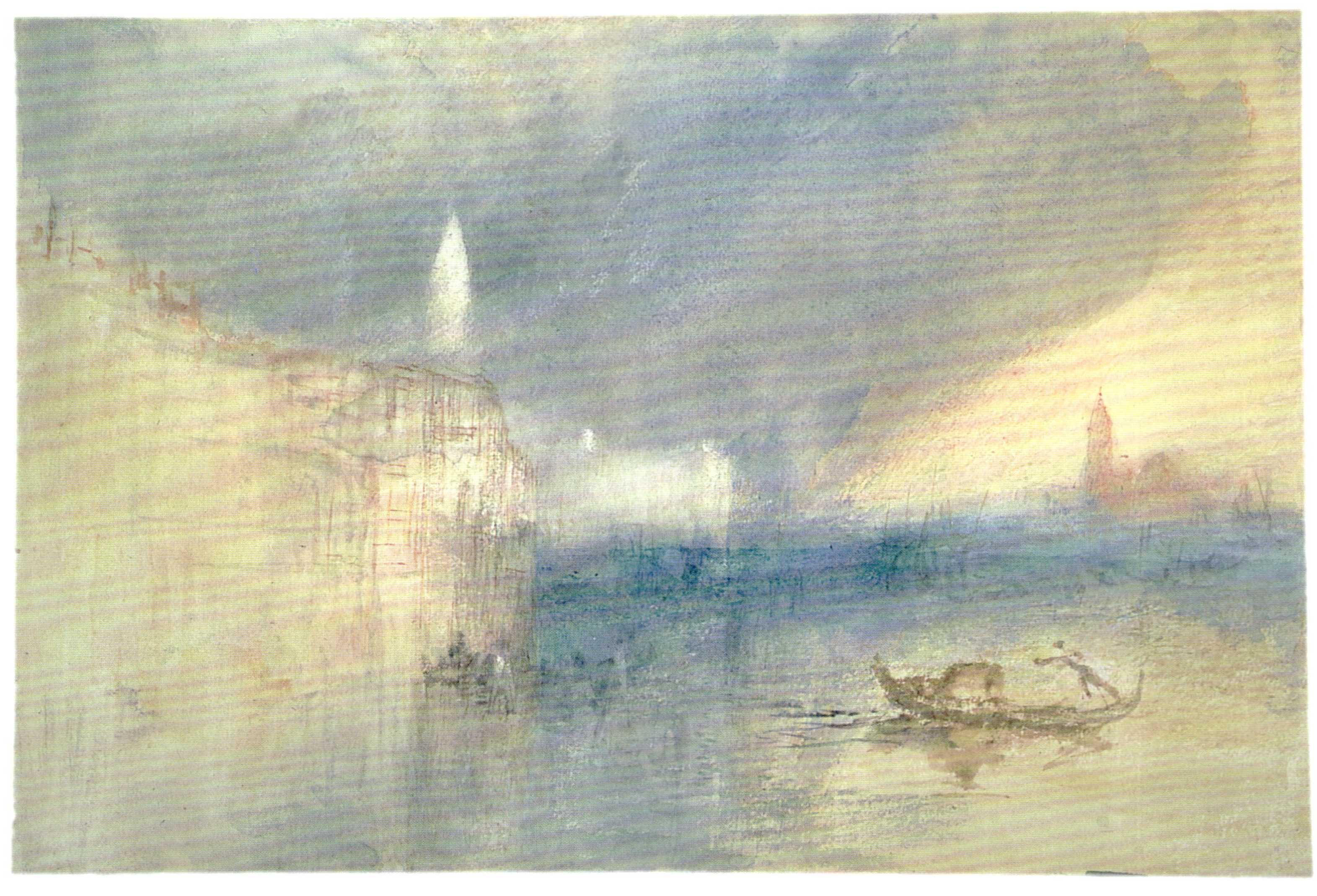

Storm at the Mouth of the Grand Canal c.1840
Watercolour and white highlights on off-white wove paper, 21.8 × 31.9
National Gallery of Ireland, Dublin

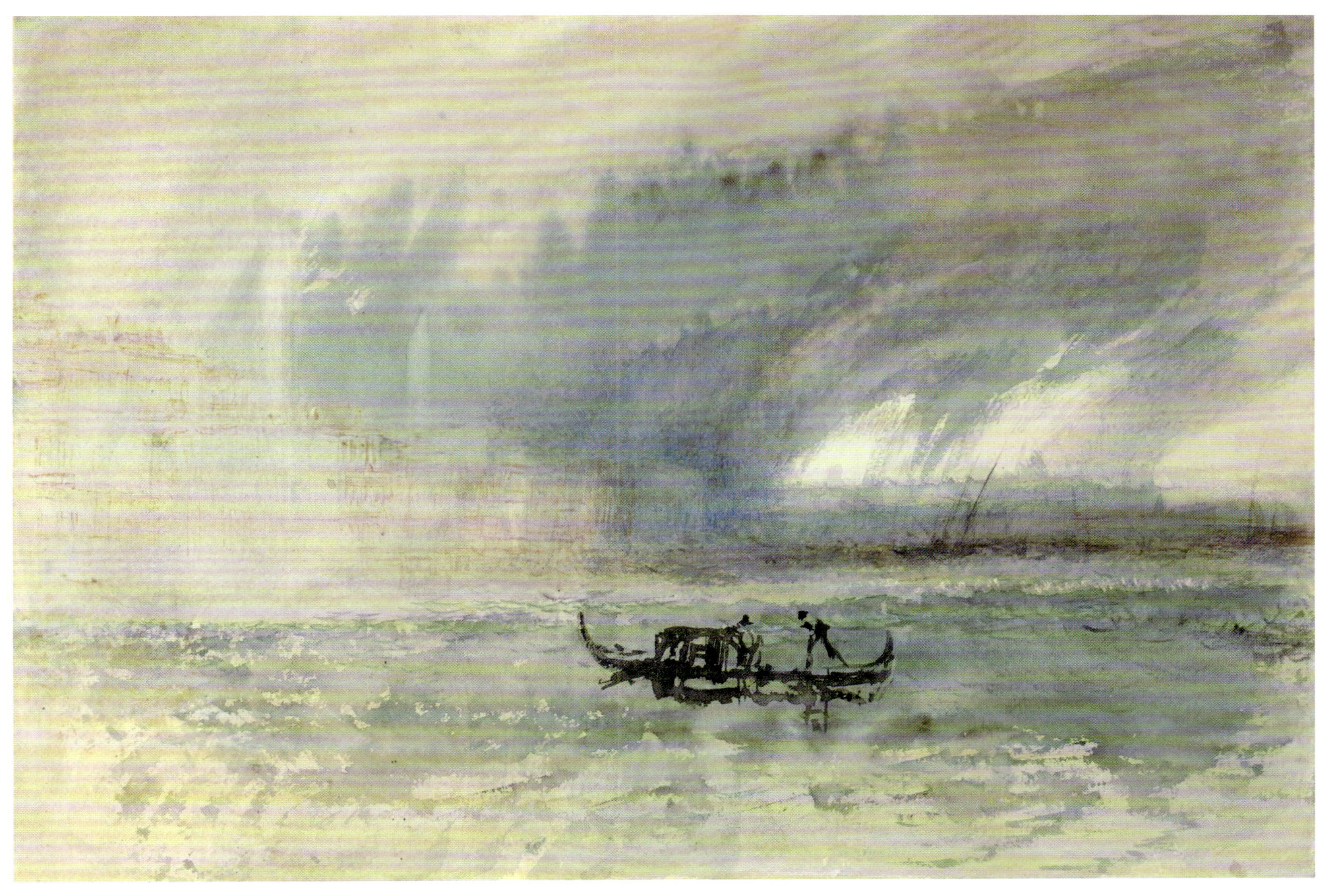

Storm at Venice 1840
Watercolour, with details added using a pen on paper, 21.9 × 31.8
British Museum, London

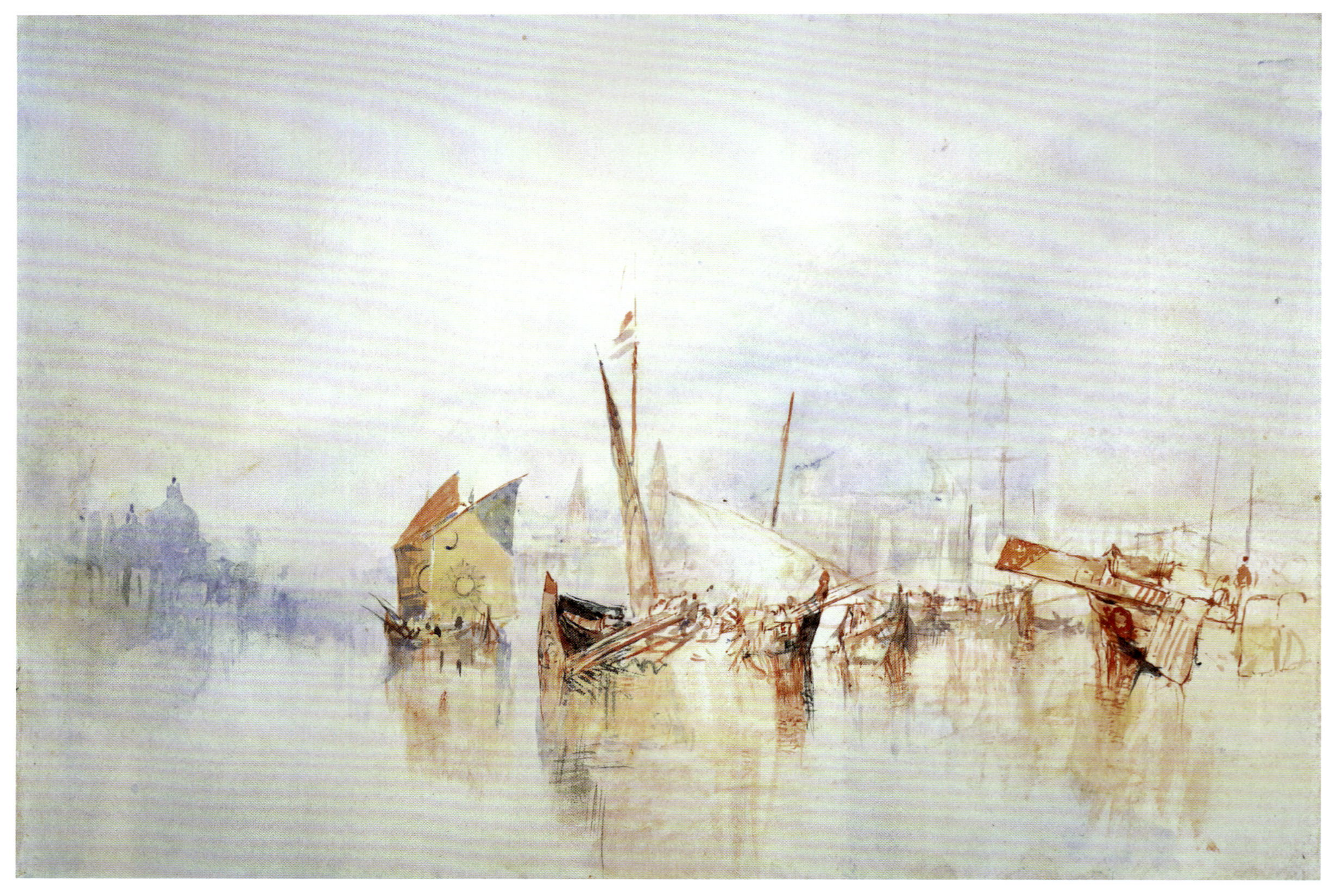

The Sun of Venice: Bragozzi moored off the Riva degli Schiavoni 1840
Watercolour on paper, 21.9 × 32
National Galleries Scotland, Edinburgh

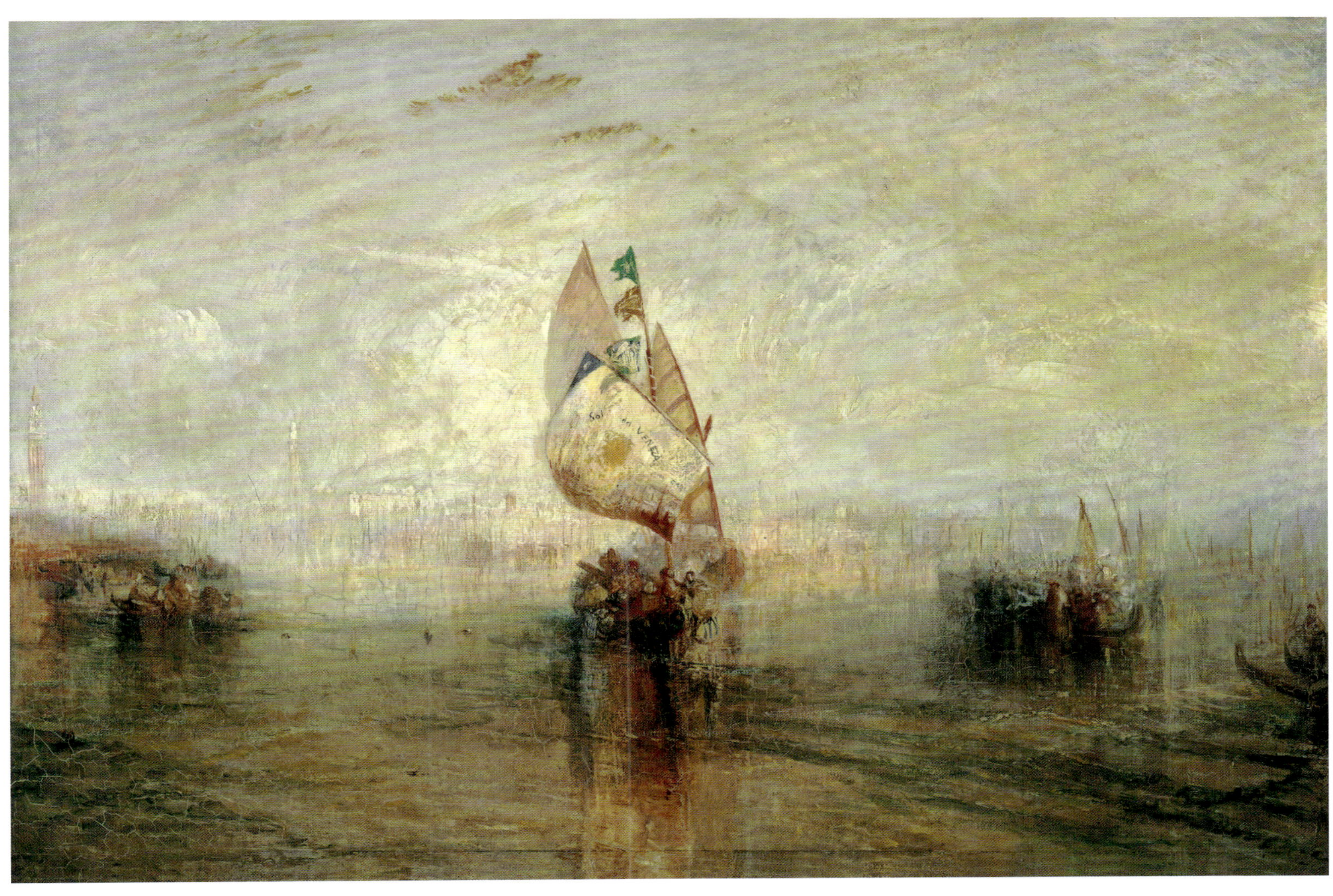

The Sun of Venice Going to Sea exhibited 1843
Oil paint on canvas, 61.6 × 92.1

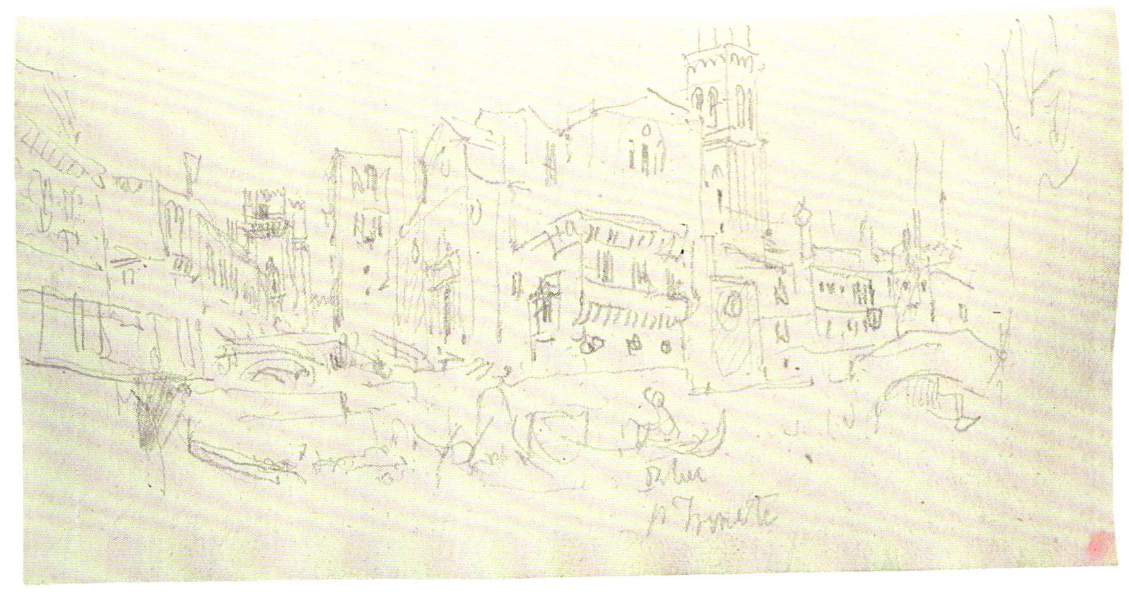

Approaching the Main Entrance of the Arsenale, with the Church of St Martino to the right from the Venice Sketchbook 1833
Graphite on paper, 10.9 × 20.3

The Entrance of the Arsenale, from the Rio dell'Arsenale from the Milan to Venice Sketchbook 1819
Graphite on paper, 11.2 × 18.5

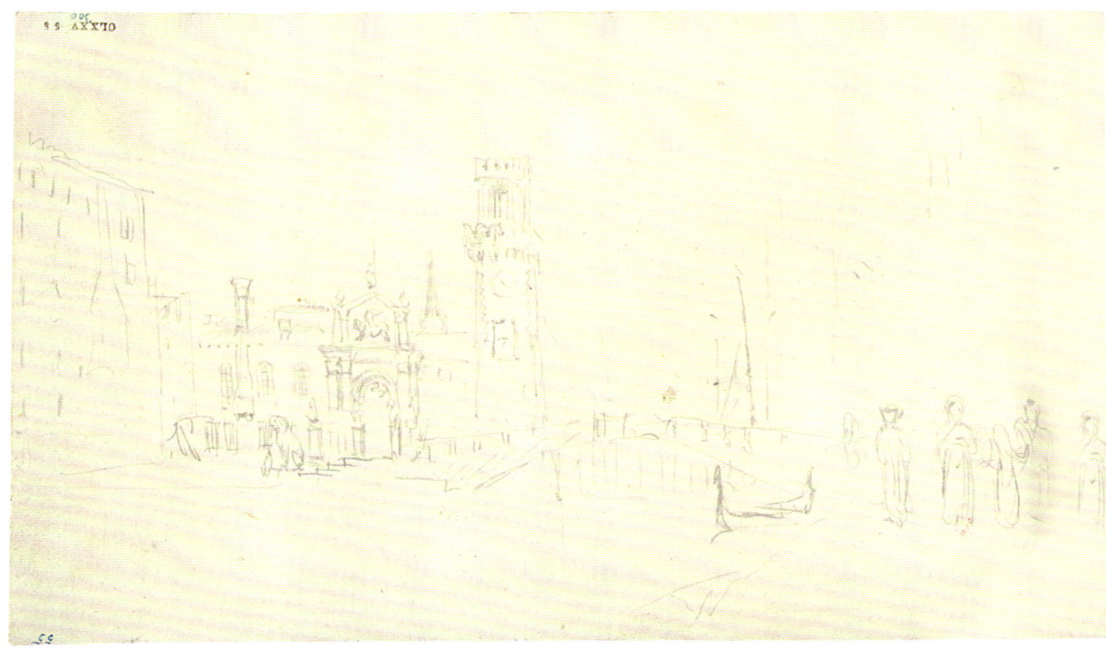

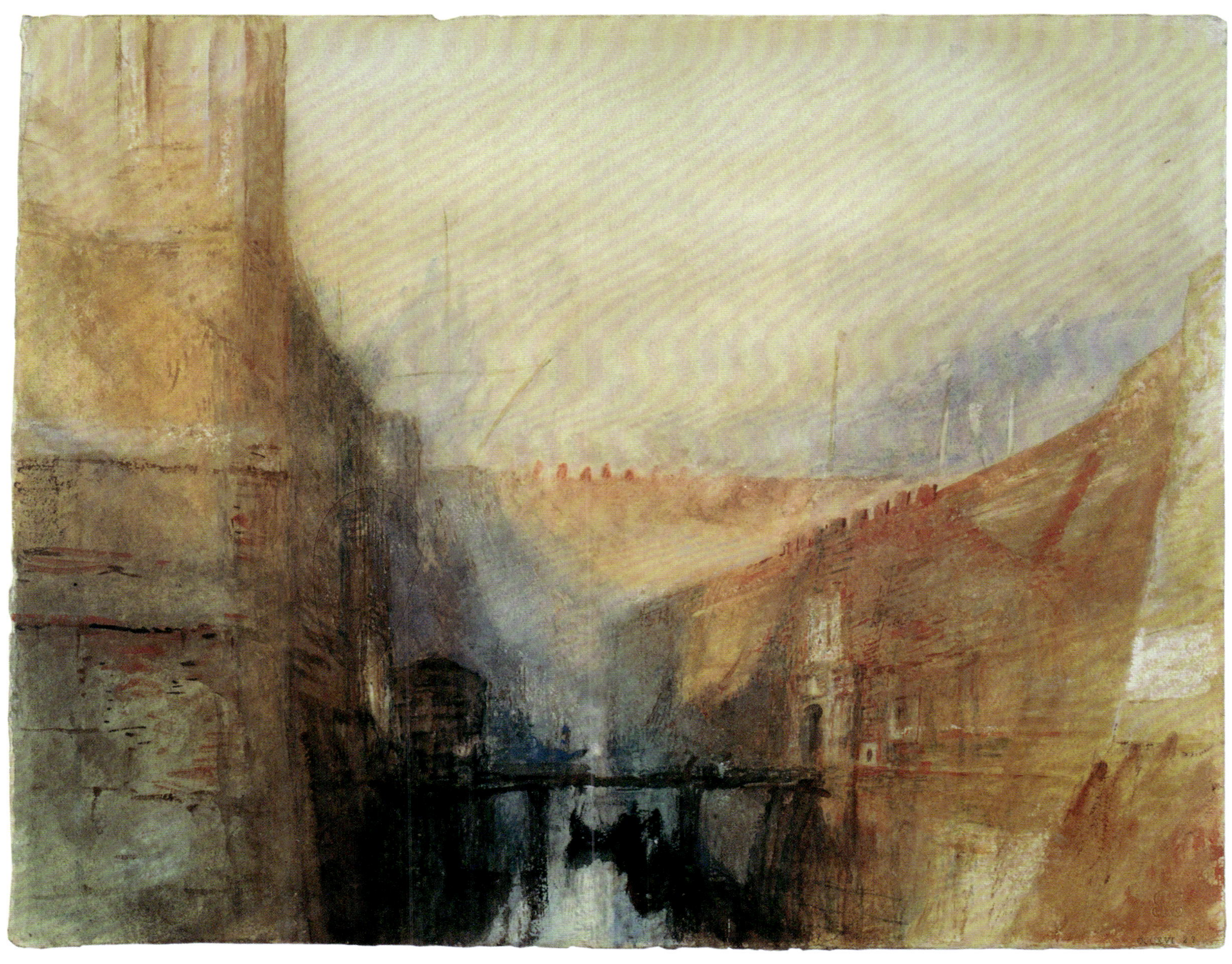

An Imaginary View of the Arsenale c.1840
Watercolour and gouache on paper, 24.3 × 30.8

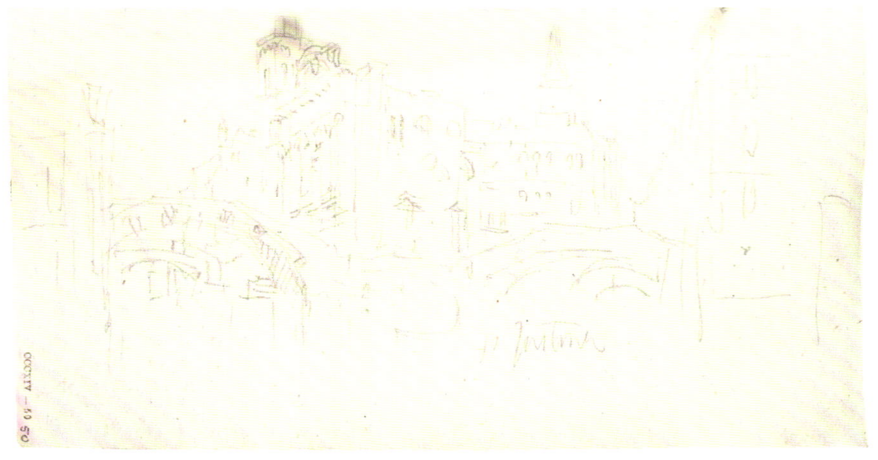

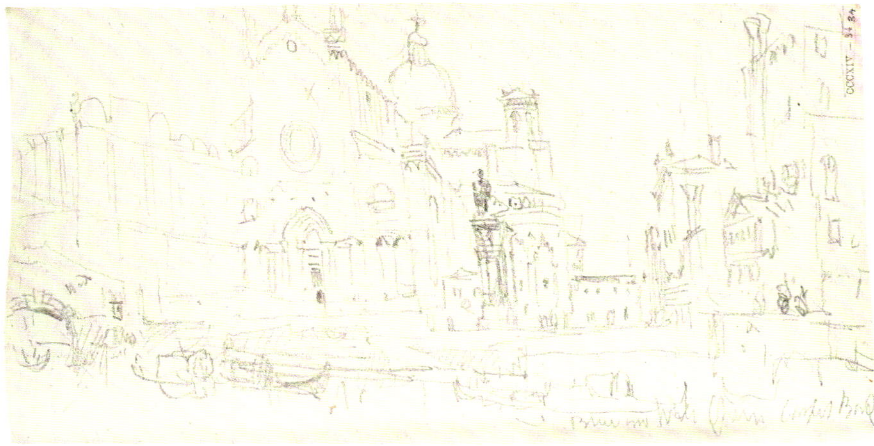

*The Junction of the Rio de Santa Giustina and the
Rio San Francesco, with the façade of the deconsecrated
church of Santa Giustina to the left and the Campanile
of San Francesco della Vigna to the right*

*The Church and Campo of Santi Giovanni e Paolo, with
the Colleoni Monument, from the Rio del Mendicanti*

*The Façade and Campanile of Santa Maria Formosa,
with the Bridge over the Rio del Mondo Novo*

All from the Venice Sketchbook 1833
Graphite on paper, 10.9 × 20.3

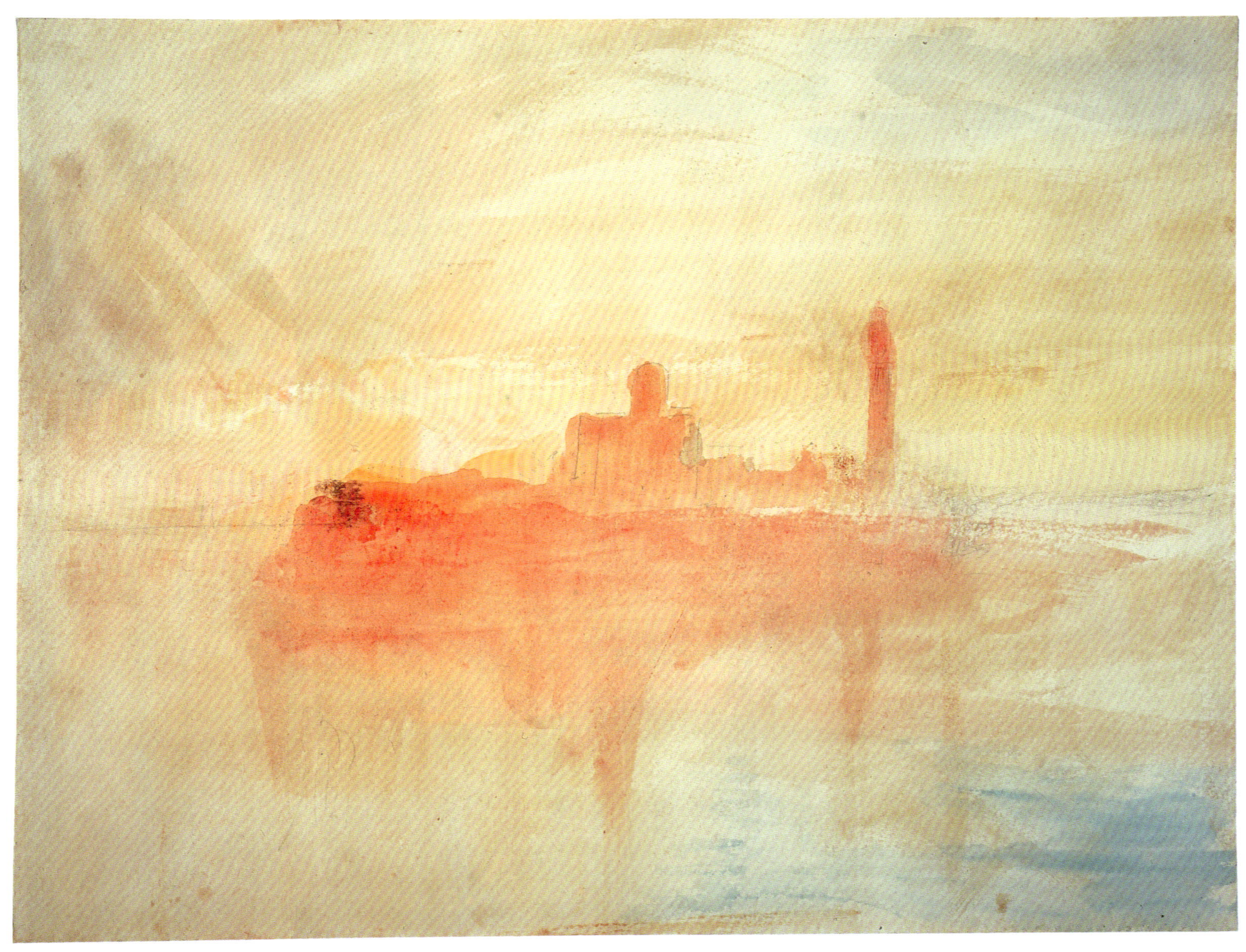

San Pietro di Castello at Sunrise 1840
Watercolour and graphite on off-white wove paper, 22.5 × 29
National Gallery of Ireland, Dublin

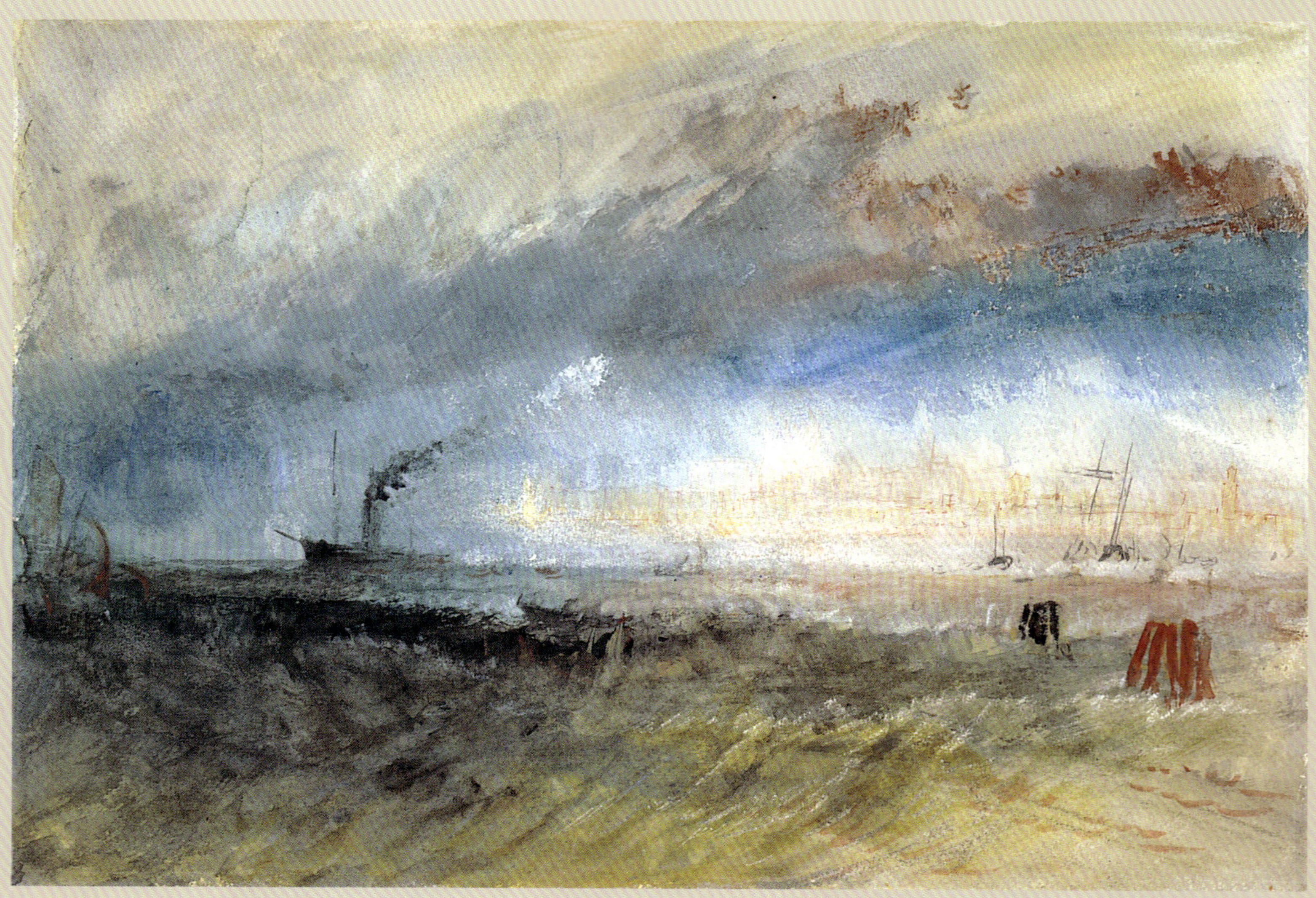

The Fondamenta Nuove and the Lagoon

Turner was fortunate in being among the last generation of travellers to experience Venice as a city that was still completely physically separate from the surrounding *terra firma*. In the first half of the 1840s, beginning soon after his third and final visit, a railway bridge was constructed linking Mestre on the mainland with the Cannaregio district, eventually bringing trains within yards of the Grand Canal, once the church of Santa Lucia was demolished. Even before this, however, Venice had not been immune to the dynamic changes of the industrial age. Steamboats were added to the array of vessels mooring on Venetian quaysides during the 1820s, and it was aboard one of these steamers that Turner set off for the city of Trieste, as he departed Venice for the last time in 1840 (see p.47).

Despite this first-hand experience of modern travel, in his later paintings he repeatedly explored the idea of the traditional, man-powered passage across the lagoon on the way from Fusina (the route he had taken when arriving in the city for the first time; compare p.4 and p.124). This was inevitably a much slower process, during which the unique character of Venice, rising from the waters, only gradually became an improbable reality; a dream made solid. Poets had always understood this. But the time spent on the open waters, inevitably acted on even the least fertile imagination, heightening the appetite for the wondrous place. Simultaneously, the journey tapped into subconscious echoes of watery crossings in myth, most obviously the transportation of souls across the River Styx by the boatman Charon. Turner focused specifically on this transformative period of expanded time in several paintings, also pairing some of his final Venetian paintings with titles that evoke the contrasting journeys of revellers travelling to the city for a ball at sunset and departing the following morning as the softer colours of dawn begin to infuse the sky (see p.101). The implication

in such narratives is, of course, that all pleasures are transient and that we must savour them while we can but, ultimately, we have to move on. Whether pessimistic or just a stoic acceptance of the nature of mortality, the intrinsic sentiment is not surprising from an artist who was entering his seventies when working on these images.

Rather than being cowed by such thoughts, the wide spaces of the lagoon were stimulating for Turner, liberating him from the constrictions of more contained outlooks within the city. Here sea and sky become as one and seem to extend without limits in a way that is timeless. Even when confronting directly the consequences of death, in the form of the new cemetery of San Michele, Turner produced one of the most stunning of his Venetian pictures, showing the recently expanded island lying off the Fondamenta Nuove (p.121). He had sketched this area and the islands to the north back in 1819 (p.118–9), and would have noted how the expanded cemetery grounds were the result of claiming and filling the space between San Michele and the neighbouring, but now subsumed island of San Cristoforo della Pace. The real attraction to this area for him, however, had been the churches of the Gesuiti and Madonna dell'Orto, the latter famous for its various canvases by Tintoretto, including his towering rendering of the *Last Judgement* c.1559–60. But if Turner's *Campo Santo* is in some way elegiac, there is no sense of wallowing sadness or the awfulness of death. Instead, the walls enclosing the cemetery shimmer with a pinkish glow, producing miraculously long reflections over the unbroken surface of the tranquil lagoon. Balancing this effect, the lateen sails of the nearby fishing boat (augmented with another depiction of the sun) catch the brilliant morning light in a way that is magical and transcendent.

A Steamer seen across the Lagoon 1840
Watercolour, pen and ink and scraping on paper, 22.1 × 32
National Galleries Scotland, Edinburgh

*A Panoramic view over the Lagoon from the
Fondamenta Nuove, with the islands of San
Cristoforo della Pace and San Michele (later
joined to form the Cimitero), and Murano (with
the bell-towers of San Pietro Martire and Santi
Maria e Donato)* from the Venice to Ancona
Sketchbook 1819
Graphite on paper, 11.1 × 18.4

*The Church of Madonna dell'Orto, with the
Palazzo Minelli Spada, and the Campanile of
the Gesuiti in the distance* from the Venice and
Botzen Sketchbook 1840
Graphite on paper, 12.3 × 17.3

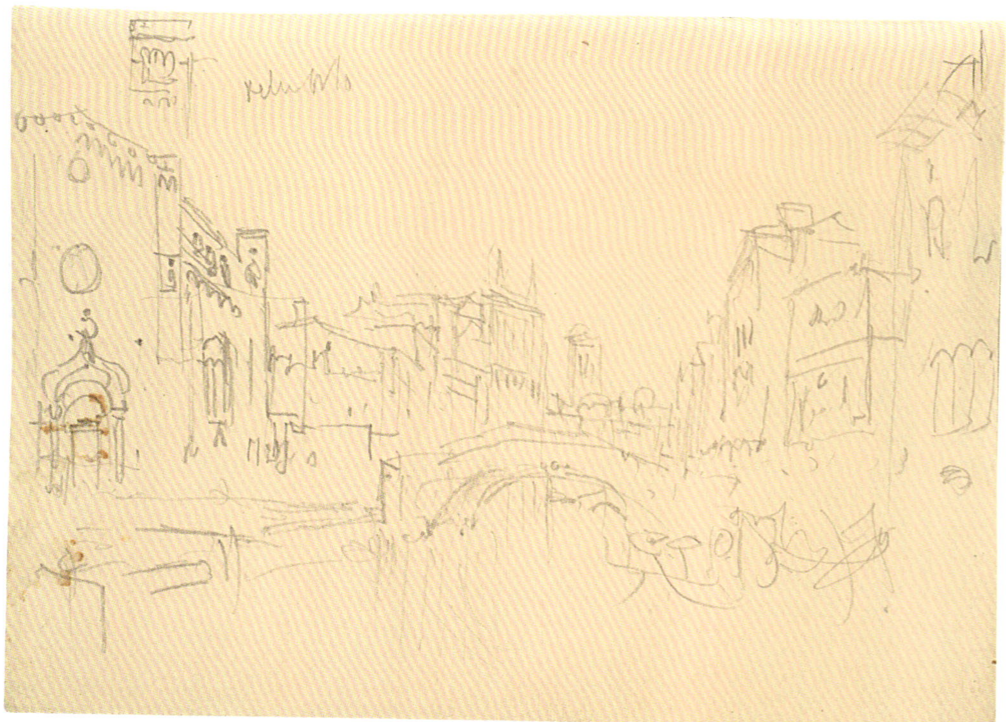

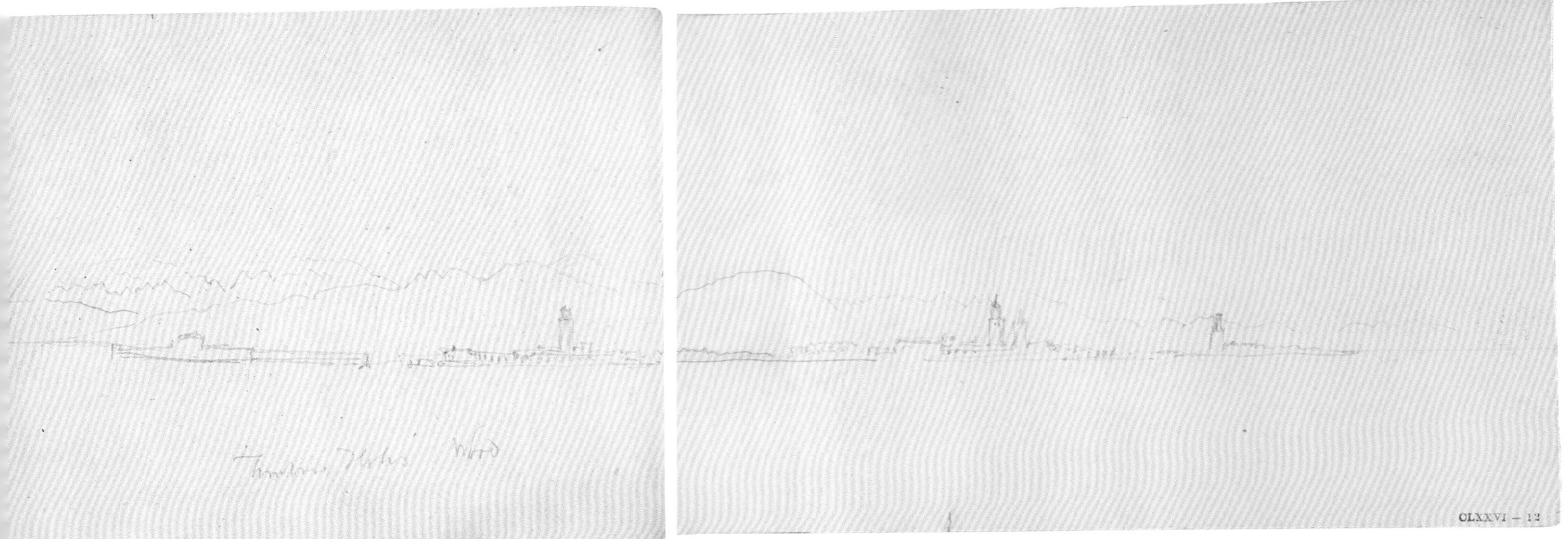

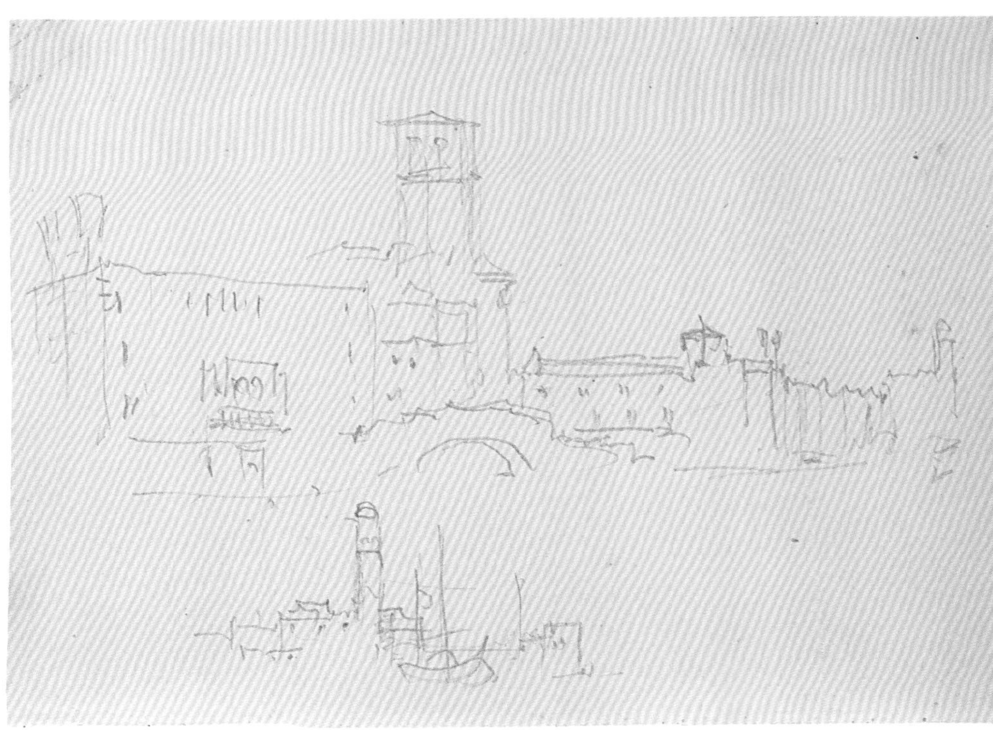

The Church of the Gesuiti and the Fondamenta Nuove, with a second sketch of Madonna dell'Orto and the Casino degli Spirito from the Venice and Botzen Sketchbook 1840
Graphite on paper, 12.3 × 17.3

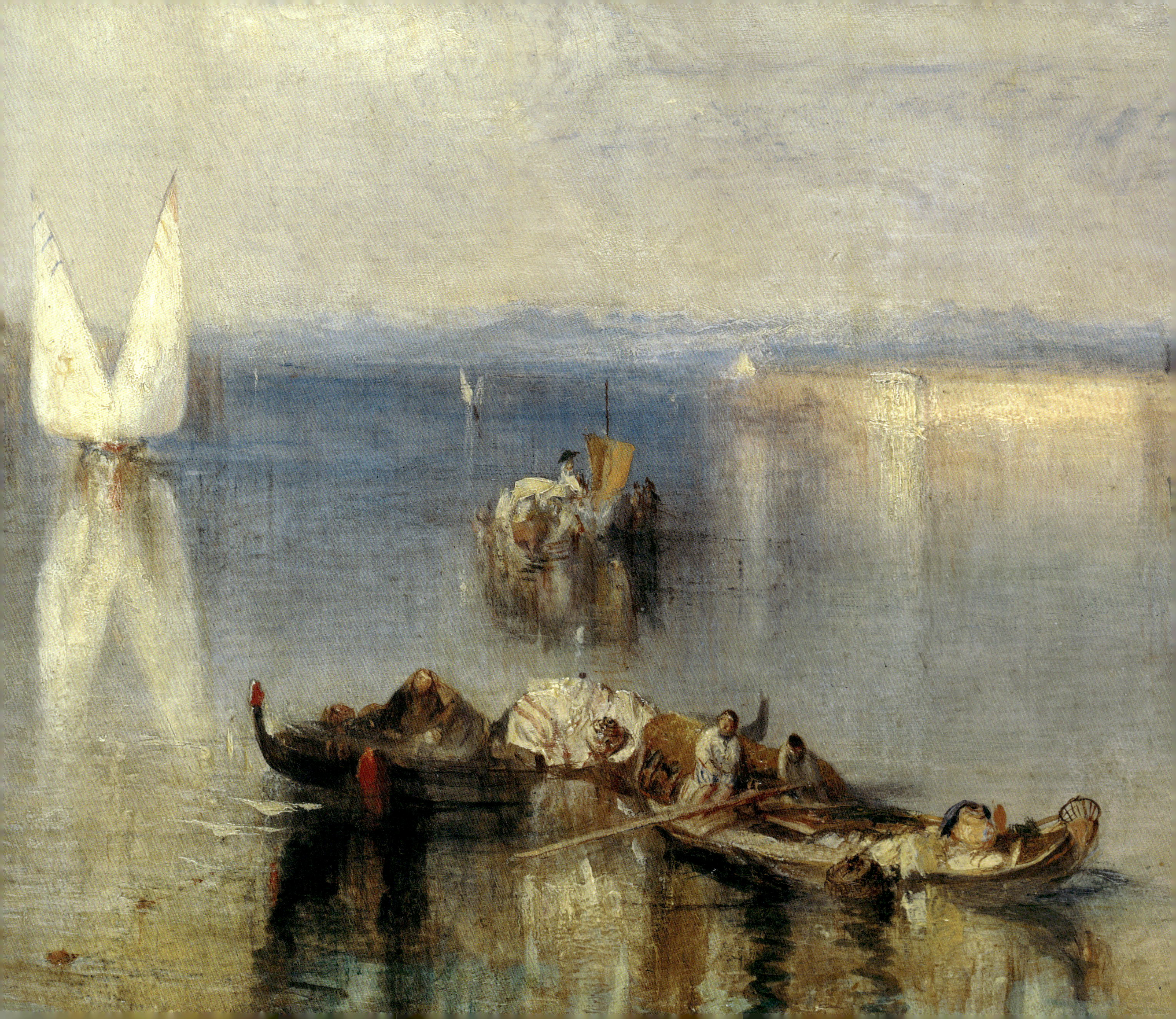

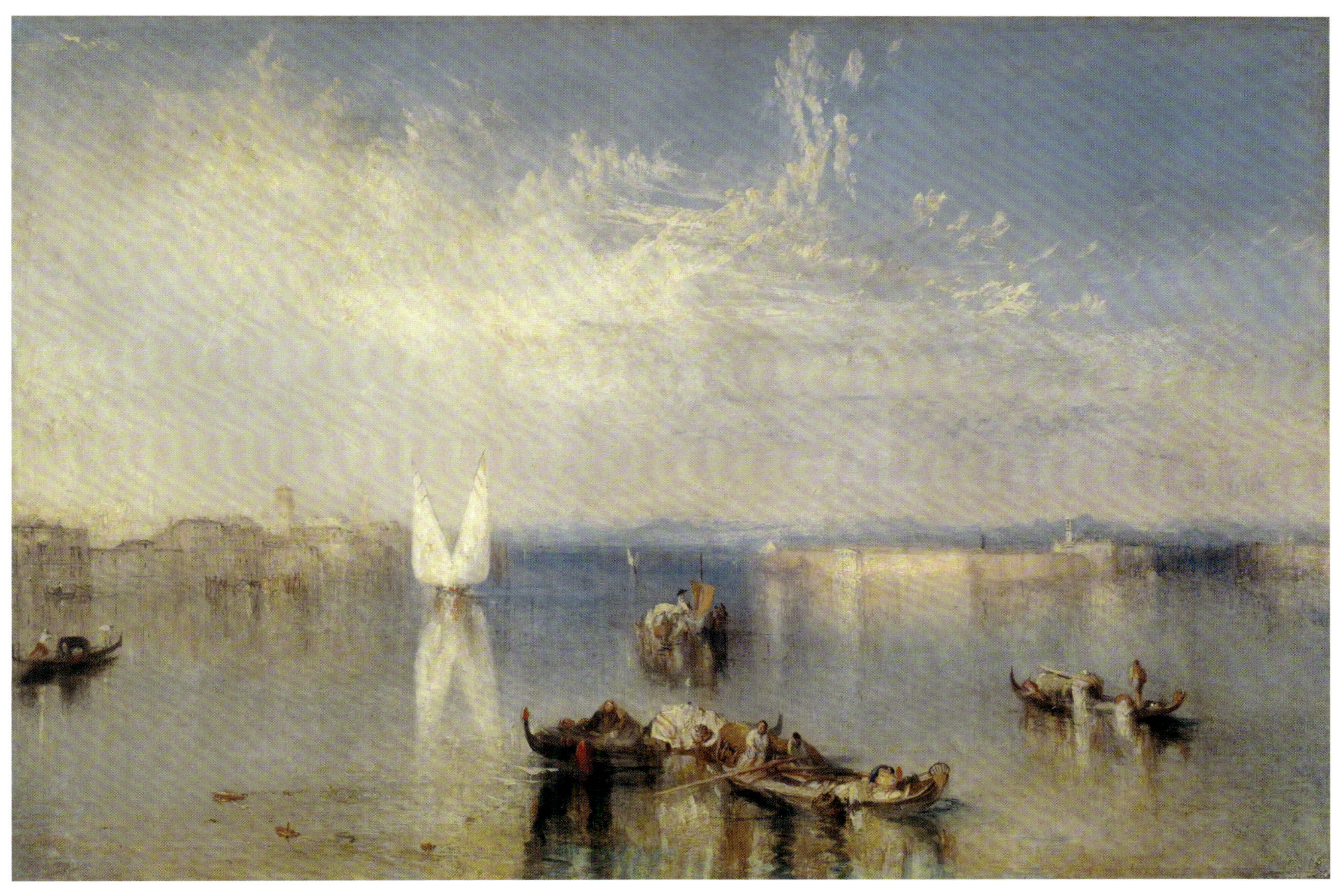

Campo Santo, Venice exhibited 1842
Oil paint on canvas, 62.2 × 92.7
Toledo Museum of Art, Ohio (detail opposite)

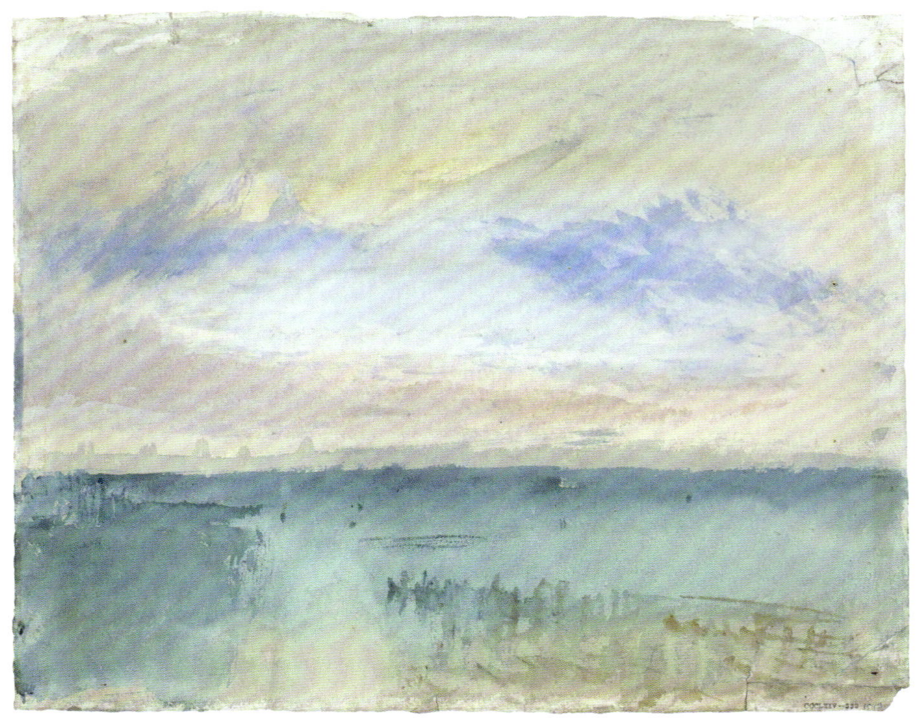

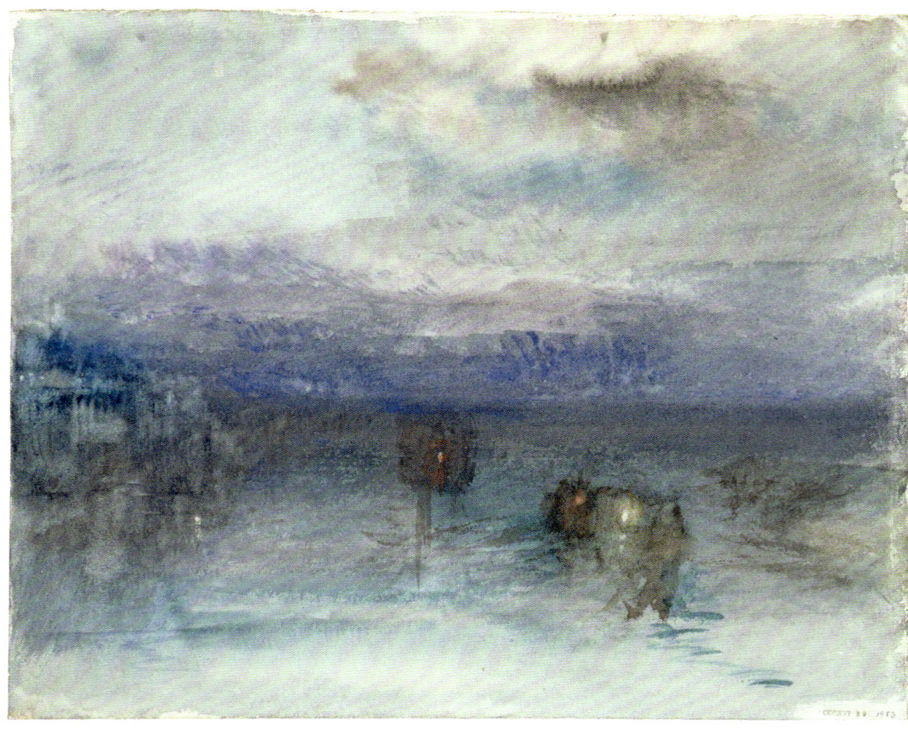

An Open Expanse of Water on the Lagoon 1840
Watercolour on paper, 248 × 307

Moonlight on the Lagoon 1840
Watercolour and gouache on paper, 24.5 × 30.4
(detail, p.126)

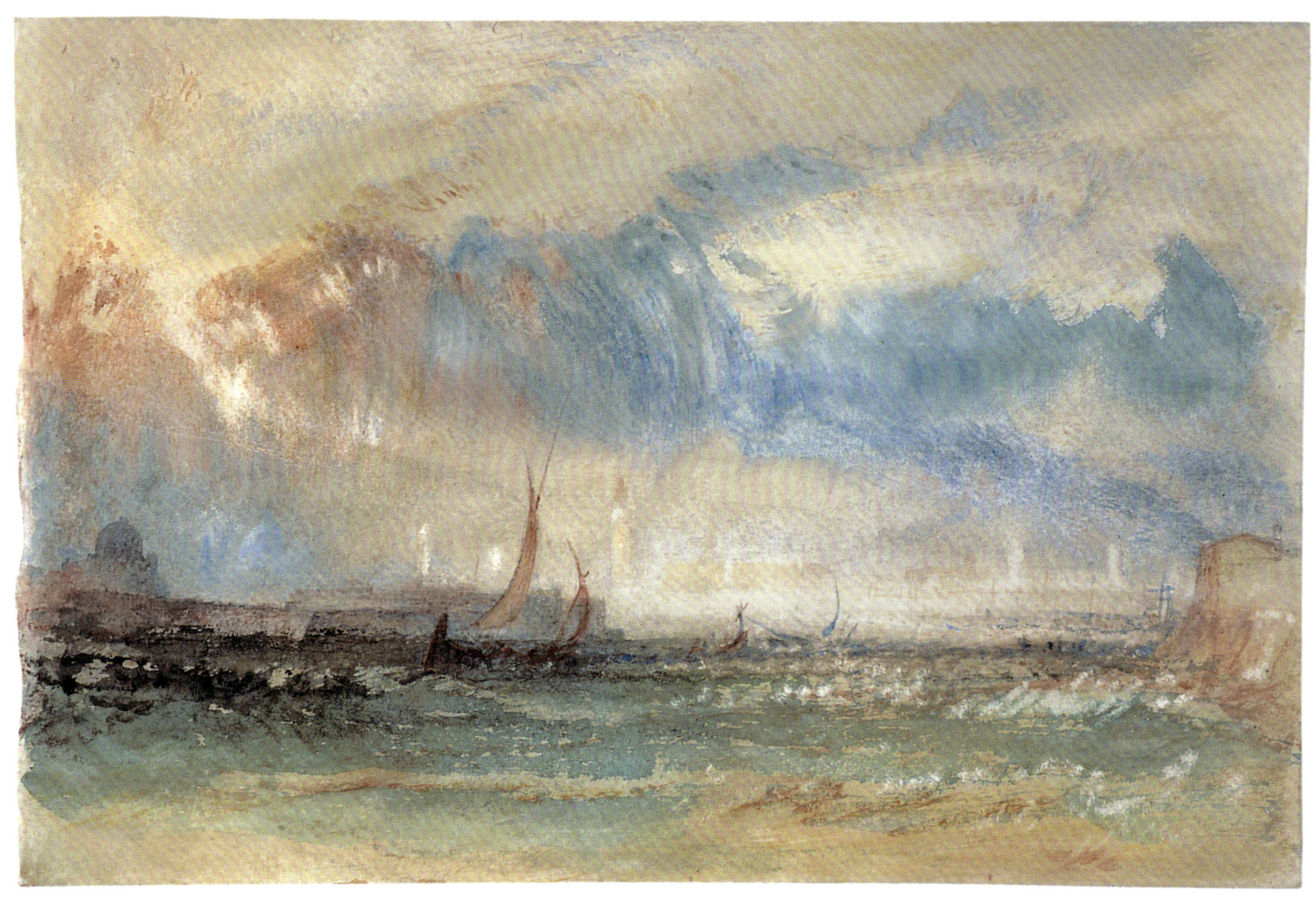

Storm at Sunset 1840
Watercolour and gouache with pen and ink and scratching-out
on paper, 22.2 × 32
Fitzwilliam Museum, Cambridge

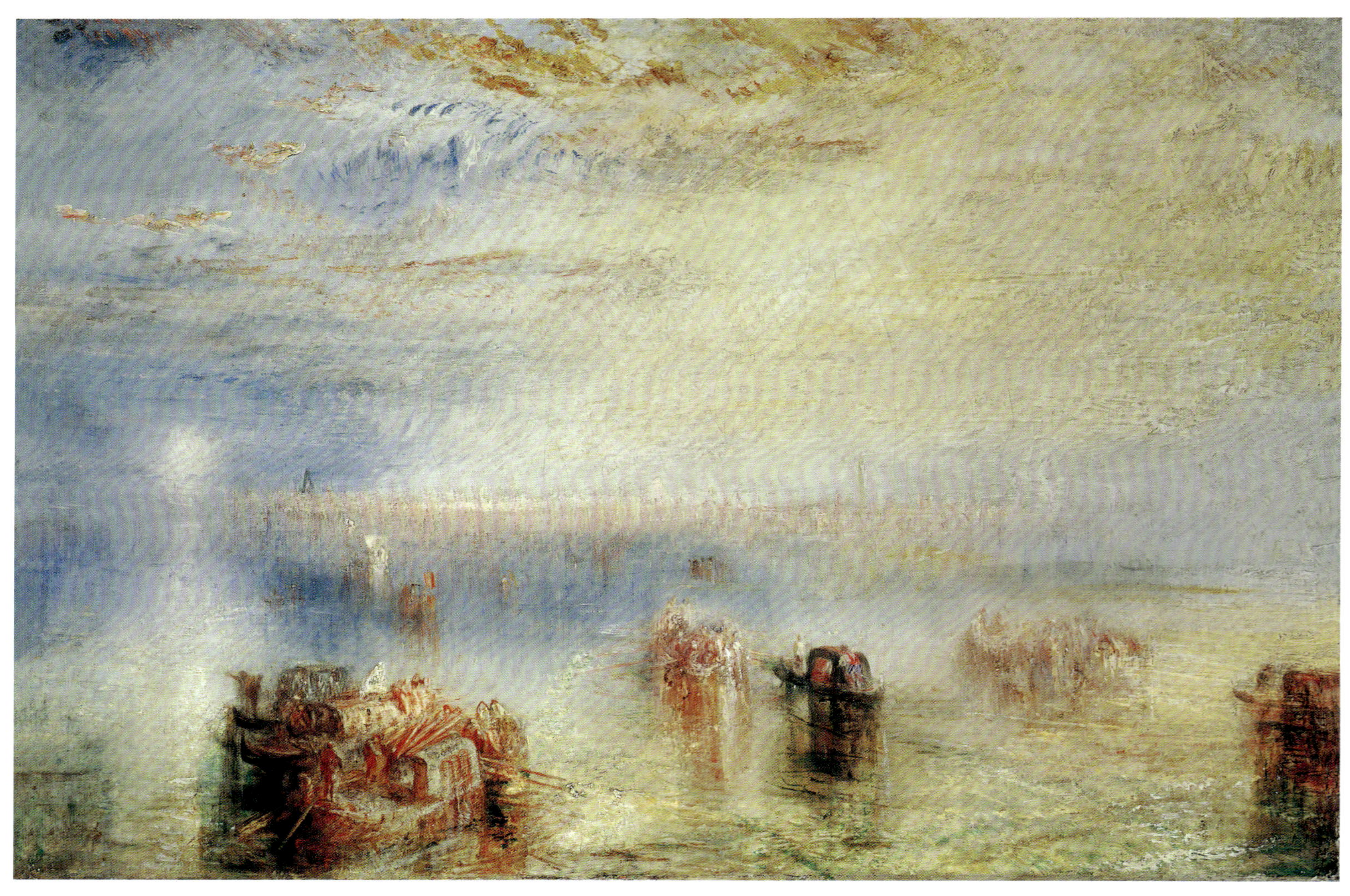

Approach to Venice exhibited 1844
Oil paint on canvas, 62 × 94
National Gallery of Art, Washington, DC

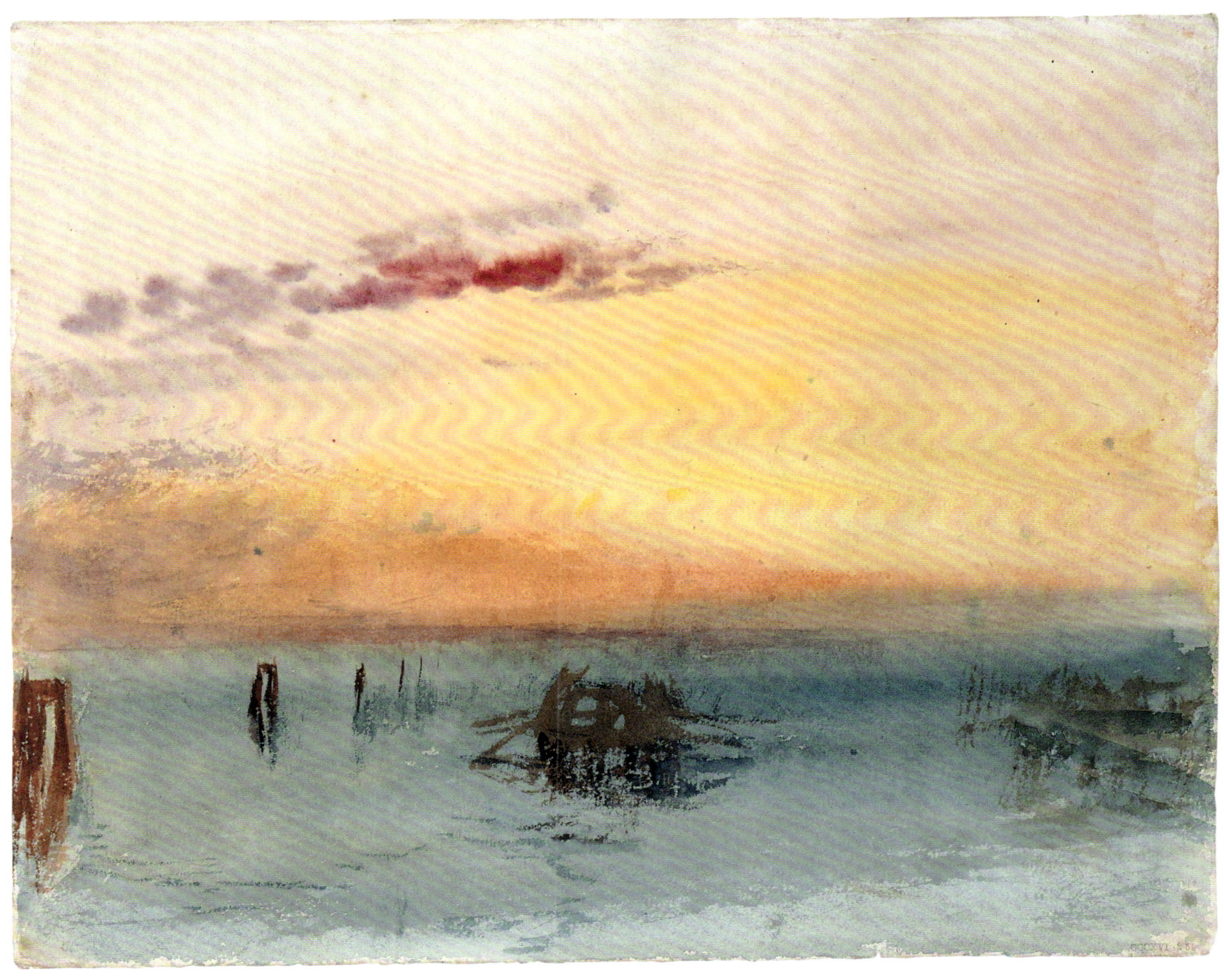

Looking across the Lagoon at Sunset 1840
Watercolour on paper, 24.4 × 30.4

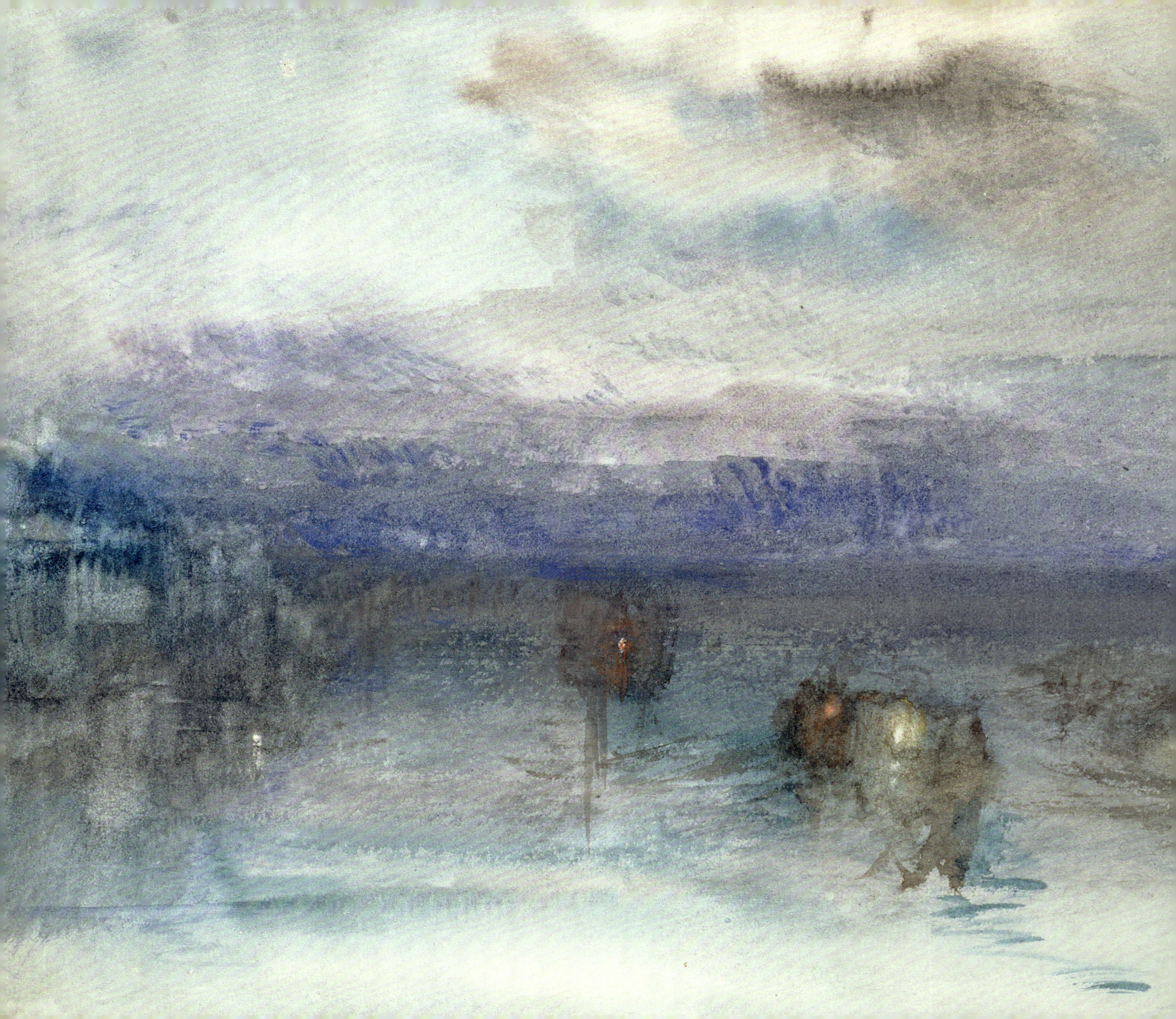

Further Reading

Christopher Baker, *J.M.W. Turner: The Vaughan Bequest*, Edinburgh 2006

Martin Butlin and Evelyn Joll, *The Paintings of J.M.W. Turner:*,
New Haven and London 1984

Federico Crimi, *J.M.W. Turner: a Milano*, Milan 2017

A.J. Finberg, *In Venice with Turner*, London 1930
—— *The Life of J.M.W. Turner, R.A.*, Oxford 1961

John Gage, *J.M.W. Turner: 'A Wonderful Range of Mind'*,
New Haven and London 1987

James Hamilton (ed.), *Turner and Italy*, Edinburgh 2009

Anne Hodge and Niamh MacNally, *The Works of J.M.W. Turner: at the
National Gallery of Ireland*, Dublin 2017

Evelyn Joll, Martin Butlin and Luke Herrmann (eds),
The Oxford Companion to J.M.W. Turner:, Oxford 2001

Nicola Moorby, 'Turner Elsewhere: Travels and Tours, 1835–45',
in David Blayney Brown, Amy Concannon and Sam Smiles,
The EY Exhibition: Late Turner. Painting Set Free, London 2014,
pp.80–3, 103–121

Franny Moyle, *The Extraordinary Life and Momentous Times of
J.M.W. Turner:*, London 2016

Sylvie Patin, 'The Last Act: Turner, Whistler and Monet in Venice',
in Katharine Lochnan (ed.), *Turner Whistler Monet*, London 2004,
pp.203–30

Martin Schwander (ed.), *Venice. From Canaletto and Turner to Monet*,
Basel 2008

Lindsay Stainton, *Turner's Venice*, London 1985

Ian Warrell (ed.), *Turner and Venice*, London 2003
—— *Turner's Sketchbooks*, London 2014

Andrew Wilton, *The Life and Work of J.M.W. Turner:*, Fribourg 1979
—— *Venise. Aquarelles de Turner*, Paris 1995

All of the sketchbooks Turner used in Venice, as well as his
watercolours, can be found on the 'Art & Artists' pages of
Tate's website (www.tate.org.uk).

Moonlight on the Lagoon 1840
Watercolour and gouache on paper, 24.5 × 30.4
(detail, see p.122)

First published 2020 by order of the Tate Trustees by Tate Publishing,
a division of Tate Enterprises Ltd, Millbank, London SW1P 4RG
www.tate.org.uk/publishing

A catalogue record for this book is available from the British Library

ISBN 978 1 84976 703 3

Distributed in the United States and Canada by ABRAMS, New York
Library of Congress Control Number applied for.

Production Controller: Juliette Dupire
Designed by Joe Ewart
Colour reproduction by DL Imaging, London
Printed and bound in Italy by Graphicom

Cover detail, *San Giorgio Maggiore – Early Morning* (p.50)

All works belong to Tate's collection unless otherwise stated.
Measurements of artworks are given in centimetres, height before width.